MICHAEL CALVIN

Michael Calvin is one of the UK's most accomplished sportswriters and a *Sunday Times* bestselling author. For his journalism he has won both Sports Writer of the Year and Sports Reporter of the Year and as an author he has twice won the British Sports Book awards.

His previous books include *The Nowhere Men*, *Living On The Volcano*, *No Hunger In Paradise*, *State of Play* and *Family*. As a collaborator he has written acclaimed books with Gareth Thomas and Joey Barton.

THOMAS BJØRN

Thomas Bjørn is regarded as one of the European Tour's greatest players, having claimed fifteen European Tour titles to date. He made his Ryder Cup debut in 1997 and appeared twice more in 2002 and 2014, experiencing victory on all three occasions.

He was appointed Chairman of the European Tour's Tournament Committee in 2007, before stepping aside in 2016 to focus on his duty as Ryder Cup Captain. In 2018 he led Europe to a famous 17½–10½ victory at Le Golf National, Paris.

MICHAEL CALVIN
THOMAS BJØRN

Mind Game

The Secrets of Golf's Winners

VINTAGE

1 3 5 7 9 10 8 6 4 2

Vintage
20 Vauxhall Bridge Road,
London SW1V 2SA

Vintage is part of the Penguin Random House group
of companies whose addresses can be found
at global.penguinrandomhouse.com

Penguin
Random House
UK

First published in paperback by Vintage in 2020
First published in hardback by Yellow Jersey Press in 2019

penguin.co.uk/vintage

A CIP catalogue record for this book is available from the British Library

ISBN 9781529110586

Printed and bound in Great Britain by Clays Ltd, Elcograf S.p.A.

Penguin Random House is committed to a sustainable future
for our business, our readers and our planet. This book is
made from Forest Stewardship Council® certified paper.

MIX
Paper from
responsible sources
FSC
www.fsc.org FSC® C018179

'We are working on the jagged edge of success, where the level of insecurity and misery pushes you into becoming better.'

Sean Foley, coach to Justin Rose

CONTENTS

PROLOGUE: THOMAS BJØRN
CONVERSATIONS IN THE MIRROR

'Why are you crying?'
'Why do you put yourself through this pain?'
'Why do you play this game?'
'Who are you?'
'Where are you in your life?'
'What do you want to achieve?'
'Do you really want to continue?'
'Why does it mean so much to you?'

These are the questions I ask myself when I stand before the bathroom mirror. It begins as a one-way conversation, framed by fear, frustration and self-doubt. I reach out to the boy who was captivated by the challenge of chipping golf balls into a birdbath in the back garden, but the mirror remains mute. I invariably see the man I have become, through moist, red-rimmed eyes.

Golf came close to breaking me. I had to hit rock bottom before the exchange became meaningful, because on the way down a golfer is conditioned to grasping at straws. It is human nature to seek a shortcut, to shy away from unpalatable truths, but my sport demands submission before remission. I stood there for hours, morning and evening, before the mirror answered back.

It spoke of love, respect and the purity of an impossible search for perfection. It helped drive away the demons by reminding me of those beguiling moments when golf is just a game, instead of a starkly defined, casually cruel profession. Innocence is lost quickly, easily. If you cannot reconnect with the sense of wonder you had as a child, then you, too, will be lost.

Every professional golfer knows what to do to improve. We are products of a remorseless sport that depends on the reproduction of technical excellence. Our lives are spent honing short, concentrated bursts of synchronised movement. Radar technology defines clubhead speed, the launch angle and spin rate of our shots, but it cannot measure strength of spirit.

We are attuned to weakness, and we understand shared pain. I've lost count of the number of players I have sat with, trying to drag them out of the shit. I talk to them about the mirror, in those private moments. They have to find the heart and soul of who they are, what they do and why they do it. They cannot continue to play with a hatred of the game, as I once did. They need to find the goodness, rediscover the things in which they believe.

In case you hadn't guessed, this isn't the usual book to which a winning Ryder Cup captain contributes. It is not a breathless memoir, or an ego trip. I wanted to work in conjunction with Michael Calvin because he casts a fresh pair of eyes on golf. He has covered just about every sport you can think of, at the highest level. He has worked with big personalities and quiet contemplators, but I knew he would scrape away our superficialities.

Golf is not a game of birdies and bogeys, of numbers and archaic niceties. It is a game of flesh and blood, heart and mind. It shines a harsh light into dark crevices. It invites obsession, teases out human flaws and reveals admirable traits. Occasionally, as in the European team's win at Le Golf National during an unforgettable week in Paris in late September 2018, it can prove impossibly uplifting.

Welcome to our world.

It's a very lonely place. You have your caddie, but you're pretty much alone on a golf course. A round lasts a long time. It is a solitary existence, because the only people you are surrounded by are your competitors. You've got to find your friends. I tell young players on the circuit not to let playing poorly interfere with normality.

People get fed up having to wait to see whether you have shot sixty-six or seventy-six before knowing whether you will join them for dinner, as planned. Eventually they stop issuing the invitation. That's how you get lonely. You retreat into a world of room service and remorse. The walls close in. You will obsess, over-analyse, underperform. It is not a nice place to be.

The Tour can be claustrophobic, but it provides a lot of common ground. It is relatively easy to strike up a conversation, but ultimately you are passing time until you have to get out there and do it again. As you get older you develop really deep, meaningful friendships, but you can never get away from the fact that you are on your own.

I've seen golf devour people, bite by bite. It is death by a hundred missed cuts, a thousand internal conversations. The game plays consistently with your mental health, because there aren't enough victories. Putting it in such terms might appear harsh, but there are a lot of us who get more miserable over the years, when we should be unbelievably grateful for our achievements.

An athlete's mental health is no longer a taboo subject, but there are still those who believe it should not be talked about, especially in a sport like golf where the upside, financially, is so big. Their reflex action is: 'He's become a multimillionaire from knocking a little white ball around. Why's he got a problem?' These people also tend to say that money isn't everything, but they can't have it both ways.

I understand the perception that we are lucky, because professional golf can be played competitively up to, and occasionally beyond, the age of sixty. But that informs the idea that the game is your entire existence. It is not as if you are a footballer, who retires at thirty-three with the rest of his life ahead of him. I am forty-eight. If I lose my game, I have nowhere else to go.

That's tough to come to terms with, mentally. I'm trained to work hard, because that is what I need to do to excel. It is a default mechanism, developed over forty-odd years. But what if I can't find what I'm looking for? I do not have the right to rely on my experience, sit back and expect things to happen in front of me. If I do that for six months, I will be out the back of the field.

Failure drives you deeper into a world that is not real. Outsiders can't help you, because they don't understand. They don't know the conventions of the locker room, the insecurities that are being masked on the driving range. They can't appreciate the competition, the constant travel. They might have a perception of what it takes out of you, but when you are down, you have to deal with it on your own.

Even your family and closest friends don't fully comprehend what you are going through, because although they pop in and out, and see certain sides of the life, they don't live it all the time. You feel their devotion, but hear that the understanding is not there. You don't doubt their good intentions, but they cannot provide the help you need.

There is a distance about players who lose their game. They detach themselves from the group. They're not pushed away, but they're at the end of their tether. They feel they don't belong and become strangely submissive. Very few stick with it. Those who do so are special characters, who come to terms with changed circumstances, before rising again.

That's not to say you don't see sadness, desperation and jealousy. You sense resentment from those who are struggling, that you are somehow unappreciative of your privileges. You imagine them thinking, 'You should be happy with the world you are in, because you could be in *my* world.' The ones who survive, and come back, deal with what is in front of them.

One of the great achievements in sport is to be good to yourself. The moment when you recognise that whatever you have done is the best you can do – that's when you begin to discover who, and what, you are. That is the basis of your story. Instead of looking at others, who are invariably world-class and have more moments when they bring their best, accept where you are at that particular time.

When people lose their way, they tend to be living as the players they once were. They're not going anywhere because they remember what they used to do, and judge themselves by those memories. If they are struggling at 100 in the rankings, on the slide after being number one, they will have difficulties if they keep measuring themselves against what they once were.

They should be using the guy at ninety-nine as a reference point. Try to be better than him. Take the small victories on the way to salvation. That's the key. The person who rationalises his weaknesses will be protected by his instincts. He may find things hard, and be driven to distraction in his everyday life, but he must wait for release.

It might only be for two holes, at first. Then it might be for six. He will begin to feel that half-forgotten sense of freedom and think, 'Whoa, I recognise this world.' He will become comfortable in his own skin and tell himself, 'Hang on, I know I can handle this.' That's why winners will suddenly win again, from nowhere.

Tiger Woods can't handle the world in which he is no good, because he doesn't recognise it. But once he gets into contention, he understands where he is and knows how to deal with it. The juices flow and the old feelings flood back. That's why, without a shadow of doubt, he will win a major championship again.

Most sports are reactional. A tennis player reacts to a shot struck in his or her direction. A footballer reacts to the movement of an opponent, and to the manipulation or direction of the ball. But in golf, the ball is immobile and within reach. You don't react. You simply do. When you are at your absolute peak, you don't think about what you are doing.

There is a feeling that follows you. You don't go through a routine of saying, 'I have to do this, this and this.' That's the habit you fall into when you are struggling. When you are at your best, you feel the shot, see it and execute it. It is unconscious excellence. It happens within you. It's there, and you just *do*. It is almost as if you are walking ahead of the ball.

It is said that when Lionel Messi receives the ball, he has about 120 different images in his head about what he's going to do with it. A successful golfer has one. I see the right one, instinctively and immediately, because it relates to my feelings. They have already told me the shot I can hit, so I see the picture of what I can do. When I am not playing well, the feeling deserts me. I think about what I should, could or might do.

Visual players, who are often the most talented ones, trust that feeling. They are the flair players: Sergio García, Tiger, Bubba Watson, Phil Mickelson. They're fun to watch because of their initiative and imagination, but when it goes wrong, it goes dramatically wrong. Seve Ballesteros was all about feel. Too much so, because when he lost the feeling there was insufficient technique to back it up. He didn't know where to go.

Others do it on pure work, robotically. They repeat the same thing a hundred times over and push their way through it. They tend to make a lot of money, through consistency and commitment, yet have a different degree of talent. They are the guys who can't go to sleep if they know they haven't done exactly what they needed to do.

Different strokes, different folks. I see golf as an art, rather than a science, because you can hit the ball from the same place, the same distance, in many different ways. None of it is correct, and none of it is wrong. Expressing yourself is an art, and science is something that is written in a book. There are very few players who get to number one in the world by following what they've read.

That's applicable across sport. Jordan Henderson leads Liverpool, my football team, through example. He plays by the book, by what he has been told he has to do. He does it very well, which makes him a very good player. But Messi doesn't play by anything he has been told. He expresses football. No manager would tell him, 'This is how you must play.' They let Messi be himself.

Part of being very good is knowing where you are in your own mind and being aware of the level of your ability at a particular moment. Your understanding of yourself – and of the environment in which you work – allows you to achieve the ultimate. The best excel when mind and body are at the perfect pitch. They respond to the moment.

They tend not to be very good in practice, but when the occasion applies pressure, they excel. Lesser players tend to be great when it doesn't matter, and fall off because they cannot contain their excitement when it becomes real. Nervousness is a natural ally, because you have to be awake and aware, but there is too much going on for them to perform.

The unique thing about golf is that your toughest opponent is usually yourself. There is nothing you can do to affect a rival's game. If someone shoots the lights out, you have to accept it was their day. Equally, if you don't fulfil yourself, because of what is going on in your head, you have to rationalise your faults and move on.

It's an interesting, occasionally illogical place to be. There are players who get something out of the day through the sheer force of their will, even if they are not in the right place, technically. And sometimes the game surprises you. You think it is going to be shit, and it turns out fine. On other days you will be feeling great, and so you become a little lazy. It doesn't turn out well.

We're all waiting for that moment when things just go. I imagine it is similar to being an airline pilot. The pre-flight checks are done and you taxi towards the end of the runway, before accelerating to that point where air flows so rapidly over the wings that lift-off occurs. Before you know it, you are on autopilot at 30,000 feet.

When you are on autopilot on a golf course, nothing punctures that bubble of concentration. I relate the situation to a baseball movie I once watched, starring Kevin Costner. As he is pitching, on the mound in a big game, with the crowd on top of him, you can hear his inner thoughts clearing his mechanism. Nothing is allowed to interfere with the moment.

It is the same in golf. The world around you becomes an energy-feeder, a battery supplying mental power, but you don't notice exactly what is going on. When you're not in that zone, you become aware of everything that can disturb your equilibrium: somebody moving, somebody screaming, a child crying.

I know, to my cost, that the margins are terrifyingly small. I hit one shot, from the elevated tee on the 163-yard sixteenth at Royal St George's in 2003, that was about three feet from being pretty much perfect. It cost me an Open Championship and defined a playing career. If that shot had landed a yard or so to the left, I would have protected or even extended a two-shot lead; instead, it rolled into a greenside bunker, from which it took me three shots to emerge.

To this day, people still make that the biggest mark they put next to my name as a player. I'm the guy who lost the Open, in that bunker. There are margins in every sport – the lucky net cord, or the fractional deflection of a goal-bound shot onto the crossbar – but golf has many more external influences to factor in. You are playing the golf course, the weather, and must deal with inequalities beyond your control.

Courses play differently at nine in the morning and two in the afternoon. Guys come through the field because they play in good weather early in the day, before the leaders are out in the pissing rain. You can go to an Open Championship in the form of your life, ready to perform, but if you are in terrible conditions on the first day, when others are luckier, your attempt to win the Claret Jug is over before it has barely begun.

If you don't react well, and turn in on yourself, you are in trouble. Perspective is everything. It took me many years to mellow, but I've been sustained by one of the earliest promises I made to myself: that if I finished in the top ten of a tournament, I would walk away without regrets, because it represented a good week. Sure, things could have turned out differently. You could have thought more sharply, executed your shots more effectively, but never forget to pat yourself on the back.

Ensure that your goals are realistic. A Danish journalist once asked me my ambition for the season. I told him I wanted to win the European Tour money list. I did well, finishing sixth or seventh, but he slaughtered me for not living up to my expectations. When he asked me the same question the following year, I simply said I wanted to keep my Tour card, because I knew that was something I could guarantee.

I've played more than 600 tournaments worldwide, and won nineteen times. That's an impressive ratio, but if winning is the only thing that matters, then I've had a lot of bad experiences. Look at it the other way: I've had 110 top-ten finishes, so that means I've gone home feeling good about myself 110 times.

A successful tennis player goes home a winner more often than not, by progressing through a few rounds, before invariably being eliminated in the later stages of a tournament. If victory is the only gauge of success, then most golfers don't have an end result. They have to find their consolation in more relative terms.

Consistent winners on Tour – and by that, I mean those who win three times or more a year – feed off the inner belief that they are better than the next guy. It is more than an amalgamation of talent, application and the insurance of surrounding yourself with the right people. It is something elemental, something deep-seated that is destined to be revealed.

A special talent is announced in whispers. Names are mentioned, scores are scrutinised, references are quietly taken from respected judges. Reputation grows before the breakthrough comes. The prodigy knows he is being built up into the next big thing, accepts the expectation and delivers. That is the source of enduring inner confidence.

Professional sport is hard work. It strips away the veneer of youth and easy praise. Respect within your new peer group doesn't come courtesy of conventional wisdom. You have to earn the right to that respect, by proving yourself under intense scrutiny. Game recognises game. An understated word of congratulation in the locker room means more than a shrieking headline.

Golf cherishes its legends, whether they are enshrined in a different era, by the likes of Arnold Palmer, Jack Nicklaus and Gary Player, or by their reputation as forces of nature, like Seve. In my time on Tour, I've seen Sergio, Tiger and Rory arrive, and knew immediately there was no way they were going anywhere but right to the top.

When they emerged, everyone talked about them. The media – as they do with any young star in any sport – pushed it to the limits of reason. Yet they just went: 'Bang! I'm here. Deal with it.' As born winners, they identified the opportunity and took it. Other players who came in with similar fanfares didn't get beyond that make-or-break boundary. They became uncertain, under the unaccustomed pressure, and succumbed to self-doubt.

Time can be corrosive. Scar tissue builds. A light went out when I lost my swing for a couple of seasons. I look at myself today and realise I don't play the game with the same love that I lavished on it as a kid. I don't run to practise, or play golf for fun with my friends. To me, it is a job, and therefore it is a short-lived thing.

I'm coming down from the huge high of captaining a winning Ryder Cup team and it is time for another conversation with the mirror. I need to retune to reality, and I don't know what the answers are going to be. I will offer insight where appropriate, but this journey is under the direction of Michael, who has walked many miles – both literally and metaphorically – in our shoes.

He has his own questions to answer, in what we hope will be taken as a study of human nature, expressed through leading golfers and the individual support teams that came together so seamlessly, for a common purpose, in Paris. The aim is to offer a balanced, nuanced and emotionally engaging view of the group, the game and their craft.

Michael's search for wisdom begins with one of my greatest friends, Martin Kaymer. If he was not a professional golfer, he would be saving lives in Africa. He is a humanitarian, who sometimes gets in the way of himself by thinking too much about the big picture. I love him to bits, but sometimes feel like telling him, 'Can you not be selfish and just think about you, and nobody else, for three months?'

He is a fantastic guy, but occasionally he struggled with the acid humour of a team room dominated by the Brits and the Irish. I advised him to speak to Bernhard Langer, who realised very quickly that he had to change for Ryder Cup week, because he couldn't expect people to change for him. He embraced the environment. He danced on the table on the Sunday night and went back to his placid, imperturbable Germanic self when he teed it up the following Thursday.

I don't think Martin really realised what the Cup was all about until he holed that winning putt in Medinah, Illinois, in 2012.

Here's a guy who has been world number one and has won two major championships, who will be remembered by most people as the man who confirmed a sporting miracle. That's the difference. Seve won five majors, but nine out of ten photographs you see of him depict Ryder Cup moments.

I told the players they would not be defined as golfers by the Cup, but they would be identified as personalities. Their philosophies, experiences, characters and approaches were different, but they responded collectively to one of the most pressurised environments in world sport. That team will never again play together, but they will be with me for the rest of my life – through that infamous tattoo on my nether regions.

I had that silhouette of Samuel Ryder's gold trophy, with the numbers 17½ and 10½, inked on in Soho just before Christmas 2018. It wasn't an entirely pleasurable process, but a promise is a promise.

Boys, we will always have Paris.

Chapter One

THE SEEKER

Nothing is quite as it seems. A midsummer sun dances through a pine forest on the southern edge of Gothenburg, lending a silver sheen to the rocky outcrops through which a golf course has been fashioned by American designer Arthur Hills. Yet rain is less than an hour away and a chilly northerly wind is the first whisper of winter.

Conservationists have installed more than 100 bird boxes in the valley, but chalets are being cleaved into the hillside to the right of the second fairway. Those on the far side of the building site, dark grey and angular, are close to completion; others are skeletal wooden frames, whose modesty is protected by garish purple sheets of insulation. Nature resents the intrusion.

On the green, below an elevated clubhouse, Martin Kaymer is practising medium-range putts from around fifteen feet. He holes one of a dozen attempts, leaving the majority slightly short and leaking to the right. Craig Connelly, his caddie, stands behind him and extends his left arm, so that it rests gently on the golfer's right ear and provides a reminder of the need for stability.

They have been through much together, in two spells over eight years punctuated by two major championship wins and a return putt from six feet that entered Ryder Cup folklore as the stroke that secured European victory in Medinah in 2012. The tenderness of the gesture is a refreshing contrast to the mechanical rituals enacted around them, but it is deceptive.

The softly spoken German and the garrulous Scot are divergent characters; though confidences are shared and respect is mutual, theirs is a marriage under terminal strain. Kaymer admits they have been 'picking on each other' since the spring. Within a month they will part, sadly, amicably. Connelly will be employed immediately by emerging Australian Lucas Herbert before linking with South African Branden Grace for the 2019 season. Kaymer's world ranking will fall to 174.

In a low-key introductory press conference at the Nordea Masters, the former US Open and PGA champion had celebrated simple pleasures, such as watching a large family greet a returning couple at the local airport with flowers and unrestrained embraces. He spoke of love and authenticity, and observed, with endearing earnestness, that he was 'on the seventh green of life'.

Not for Kaymer the usual regimented recital of swing thoughts and summaries of prevailing conditions. He is a man of light and shade, combining traditional Teutonic reverence for efficiency with a thirst for adventure that led to him breaking three bones in his left foot in a go-karting accident in his adopted home town of Scottsdale, Arizona.

He seeks enlightenment through experience, and agrees to an extended conversation because he hopes he will glean something new from the lessons of a stranger's life in sport. He is thirty-four and has won more than £22 million in official prize money, a sum that can comfortably be doubled when external earnings are taken into account, yet acts as if both numbers are irrelevant.

Kaymer's thought processes are clearly as broad as his shoulders. So why, in metaphysical terms, has he yet to complete life's front nine? A slow smile: 'You need some time to get to know and place yourself in the world of golf. In the beginning you can't know, you have zero experience. Then you play around the world and measure your game with the best.

'Then you see good results and, in my case, underestimate yourself a little. All of a sudden you win a major, you play a vital role in Ryder Cups, you win your second major. Then you need to adjust, because it's sometimes overwhelming and not understandable. It cannot only be talent. You need to ask yourself how you actually got here.

'If we are talking the language of Buddhism, it's really about the happiness of the journey. I know this from experience. When I was number one in the world, it took me such a long time to understand why that feeling was so empty. There was so little satisfaction it felt meaningless. I had never felt so lonely.

'About a year and a half later I realised I was not proud of reaching number one, but I was so proud and happy about what I had done to get there. Those very private and intimate moments you have with the sport, developing and creating on your own, that's the beauty of what we do. The success is just the outcome.

'Of course that matters. We all need success for our egos. But for motivation to continue, you need some reflection. To become better, you need a vision of what is right for you. Sometimes that vision is a bit cloudy, so you need some people – not too many, but one or two – who will open the door a little bit for you.

'Fortunately I've always been brave enough to walk through that door, because it felt right. You almost don't have a choice, because you're committed. You know this is the way, and it always leads to success. It's just a question, then, of timescales. You need to be patient. And you need to be conscious of what you are doing, and where you want to go. It is good suffering.'

Belief is the bedrock of professional sport. It took inordinate faith for Kaymer to challenge convention when he missed the cut in his first four appearances at the Masters. More than seven years later, he is still being asked why he resolved to reconstitute his swing, despite being ranked as the best golfer on the planet.

Others with less equitable temperaments would have snapped, screamed or yawned in theatrical boredom when the question was posed by a Swedish TV reporter who seemed unaware of his lack of originality. Kaymer has come to loathe that line of enquiry, but patiently contextualised his determination to master a right-to-left draw shot, deemed essential at Augusta.

'I'm still amazed that people say I changed my swing,' he said, in a firm, even tone. 'I was not able to hit a draw because of my swing plane, so it was a matter of adjusting a few things. The way I played, I never had the chance to win the Masters. In 2011 I was number one in the world and went to Augusta knowing I can't play the golf course the way it is supposed to be played.

'People say that Jack Nicklaus won there with a fade. Yes, but there were not that many trees, they were not so high, the course was shorter. I had a huge disadvantage and I could not live with that knowledge. You need other goals, other visions. If you don't have goals, you're just swimming around and you don't go anywhere. I'm glad I took that chance, even though I got criticised.'

It is difficult to detect the aggression that made him a sought-after centre forward in youth football in Düsseldorf in his mid-teens. He has inherited his late mother Rina's gentility, poignantly expressed by the sunflower he carries on his golf bag as an act of remembrance of her passing, in 2008, from cancer. His father, Horst, had an accountant's fondness for order, and disciplinarian rigour.

Martin was nine when he and elder brother Philip were enrolled at the golf club in Mettmann, Germany's most heavily populated rural district. It is a distinctive institution, which stages quarterly art exhibitions and celebrates the 'fascination and tension' of bridge every Wednesday afternoon. Rina Kaymer was uncomfortable with the inevitable sibling rivalry, but Horst encouraged competition.

He preached practice with a purpose. His sons were made to use the back tees. They were not allowed to use tee pegs until they played in a tournament, because the game would feel easier when it mattered most. When they faced each other in the final of the club's junior championship, Martin four-putted the last green, to hand victory to his brother. No one was entirely sure of his intentions; he compensated by winning the club's senior title at the age of fourteen.

Self-sufficiency was a feature of his emergence on Germany's third-tier tour, where he played every practice round on his own because 'there was so much bullshit being spoken'. He told the European Tour's podcast that he 'felt I didn't belong' when paired with Lee Westwood and Pádraig Harrington on his debut in Hong Kong, but became the first German to be named Rookie of the Year in 2007.

His victory on home soil the following year, at the BMW International in Munich, was a rite of passage, personally and professionally. Aware that his mother had little time left, Martin squandered a six-stroke lead in the opening eleven holes of the final round, before rallying to beat Anders Hansen in a play-off. He deliberated publicly on the power of the mind and dedicated the win to Rina, before dashing to her bedside.

The family unit became a place of certainty and sanctuary when fame engulfed him, since 'the only people who treated me the same were my dad, my brother and my coach'. His status as a major champion led to him being stalked in the street; fans and local media laid siege to the family home. When 'people who once changed my diapers' craved souvenir photographs, he knew he had to recalibrate.

'People say you should not change when you become successful, but you have to. It just depends on how. I never understood why people treated me the way they did. They saw me as some-one else. That's weird. It's hard to describe, but you have to make a mental adjustment to who you are, what you do, what kind of life you live.

'People see you not for who you are as a person, but as the athlete, the guy who makes a lot of money. I didn't want to be treated that way, because I was raised differently and wanted to be normal. It took me a long time to understand you are not normal when you do what I did. That's the tricky part.

'With friendships, you need to look out for the real person. Say you go into a love relationship with a girl. It takes a long, long time to trust that person, and it depends on the little things they do and say. I became careful. It doesn't mean that a relationship means two different lives, but you need respect and distance. That's the best way: give each other room and get to know each other on the same level.

'Golf defines me in some ways, for sure, because I have a lot of passion for the sport and I really love what I do, but ultimately it should not dictate how you feel about life. If you narrow your-self down, it adds a lot of pressure – not always consciously, but subconsciously. I've always thought when you are happy off the golf course, you will do better on it.

'You need to see the bigger picture in order to be okay with yourself. Don't make your success related to your happiness. For-tunately, when I have a bad round, or a bad tournament, I don't carry it with me. I understand that we just play a game. It is important to appreciate how unimportant golf can be.'

There's a process of intellectual osmosis going on here, as we sit on stools across a small white circular table. Martin's com-ments suggest a spiritual affinity with ancient-Greek philosophers whose emotions were linked to belief systems and interpretation of the world around them. Epictetus, a liberated first-century slave, suggested that 'men are disturbed not by events but by their opinion about events'. Seneca wrote: 'What is the point of drag-ging up sufferings that are over, of being miserable now, because you were miserable then?' And Socrates tried to educate his fel-low Athenians to ask themselves pertinent questions. Good luck trying that on the modern golf circuit, because too many players would be scared by the starkness of the answers.

At Kaymer's elevated level, dislocation is literal and meta-phorical. He spends only twelve weeks a year at home, either in Mettmann or, more usually, Scottsdale. A product of a globally focused lifestyle, he admits to feeling only '50–50' German, in a cultural sense. Some players never come to terms with the soli-tude and the contradictions of being constantly on the move.

'I haven't understood the life yet. Fortunately and unfortu-nately, I'm that guy who is sensitive to certain circumstances. I try to make sense out of many things, but I've also learned that some things are not meant to be understood. I keep having to remind myself to just go with the flow.

'It's a very complicated life, especially with social media and the superficial world that we live in – the circus. I try to stay away from it, but I can't because I'm in it. So somehow you need to find a way to take it as neutral, something that doesn't bother you, or affect you in a negative way. This, I haven't really found yet, but I'm actually quite fine with myself.

'You see people and think, "Why are they so happy? Why don't they have issues, problems in life?" It's human nature to under-estimate how well you handle things and, as an athlete, you are conditioned to improve. Sometimes you never enjoy what you have created because you are already onto your next journey.

'That's what I did wrong. I never, ever celebrated a win, so I didn't know how good certain wins were. That might be healthy for your career, but not for your own satisfaction. I know my approach needs to be to finish one thing, relax and then start again. You have to see it for what it is, and not see it so seriously.

'I got asked on a TV show how I felt as a kid when other guys went out on the weekends and I went to the golf course. I didn't want to do anything else. For me, that was my happiness. Get up in the morning when it's snowing outside, and you go to the driving range? I never had to ask myself that question. That's the beauty, a great indication you are doing the right thing.

'Don't over-think it. Golf is a game of variables and we try to over-prepare, try to be ready for every circumstance. Eighty per cent of the guys playing here this week can win, if we take their brain out. Maybe only ten per cent can win with their brain intact. That's just how it is. It is part of the sport.

'We play the tournament until Sunday. Then everything is going to be gone, and nobody gives a shit about anyone. There's the tournament in Prague next week, and the same thing happens then. There is so much for me in enjoying the little things that come with it. You know, this chat that we have now is quite good. I like it because I have to think a lot.'

Elite athletes are intrigued by the principles, philosophies and personalities of successful figures in other sports. Kaymer's curiosity extends to a study of body language – an appreciation of the fusion of physical and mental energy. His favourite place for people-watching is Wimbledon, a venue synonymous with a principal role model, Roger Federer.

'I guess you look for something, but not consciously. Tennis is so similar to golf, because they are always one hundred per cent committed on the shots. There is a lot of fight, a concentration of mental strength. You can learn a lot from tennis players about not holding back. That's one of the greatest things in sport, when you fully commit and get to your highest potential.

'You don't become a great player without confidence, but sometimes you get distracted by outside circumstances and forget why you actually do what you do. You lose a bit of passion, your confidence goes down because you are not as successful, and you are trapped in a spiral. Watching the best at their best is inspiring, because it reminds you a little bit of where you come from.

'When you look back to when you were a child, why and how you played the sport, you didn't think it was difficult. It was not complicated, because you enjoyed it. You just played the game. You didn't try to control the game. But when we grow older, we want to control, because we are scared of losing. We are not born with fear. We are born with happiness. We learn the other shit that really distracts us from reaching ultimate success.'

He admires Federer's family values and his grace under pressure. He retains focus on Michael Schumacher's achievements, while remaining moved by his plight. He respects German basketballer Dirk Nowitzki for the strength of will it took to travel to the United States with $800 to his name, enter the NBA draft and forge a storied twenty-year NBA career with Dallas Mavericks.

Outside sport, he regards actor Will Smith as 'incredible'. Kaymer identifies with his spirituality and urgency, his 'full-on approach to life'. Closer to home, in golf, he cites Thomas Bjørn and Günther Kessler, his coach for the past eighteen years, as important influences. Bjørn's impact has been practical, helping to improve his short game, but also philosophical; the Dane's reflection during a practice round in Italy in 2015 – 'Don't forget how good you are' – has stayed with him.

Intriguingly, Kaymer disagrees with Bjørn by insisting that he responded to the diverse cultures of a Ryder Cup team room. The arch-individualist found solace in the honesty required to fulfil collective ambition and goes so far as acknowledging, 'I didn't know until I got to the Ryder Cup that individual sport is not really me.'

Epiphany shines from his hazel eyes as he leans forward in an attempt to amplify the point: 'It was a relief to know finally that this is what I like the most. You are playing in the same team as your opponent. You need to talk to that guy – your partner – about your weaknesses, to see if they match his strengths.

'You play the golf course a bit differently and need to be very open. I found I didn't mind my weaknesses, because I had enough confidence in my strengths. That was huge for me. It's not usually your place to help each other. If you are really honest, you see guys struggle on Tour, know what they are going through, but do nothing to help because no one is helping you. You have to figure out your own stuff.'

He views Medinah as a dream sequence. Since 'everything was moving so fast', he consciously paused for ten seconds on the final tee of his match against Steve Stricker. He was puzzled, momentarily, by the memory of high-fiving an indeterminate figure on leaving the previous green (it turned out to be Graeme McDowell).

He aimed his drive at a stripe on the fairway, cut into the grain, but found a bunker. Assured by Connelly that his second shot was a 'perfect' eight-iron, he used the wind, coming off his right, to hit a high draw, the shot he drove himself to master, past the flag. His senses were scrambled; the crowd was a blur of humanity, yet he spotted his brother, standing out in an abstract confection of colour.

Clarity – he felt as if he could identify individual blades of grass, though he was slightly misaligned, on the approach putt – was replaced by certainty. It 'never crossed my mind' that he would miss the decisive putt, uphill and right-to-left. He knew it was in, two feet from the hole, exulted and spun round to leap into the arms of another indeterminate figure, which turned out to be Sergio García.

'It was all up to me,' he remembers, wistfully. 'I mean, how cool was that? I wanted the ultimate feeling. There are so many feelings in that moment. Eventually you realise you are so tired. You are done physically. I didn't watch it until two weeks later, at home in Düsseldorf. I was more nervous then than when I was playing, and I knew how it would end. Crazy.'

Walking through the fire has not insulated him from the vagaries of form or fate over six subsequent years, but he draws strength from his purity of purpose. Kaymer has assembled a seven-strong support team, including his brother, who acts as his manager. Trust and respect must be mutual, though the golfer's devotion to Kessler, who first coached him in a regional junior team, is touching.

'He is a guy who explains difficult things very simply. He can explain the same thing in ten different ways. One way works for you and one way works for me, and he is very talented in knowing what that individual needs. That's why we don't need to speak much, because he trained me and developed my swing so that I can help myself most of the time.

'We don't see each other often, maybe ten, twelve times a year, and that's enough. I wish he would speak good English, so that people could understand and know how good he is. I really value the knowledge, not only of the golf swing, but also of the science behind the body. My sport has become so intense, because of the travel, that it is sometimes nice to be used as a tool, and not to think about things.

'When I go to the gym, I like to have a trainer who takes my body and just uses it for an hour, before letting me go. It clears out my mind. Fortunately, we make enough money to pay people to make us perform even better. The game has changed. Courses are set up differently; it's a lot about hitting the long ball. I still play an old-school game, and need to change my body to compete on a daily or weekly basis with the best.'

He employs a strength-and-conditioning coach, but studies basic biomechanical programmes to enhance his understanding of the logic of developing muscular speed and core strength in his legs and backside. When he arrives on the eighteenth green of life, to use his analogy, he would 'love to have a couple more major wins, just for my ego. We all have one – some bigger, some smaller.'

He is already forty minutes late for his next appointment, but happily accepts a final question: how would he describe himself? Kaymer instinctively furrows his brow, like a schoolboy studying a newly presented examination paper: 'I would like to say I was brave enough to keep developing, that I didn't stick to one safe way.

'I'm a very reflecting person, calm, sometimes sickeningly determined. That can be good for the sport, but in other things not quite so good. I'm quite radical in certain ways. I suppose I would like to know how others see me. That's very interesting, because they always see you very differently to how you see yourself.'

I tell him I regard him as a seeker, a searcher for truth that may never be revealed.

'Is that a good thing?'

'I think so. In your game it is. You're seeking perfection, which never comes.'

'Yeah, because why does Tiger Woods want to win eighteen majors? He becomes the greatest, so he goes for the absolute maximum. Does it mean he's perfect when he wins nineteen? Probably not. You need to go high, very high, almost to the point where you think, "It's too much, I'm not going to make it." I reached that height, and thought, "Shit, that's too early. I'm not supposed to be number one in the world when I'm twenty-five years old." But I was, and there was a bit of a problem . . .'

Chapter Two

CHASING RAINBOWS

It was the equivalent of employing a poet as a bodyguard. Thomas Bjørn sensed he needed someone to protect him from himself, and so he appointed Robert Karlsson as the first of his five vice-captains, sixteen months out from the Ryder Cup matches in Paris. Intelligent, sensitive, quietly determined and deep-thinking, the Swede set the tone of the European team room.

At the age of forty-nine, and in his thirtieth season on Tour, Karlsson had, by his own admission, been playing 'really poorly' for seven years. He was dealing with the fear of competitive insignificance and, sustained by sporadic stellar rounds, methadone shots that eased him through his addiction to a game in which 'you create misery for yourself'.

No one had a better grasp of life on the road, and the psyche of the modern golfer. Tall, athletic and looking a decade younger than his age, he was in his element in yet another bland, white-canvassed players' lounge, constructed behind the final green on the links at Ballyliffin, in towering sand dunes on the north-western tip of County Donegal.

The last of his eleven tour wins came in the Dubai World Championship in 2010. 'I can kind of sniff it sometimes, and I want more of it,' Karlsson said, looking through a picture window towards Tullagh Bay on the Atlantic coast of the Inishowen Peninsula. 'At the moment I'm going through some really, really tough times. I like playing, though not all the time, and I still love the challenge.

'Golf is almost like a miniature life. If you're good enough, and learn to know yourself, you can create serenity. If you let your mind rush, you can create hell. It doesn't matter how well you are playing, you're going to miss some shots, get the odd bad break and the odd good break. For me, the guys who win tournaments are the ones who handle that best.

'I see plenty of players on the range with great technique. Everything looks perfect. But if he is not emotionally stable, he's not going to be able to use that technique out on the course. He's going to have to deal with different lies, the wind in his face, different circumstances. How does he handle what is happening to him, so that he can use his tools? The more in harmony he is as a person, the easier it will be.

'When I had the best period of my career, between 2006 and 2008, outside things didn't disturb me. I learned that it doesn't matter if the plane is late, or the baggage isn't coming, or there's a queue on the way into the golf course, or if I hit the ball into the water hazard. I can't do a thing about it, but if I allow myself to be pissed off, and caught up in it, I'll keep spinning and spinning and spinning.

'It's all about self-worth. How much do you love yourself? How much do you love everything that is around you, even when the weather is crap? How do you relate to your so-called luck, when the rest of the field has had a nice calm morning and you're stood on the first tee in a thirty-mile-an-hour wind with hail? It's not about being calm, or dead inside. It's about being content.'

Temporarily lost in thought, Karlsson pushes a solitary poached egg around his breakfast plate, slicing it laterally before spreading it onto a bread roll. He remains receptive to a deeper analysis of adversity, but the brief pause prompts a mental image of Bjørn, explaining himself to me with trademark deliberation.

'I needed somebody that would tell me the truth about me,' he had said the day before. 'Robert might not necessarily say it when everyone is there, but he will take me aside, look at me with those eyes, and go "This is what I see. You're pissing into the wind. Take a step back and make sure you have covered everything, because this train is running at two hundred miles an hour. Don't rush it."'

Karlsson laughs when I pass on the compliment: 'He told me, "You're strong enough to hold me back when I'm about to say something stupid to the press, because I can be emotional." That's true. I'm pretty good at reading that. He might have thrown in a few "Fucks", but he also said I was the least annoying person he knew. I'll take that.'

Karlsson's search for perspective took him to the village of Vuollerim, just south of the Arctic Circle in Swedish Lapland. Home to 800, it is situated at the confluence of the Lule rivers and is known, in the local dialect, as 'the place where everything and everyone meets'. Surrounding forests and cloudberry marshes, populated by the indigenous Sami people, have featured in human settlements for 6,000 years.

In the midst of the second existential crisis of his career, at the end of the 2004 season, when 'I kept my card, but only just', he met Annchristine Lundström, an entrepreneur who had rebalanced her life in the mid-Nineties. Director of a so-called 'Reality Center' operated by the SVC Foundation, she espoused an experience-based approach to personal development, to which Karlsson immediately related.

She promotes separation 'of the issue and the individual', in an egalitarian programme that seeks 'to increase awareness of the weight of our individual choices'. The aim is to build 'on

openness, reflection, awareness and a constant growth by learning from the different situations in life'. Peace of mind is the-
oretically created by taking responsibility for your own thoughts,
words and actions.

Lundström argues: 'As long as you judge and point a finger at
others, nothing gets resolved. You will continue on a path of
ingrained patterns, familiar habits and the same old playing of
games. However, when you choose to go down another road and
change your approach and attitude, and consciously work on getting rid of judging yourself and others, life will get fun. You will
find yourself on a comfortable course, working well with both
yourself and your surroundings. '

Karlsson acknowledges, 'She took me to another level of thinking, where you see everything as part of a learning process. Whatever happens, how do you relate to outside stimuli? How do you
relate to what is happening around you? A sports psychologist
might have different words and different angles, but at the end of
the day it is pretty much common sense.

'Say you have a three-year-old who spills his milk. If you're
really pissed off with him, you know that next time he goes to
drink he is going to be afraid, and he'll probably do it again. It is
the same in golf. If you beat yourself up really badly when you're
on a bad run, you're not going to feel very comfortable standing
on the first tee the next time you're out there.'

He began accumulating scar tissue in 1996, when he made
only five cuts in nineteen tournaments and 'borderline couldn't
play'. He remembers standing on the first tee at Druids Glen in
the Irish Open, when 'The fairway suddenly disappeared. Whatever I did, my ball was too big to fit on it.' He traced his problem
to the previous year, when an early win in Spain and a third-place
finish in Morocco installed him as Europe's number one.

'It didn't mean very much, because the big players at the time
– Faldo, Woosnam and the rest – were playing in the US, but I

got sucked into the money list and forgot what I'd done to get there. I was chasing rainbows, chasing money and rankings, and it drove me insane. Everything was mental. I had the wrong attitude, the wrong focus.'

Any professional golfer with a long-term career learns to cope with the game's inevitable peaks and troughs. Karlsson looked around the European team room at Le Golf National and identified fellow survivors. Henrik Stenson, his friend and fellow Swede, had dark moments during two slumps in form. Paul Casey had come through a sustained struggle.

Karlsson identified most closely with Sergio García because he, too, had gone through the visceral experience of suffering from full-swing yips. Golf's greatest terror essentially involves being stuck in the address position, unable to draw the club back because of what Karlsson describes as 'brain freeze'. In layman's terms, he couldn't pull the trigger.

Something so natural, supposedly ingrained since childhood, becomes artificial to the point of perceived impossibility. It is the sort of neurological dysfunction, more usually identified with the putting stroke, that can end careers. Little wonder that 'yips' is regarded as the game's most vile four-letter word. It has the same effect on golfers as 'Macbeth' does on actors.

'I really don't like that word, because so many people think so many things about it,' Karlsson admits, bracing himself for an extended explanation of his decision to withdraw, less than twenty-four hours before the 2012 Open Championship at Royal Lytham & St Annes. It had taken him more than a minute to hit the ball after addressing it on the first tee in an initial practice round that lasted two holes. He returned the following day and managed seven holes before walking off the course in despair.

Anxiety, which began to build at the US Open a fortnight previously, where he finished with three successive bogeys and 'took two minutes to get the club away', consumed him. Karlsson then consulted Lundström, recalibrated his personal life and took four months to rediscover his confidence. He began by convincing himself it didn't matter if he missed the ball when he chipped it off the tee.

'Without sounding too much like Churchill, the battle was won, but the war was lost. I got through the US Open, but it was just too painful to deal with. Gradually, the picture became clearer. It was like, "This is something I have created." Annchristine and I sat down and talked about all the fears, the thoughts connected to it.

'This was not the yips, because when you have the yips you can't do anything about it. This was something that, unconsciously, was my own doing. It was cumulative. I felt I was playing worse, I didn't like the situation, and there were things outside of the golf course that were bothering me. I was stood in the rain thinking, "I'm hitting it rubbish."

'I'm taking new balls, thinking, "How am I going to hit this one?" I started standing over the ball, taking decisions, instead of making them behind the ball. That's how it started, being unclear. I'm not doing a good routine, the routine gets worse, one thing leads to another, and I'm wondering if I will ever play this game again. It's a spiral.

'I talked to Sergio. His problem was that he didn't know where to put his thumb on the club. It didn't feel right, so he changed its position, constantly. There was no place that it was good. He had to create that place, so he taped his thumb to the club. He told me it didn't matter if he hit five thousand shanks from the tee peg, or if he missed the ball five thousand times, that thumb had to know its place.

'I related to that. I had a very long routine over the ball, which was a big problem because I never felt ready. It was almost like when you go to catch a train. You stand on the platform, the train comes, the door opens and you think, "Oh, I should go in now, otherwise the door will close. Oh crap, the door closed, the train has gone. I have to start again to wait for the next train." I went through that same cycle of concentration and frustration.'

Empathy is painfully acquired, and not usually expressed until it is too late. Karlsson attempts to convince young players not to make golf their world, but admits, 'It's a hard sell, because it is like telling a fish, "Get out of the water, you'll be fine." It's painful when you are around people who are playing well when you are playing poorly, because it reminds you of your own failure.'

Occasionally, sympathy mutates into alarm. He recalls, with brutal clarity, the plight of an Asian player with whom he once shared a management company: 'He hadn't made a bean in two years, was playing with injuries and had a very complicated relationship with his parents. We get to the fifteenth at Wentworth, and he is on his way to shooting eighty-seven.

'He drives the ball a hundred yards, straight through the bushes and into a car. One of the guys in our group whispered, "Just take him out. He is destroying himself." You know when someone is really struggling. You can see it in the way they walk, the way they spend a long time over the ball, but when they hit such a bad shot that it is off the planet, you know there is something else going on.'

That player has disappeared into a vortex of confusion and self-loathing. Karlsson's wider value to the Ryder Cup team lay in his ability to combine experience, intuition and an analytical approach to what is an emotionally intense game. Recognising this, Bjørn gave him the additional responsibility of being the bridge to the statistical support team, led by Blake Wooster and Duncan Carey.

Wooster heads up 15th Club, an analytics company that operates similarly in football, where they advise clubs on managerial and player recruitment. The aim is 'to apply intelligence and context to performance data'. Their advisory services are used independently by around thirty players, including Rory McIlroy, Thorbjørn Olesen and Danny Willett, who used personalised performance software, in conjunction with his caddie Jonathan Smart, in winning the Masters in 2016.

Golf's analytical revolution, similar to that prompted by Bill James and popularised by Billy Beane in baseball, satisfies the traditional priority of a professional athlete: it shows them the money. It was inspired by Mark Broadie, a Professor of Business at Columbia Business School, who questioned conventional measurements of efficiency, such as greens in regulation and putts per round, through analysis of 4,000,000 shots on the PGA Tour between 2003 and 2012.

Wooster warns against regarding analytics as a 'silver bullet', but research has shown that if a professional golfer is able to reduce his score by an average of half a stroke per round, his earning potential will increase by 73 per cent. Such statistical probability gets people's attention, and although it is not directly relevant to the Ryder Cup, where players are unpaid, the general principle applies.

'Broadie taught us there was a better way of measuring the game,' Wooster explained. 'That's infiltrated a lot of the work we do. Irrespective of the data, it comes down to decision-making. I would rather have a team of smart decision-makers using simple data. We've had great interactions with the likes of Robert, the other vice-captains and Thomas, who leaves no stone unturned and knows when to say no, and how far to go with it.

'We try to give them the confidence to make brave decisions based on research, but know we are just another voice in the room. We don't have the experience of a Robert, a GMac, Luke or Westie. Historically, in sport, there has always been this kind of tension between gut feeling and data, but its bollocks, really. Conflicted opinions are fine, but in any good team culture in a high-performance environment people understand there's another perspective.'

Karlsson, who oversaw an informal exchange of information on a WhatsApp group that included Bjørn's closest advisers and senior members of Wooster's team, was intrigued, though he quickly realised the limitations: 'The sample size is small, and numbers are going to be taken in an environment that has nothing to do with the Ryder Cup. Numbers can be your guide, not the be-all and end-all.'

Analysis of Cup matches from 1999 onwards identified two of the worst-performing groups as players ranked above forty-five in the world and those ranked between one and five in the world. The former was logical, and the latter was skewed principally by the inability of Tiger Woods to respond to team competition, but it provided food for thought. Calculations are multi-layered and nuanced. The 15th Club utilises a metric called 'performance indexing', a more accurate indication of form.

Wooster clarified, 'Like a League table in football, the world rankings in golf can give you a distorted view. Say someone wins in a play-off. He gets a disproportionate amount of points compared to the guy who comes second, who may have been beaten by a bad bounce or the spin of the ball. We can calculate his underlying performance, which is predictive of what he may do in the future.

'On Tour, our role is not just around the performance piece. It's also about trying to encourage them to keep calm. Much like a football club will sack their manager after a couple of bad defeats, a golfer is inclined to sack his coach or caddic on the back of a couple of bad performances. There's a kind of blame culture. They immediately think something needs to change. A lot of the time our job is to peel things back, look a bit deeper than the result.'

The 15th Club developed a projection model for the Ryder Cup, early in the selection process, to calculate the eight players who would qualify for the team automatically. They had advised Bjørn to press for four wild-card picks, and assessed the relative merits and real-time form of potential candidates. Presented in a dashboard format, this was based on an algorithm that took into account accumulation of qualifying points, specific performance data and scheduling plans.

It was augmented by password-protected personal information, entailing family backgrounds and personal preferences. Planning tools, based on course characteristics and inclinations of performance, allowed the team to run scenario-planning for specific partnerships. Inevitably, in such an individual sport, there were distinctive levels of buy-in from the players.

The most receptive group were open-minded, detail-oriented individuals who had typically grown up with the trappings of new technology. The outlier, given his age (forty-two) and his exhibitionist streak, was Ian Poulter, who complemented his passion for the event with natural curiosity and a desire to delve into the minutiae of his craft.

Jon Rahm, Spanish by birth but a creation of the US college system, typified a second group: instinctive 'feel' players, who were not necessarily as hungry for information, but acceded to the wishes of their caddie or coach to study the data. A minority preferred to remain true to their normal preparatory rituals.

Athletes are not inanimate objects, products of a cold, impersonal process of discovery and development. They have their faults and foibles, and tend to reflect their working environment. Perhaps it was a result of proximity to a man of Karlsson's inquisitiveness and sensitivity, but Wooster grew to appreciate golf's human dimension.

'It's a very long and very lonely season. Unless they miss the cut, the guys are typically playing from Tuesday, when they tend to arrive at an event, to Sunday, and travelling on the Monday. They're spending at least half of their lives in hotel rooms, speaking to their wife and kids at home, or being sat there on their computer.

'It seems they don't spend that much time with their caddies, outside the course, so the caddie is probably equally as lonely. There's a weird class-divide thing going on. This certainly isn't my language, but I've heard caddies referred to as "the rats". Some of the players also suffer from a weird kind of tension between having to focus on their golf and their families.

'They're struggling to get the balance right between bringing the family on the journey, because they're not seeing them, and having them around. When the kids are there, and crying, there's a conflict because the player feels unable to focus on his performance and he probably plays worse than when they are not around.'

This is straying into unspoken territory, highlighting uncomfortable truths that are usually suppressed. Karlsson is sufficiently worldly and well adjusted to appreciate such candour, since it poses an implicit challenge to the individual and highlights the central challenge of a player owning his own reality.

'Everybody has bad results. Henrik [Stenson] is a pretty good gold player, but he's been through the deepest of lows a couple of times. Look at Westwood – he was pretty awful for a while. Look at Tiger. Everybody is going through these sorts of things, but if you are afraid of it and don't tell the truth to handle it, you don't really want to face it. Then you have a problem. You're more likely to disappear.

'But if you have a support system, or other players, or you have someone to talk to and understand it, and if you're maybe strong enough and clever enough to open up, it's no big thing. Look how many people are going through tough times in life. How many people are getting divorced? It's happening all the time, and

we're not immune to that, far from it, because we expose ourselves to the worst of the worst all the time.

'I mean, we are right there on the edge every week, trying our
best. Everyone who goes out on the first tee is exposing themselves, almost like they are onstage at a rock concert. You are
playing with your heart and your soul. In normal life you can get
by not exposing yourself fully, but if we are going to do any good,
we'd better be fully committed. That's our normality. We become
a bit weird to live with, sometimes. I've been told that,
frequently . . .'

Karlsson laughs easily at himself – a natural protection mechanism honed over many years and more than 600 tournaments.
He questions himself regularly, reads widely and reappraises
what 'makes me tick'. He consciously seeks what he refers to as
'calmness under focus, and under pressure'. It is often a question
of perspective.

'You never, or very rarely, hear a good athlete say they are
nervous. They are always excited. Same thing, but different
words, different meaning. During that excitement you know
that you will snap if you take one wrong step, so you are so
much more aware. When awareness is high, keeping serenity,
focus and all those good things, you're going to be better at
what you do.

'Nothing should bother you. It should be normal, like the drive
to work on a Wednesday morning in the middle of October. In
the beginning, the buzz is to become better, result-wise. When
you win your first tournament it is a huge buzz, the second a
little less, the third even less. When I hear a guy saying, "When I
win one tournament, everything is going to be good", I'm thinking, "Oh dear, you've got a long way to go."'

His search for contentment is both mental and literal. He
retreats to a small summerhouse in Porjus, a village in Swedish
Lapland whose population increased by fifteen, to 343, in the five

years leading up to the last census, in 2015. It represents civilisa-
tion's last gesture before entry to a UNESCO World Heritage
Site that features four national parks.

The local hydroelectric power plant, built principally to service
a railway that shipped iron ore a century previously, has become
a museum, an unlikely tourist attraction alongside a gallery
renowned for its collection of photographs of the aurora borealis.
But Karlsson gravitates to a unique nine-hole golf course, which
incorporates the Lule river and runs alongside a dam.

He is caught in the moment, transported from an unseason-
ably warm morning in Ireland to a place where his mind is as
clear as the Arctic air. 'If I can walk up the ninth hole there, feeling calm, quiet and content, with the peace of mind I imagine
I'd have if I was walking up the eighteenth hole at Augusta with
a one-shot lead, then I have succeeded. I will have found what
I'm looking for.'

His best performance in six appearances in the Masters was
tied eighth in 2008, the year he became the first Swede to win the
European Tour Order of Merit, so the Augusta experience is
strictly theoretical. He came closest to his perception of perfection in the Ryder Cup at Valhalla Golf Club in Louisville, Kentucky, that September, when he made six birdies on the back nine
in partnership with Henrik Stenson.

Karlsson speaks slowly, with an audible sense of wonder. 'We
are the last game of the day, behind and chasing. The eighteenth
is a par-five uphill. I hit my second shot from two hundred and
thirty yards and think, "That is perfect." I look up and the ball is
straight at the flag. It almost looks as if it goes in. It disappears,
because of the contours of the green, and then starts to roll back
from a bank.

'Everyone was there. Our whole team was behind us. There
were thirty thousand people around the hole. As I walked up,
through the shadows of the fairways, with the crowds all around,

it was like, "Yeah, I've found golf nirvana." That split second was an unbelievable experience – my strongest memory in golf.'

Karlsson feathered his eagle putt, from ten feet, but missed to the left. He holed the return, so their fourball against Hunter Mahan and Phil Mickelson was halved. Europe went on to be comprehensively beaten, under the disruptive captaincy of Nick Faldo, 16½–11½. In golf, you don't tend to get what you want. You must find beauty amidst the beastliness.

Chapter Three

CARELESS WHISPERS

'*Hey. Look at that ocean on the left-hand side. Isn't that great?*'
'*Be quiet.*'
'*Imagine what it would be like to hook that ball into the ocean
and make seven.*'
'*You're unbelievable.*'
'*Just think what it would be like to lose the US Open.*'
'*You are really illogical and very silly.*'
'*They'll say you couldn't get it done. You couldn't win your first major.*'
'*I know how to deal with you. My questions are my answers.*'

Millions were watching Graeme McDowell, unaware of the
intensity of the internal struggle being conducted as he prepared to play the most important shot of his life, a drive down
the sweeping left-to-right eighteenth fairway at Pebble Beach
on the Monterey peninsula in California. The rugged splendour
of the Pacific coastline belied the threat posed to a childhood
fantasy.

He led, on the seventy-second hole of the 2010 US Open, by
a single stroke. Tiger Woods, Phil Mickelson and Ernie Els, legends based on the collective accumulation of twenty-three major
championships, had fallen spectacularly away. Ahead, on a green

guarded by a 100-yard bunker, Frenchman Grégory Havret had an eight-foot birdie putt to tie.

McDowell had to think clearly and take the correct decision under unaccustomed pressure, the essence of elite sport. He had to hit his ball as close to the water as he dared, because aiming it to the right, away from obvious trouble, exposed him to possible entrapment in the trees. But he had, first of all, to conquer himself.

'That inner voice is incredible,' he says, in an unmistakable accent that hovers between Northern Ireland and Naples, Florida, as eight years are melted by memory of the moment. 'My mechanics – and it is a mechanical process, because it is a learned technique – involve laughing at it, telling it that it is ridiculous and replacing it with the question "What am I trying to do with this shot?" The question is the answer.

'There's my target. There's my shape. There's my swing rehearsal. Now let's get over the ball and do what it is we're trying to do, because the inner voice will tell you what you're trying not to do. That's any given shot, any given day. We're no different from amateur golfers; we see trouble, we see badness, we can hit bad shots. Being able to acknowledge that voice, put it in the bin and replace it with good information has always been very effective.

'It doesn't always happen, of course. Sometimes, when I attempt to get him to shut up or laugh at him, he gets louder. Right before you're about to pull the club away, or in the middle of your backswing, there he comes again. Being able to fill your mind is a big thing, especially in your pre-shot routine, because this sport is very complex.'

Yet it also has educational symmetry and simplicity. Golf offers current players a glimpse of the game's greats in a way that football, another abiding love, cannot. As a fervent Manchester United fan, McDowell regards Sir Bobby Charlton, at eighty-one, as an iconic but inevitably historic figure; Jack Nicklaus, at seventy-nine, retains greater relevance as a contemporary example of excellence.

'I remember watching Nicklaus on the range. It was just the way he stood over the ball and looked up at the target with an intense focus. He spent two seconds longer sizing it up than any other player. The guy who is quicker is more interested in what is happening technically and forgets what the main goal is, which is to hit the target.

'So, because of Jack, I concentrate on what I call quality looks. Our bodies are incredibly instinctive machines, and if we give them target-orientated thoughts, athleticism kicks in and we are very good at reacting. But if we become obsessed with the how, as opposed to the what, things become clouded. If you want to work only on these beautiful mechanics that you have to make the ball do something specific, success will become very sporadic.'

He returns to Pebble Beach for the 2019 US Open as a former champion. Havret missed that birdie putt; McDowell safely negotiated a par five and became the tournament's first British winner since Tony Jacklin in 1970. He was swept up in an embrace on the final green by his father, Kenny, who had introduced him to the game at the age of seven on the par-three course at Portrush.

McDowell was academically adept, gaining three As and a B at A-level. Core competencies in mathematics and physics led to a degree course in mechanical engineering at Queen's University Belfast, held in abeyance after a year and subsequently abandoned when a scholarship at the University of Alabama steered him towards professional golf.

His analytical mind is suited to a game in which the best 'are able to break all the numbers down into a workable, tangible methodology to get better'. He describes the modern player as 'CEO, manager and coach' and oversees a performance support team in a technocratic manner, yet acknowledges human fallibility as a fact of life.

'There is so much more information available to the golfer these days, with regards to performance analysis. A footballer has his heart rate, distance covered, data on how is body is reacting to the loads being put on him, but we have so many metrics, from ball speed to heights, to chipping and putting numbers, driving accuracy, degrees of shoulder rotation, supination and pronation of your wrists, 3-D stuff, statistical analysis and golf-course breakdown.

'There aren't many more complicated games, but I tell young players that resiliency is very, very important. It is not all going to be plain sailing out here, so you have to build your brain to deal with the tough days, learn from them. I made a lot of mistakes when I was young. I'm not talking about hitting a bad seven-iron. I mean playing an event when I wasn't feeling ready, not preparing properly, maybe having a wrong mental approach.

'I made two huge mental mistakes in major championships on the back nine, in the last group on Sunday, both in 2012. At the US Open at Olympic Club I went into the final round tied for the lead with Jim Furyk. It is an interesting feeling, as a competitor, playing alongside a guy and thinking to yourself, "It's this guy's day. Let's just do the best we can. Maybe we can finish second or third."

'It happened again, at the Open Championship at Lytham. Instead of thinking, "I can catch this guy", I could see Adam Scott's name written on the Claret Jug. I had that same feeling of deflation, a feeling I was out of it. He was hitting all the shots, holing all the putts. It wasn't that I'd given up, but I'd lost the edge, and I was trying to get out of there in one piece. Deep down, I was telling myself, "You're the sideshow. He's the winner."'

Yet the self-destructive, disloyal inner voice does not have a monopoly of wisdom. On both occasions, it failed to identify the champion. Furyk who, like McDowell, had the chance to force a play-off with a birdie, bogeyed the final hole to allow Webb Simpson his maiden major title. McDowell parred it to finish runner-up, and went on to implode with a last-round seventy-five at Lytham. Ernie Els, whom he had led on the front nine, profited from Scott's collapse over the last four holes.

McDowell works with two psychologists, Bhrett McCabe in the United States and Karl Morris in the UK. McCabe has a background in clinical psychology, with an emphasis on behavioural medicine, and operates across sports as diverse as baseball, basketball and mixed martial arts. Morris, a self-styled performance enhancement coach, accepts that golf 'has too much thinking time' and teaches clients 'not to make decisions based on high emotion'.

The mental discipline they help to instil enables McDowell to switch back into the moment, following the inevitable lulls in a five-hour round, which he condenses into 'pockets of concentration spanning from thirty seconds to a minute and a half, if I'm doing a little extra analysis of a particularly tough shot'.

He likes to 'shoot the shit a little, engage the crowd, or talk to my playing partner or my caddie' before 'flicking the on-switch'. In a hint of McCabe's influence, he uses a similar trigger to baseball-hitters during a pitching sequence, where they unfasten and fasten the Velcro wristband on their batting glove, before settling in their stance.

'A few of the South Africans – Ernie Els, Louis Oosthuizen and Branden Grace – also do it. When you pull the club out, and engage in your routine to the moment of impact, there's probably only twenty, twenty-five seconds, so fastening the glove is a physical switch-up. Now it's performance time; time get into the zone.

'I feel like once the club leaves the bag, I'm into my bubble of rehearsal, pre-shot mental rehearsal, into impact. Even after that, there's a post-shot review. Was the shot successful, technically, and emotionally? If not, okay, well, why wasn't it successful? Was it misjudgement, a bad swing? What was specifically wrong with the swing? Okay, well, I'm not going to do that again. Let's do this instead. Club goes back in the bag. It's over. Move on. Switch off.

'My most lonely days are when I'm having a bad day on the big stage. My expectation levels have not been matched. The brain is not really communicating with the body, you know? Or maybe I'm thinking well, and the body is just not responding. You're out there for five hours, alone with your thoughts.

'I've had the same caddie, Ken Comboy, for over twelve years now, and I've got better at verbalising my feelings with him. He knows me so well, I'm not sure I could surprise him any more over the things I say. When I was really playing well, in the window between 2008 and 2013, I would write things down in my yardage books. I'd have conversations, along these lines . . .'

A brief and almost imperceptible change came over him. He had been aware of others' presence while we spoke, over the preceding half-hour, in a hospitality lounge overlooking the practice ground at Gullane, the Scottish links on which he was trying to qualify for the following week's Open Championship at Carnoustie.

His eyes had followed familiar figures on the far side of the room, without distraction or causing offence; he had taken delivery of his newly cleaned white golf shoes for the day's pro-am from his manager, and dealt briefly with ticket requests. His voice softened suddenly; it was as if he was lost in the articulation of private thoughts.

'Those conversations went something like this . . .

'I'm leading by two today, but I'm really scared I'm going to lose. I'm scared I'm going to mess this up.

'All right, well, that's a legitimate thought. So let's break that down. What's the worst thing that could happen today? You shoot seventy-five, you lose. You're going to wake up tomorrow morning. You're going to be fine, right? You're not dead. It's not your last chance. There will be more of this – you're playing great.

'Today is not the last opportunity of my life.'

He snapped back into the present: 'Today is just another opportunity. I always liked that one, so I wrote it down. Better than putting the emphasis on "Today is the day. If it doesn't happen it is going to be a disaster." Go and enjoy it. It's one of those clichés. Just go and have fun. Fuck, go and have fun, yeah. Sure. If I shoot sixty-five I'll have fun. If I shoot seventy-five I probably won't.

'What does that mean? Go and have fun? You should go and control what you can control, which is your body language. So I might write that down. "Good body language. Whatever happens, keep your head up, keep your chest out, walk around like you mean it." Then I might write down a couple of swing thoughts that I have for the day.

'You know, "stay smooth", or "pick a great target", or "quality looks" – phrases that have been clicking with me a little bit. I'd pull that yardage book out the following year, and it would be kind of funny to read some of the little notes I sent myself.'

There was a hint of vulnerability, a shimmer of self-doubt. I recalled our initial meeting, in Ireland a week previously, when McDowell had admitted to a lack of confidence and had spoken of 'just looking for that X-factor, belief, getting into the mix and getting the old juices flowing again'. He was insistent that he was 'not up against the clock', but thirty-nine is a symbolically dangerous age for a former champion looking for his mojo. His humility and honesty were impeccably judged.

'It's that little bit of scar tissue that builds up. You see guys that are better than you at the moment. The best players in the world on top form just seem to cruise. You know, you play your best golf when you don't care, when you practise really hard and really intensely and you get on the golf course and let it go. It's hard to do that when you've had three or four years of not playing well.

'You need it too badly. You want it too badly. It matters too much to you. The X-factor, for me, is finding that balance between knowing it matters in the back of my mind and consciously tapping into a carefree nature. I feel like I'm one result away from having a lot of great results, but I can't get that result under my belt. I'm starting to be like my old self again, but still can't get across the line.'

The loss of his PGA Tour card at the end of the 2018 season was manageable, since he retains playing privileges on the European Tour, but his world ranking slid to 218. Luke Donald, his fellow vice-captain at the Ryder Cup in France, was down among the dead men at 491, having endured a six-month absence from the game, rehabilitating a herniated disc in his back.

McDowell was suffering from intermittent discomfort in his wrist at the top of his backswing and on impact with the ball, a common complaint. Donald's problem was of another magnitude. The rotational stresses of the swing, exacerbated by its speed and the repetitive nature of practice, place enormous pressure on the spine, ligaments and soft tissues.

Golf Channel analyst Brandel Chamblee warns about 'turning the body into a time bomb'. Michael Duffy, an orthopaedic surgeon at the Texas Back Institute, where Tiger Woods underwent spinal fusion surgery, has identified a condition known as 'golfer's back'. This tends to afflict the two lowest spinal segments in the lumbar region, referred to as L4–L5 and L5-sacrum (S1).

Sean Foley, Justin Rose's coach, told *GOLF* magazine: 'I won't try to boil it down to a single issue because there's so much going on, and I prefer to take a holistic approach. But with all the money in the game, look at the players you're pulling in. I was on the range the other day, and there's Jon Rahm, Adam Scott, Justin, DJ [Dustin Johnson]. We're talking an average of six foot two. That used be to a linebacker in the NFL. We know that force equals mass times acceleration. All that force these guys are generating, their bodies have to deal with it, too.'

Donald, five feet eight inches in height and a little more than eleven stones in weight, is a light aircraft in an age of Stealth bombers. His fifty-six-week spell as world number one from 2011, when he became the first player simultaneously to win the PGA and European Tour money lists, remains a remarkable testament to the strength of his will and the delicacy and accuracy of his short game.

The mental stresses are onerous. Donald hinted at retirement in an interview with *The Daily Telegraph* in 2015, and workedwith Michael Gervais, the psychologist who assisted Felix Baumgartner, the Austrian skydiver who became the first person to break the sound barrier without vehicular assistance in a twenty-four-mile plunge to Earth from a helium balloon in the stratosphere.

We met at St Andrews, scene of his comeback in October 2018. Donald had the initial PR polish often associated with players more accustomed to the bland country-club customs of American golf, but the nature of our discussion scoured superficiality. It quickly became clear that his inner voice had been active during the recovery process.

'What makes a top player?' he repeated, as we shared a golf buggy on the way to the range behind the Links clubhouse, 'talent, grit, strength of mind and work ethic. Being out gives you a sense of perspective. I enjoyed some time with my family, but at the back of your mind you always want to be out there, having a chance and getting those feelings of being in contention.

'You miss being in that zone, where things happen quickly, everything is a blur and you are just going on instinct, almost operating subconsciously. There is no better feeling for a sports person, and when that is denied to you, the uncertainty can get to you. A lot of things are rattling around in your head.

'Is it going to be good? Am I going to get better? Am I going to play golf again? It is easier to switch into that negative mode. To stay positive, and train that inner voice, takes practice and skill. Hopefully my back will last for a long time and I can win some more tournaments. Is it one hundred per cent? Probably not. Can I cause more damage? The medical advice says no. I need to get a feel for how my body is feeling.

'This is what I have done all my life. I have to have hope. I've seen a lot of guys sliding down the rankings. Poults, Westie and Henrik have all dropped down and come back. They show me what is possible. That gives me motivation to kick on and do the same. You miss the joy of seeing hard work pay off and knowing that, under pressure, you can perform.'

At forty-one, Donald is seventeen months older than McDowell. He retains his boyish, fresh-faced features and is estimated to have a net worth of around £40 million, some £10 million more than the Northern Irishman. Each has the broader perspective of having had two children and adapting to the sort of financial security that can diminish desire.

'My motivations are different, but the desire's still there,' McDowell insisted. 'We make a great living. You create a lifestyle for yourself and want to maintain it. It's such a cliché, but it's not about the money. I was lucky things came easily enough and early enough in my career where I could focus on trying to be the best I could be. I suppose I'm still trying to do that.

'You definitely become more reflective in later years. Why am I out here? Do I want to keep doing this? Do I want to hole six-footers for the next ten years? Hopefully I'll hole a few of them. It's a hard sport, especially when it's not going well. Like I said earlier, that starts to take its toll a little bit. But the boat has bounced off the bottom and is starting to float back up again.

'I don't want to go out like this. I'd really like another two or three years at the top of the game, so my kids can see me at my best. I have that vision of having them run onto the seventy-second green of a tournament. I want to show them that I am a great player, so that I don't have to pull out the old DVDs – if they know what a DVD is. My kids probably don't. I'll have to pull it up on YouTube.'

He laughed so easily, and was so obviously sincere, that I forgave him the casual pomposity of using the L-word – legacy – during his self-assessment. An anecdote shared by Pete Cowen, his long-term swing coach, seemed appropriate. It related to a lunch they shared at a restaurant overlooking the seventeenth hole at Pebble Beach on the Sunday before the 2010 US Open.

'As we watched Lee Westwood win the St Jude Classic on TV, Graeme grew rather quiet and seemed to be taking something from it. After the first round of the Open – Graeme shot seventy-one, only two shots back of the lead – I casually mentioned it was too bad he didn't get more out of the round, because he'd hit the ball great. Graeme spun, looked me in the eye and said, "I've got a big one in me, you know."

'Over the next three days he put on display his particular gift, massive balls. Graeme is absolutely fearless. He hits the right shots at the right time, and if it happens to be a demanding one with dire consequences if he misses, he won't hesitate. When Graeme is on, his courage and self-belief are unreal.'

Cowen, who has also helped Henrik Stenson, Darren Clarke, Louis Oosthuizen, Danny Willett and Brooks Koepka to win major championships, reflects that 'They're gifted in varying ways – physically, emotionally, temperamentally and ambition-wise.' Most players utilise the widest possible support team, in the knowledge that, to use McDowell's acerbic admission, 'If I have a bad couple of weeks and I'm looking around for who to fire, the new expert I've just brought in has no job security.'

His entourage incorporates Cowen, putting-coach Mike Shannon and personal trainer Kevin Duffy. He also employs two psychologists, a statistician, a nutritionist and a personal assistant, as well as an agent, accountant and lawyer to deal with 'outside-the-ropes shit'. He is considering taking on a performance manager, to pull things together.

'It's sort of the Sir Alex Ferguson role, sitting above everything. The concept is that here is someone that helps you filter the information, the people, making sure you're working with the best guys available. That creates a framework, rather than the player having to manage all the data that's being thrown at him, making head or tail of it, and taking it to the range.

'The modern player can be overwhelmed by numbers. We have all these platforms that allow us to know a lot about what we're doing. The accuracy of the data is key, but the translation, interpretation and simplification of that information is a hard transition to make. In many ways it was an easier world twenty years ago, when I was setting out.

'It was a very simple process. You used your eye, saw what the ball was doing and tried to make your golf swing better. Nowadays it's a minefield. I'd tell a young player right now to have a team around him that he trusts, inherently, to help him filter all the data and to give him only what he needs to get better.'

McDowell particularly admires the independence and coherence of the strategic model adopted by Tom Brady, the New England Patriots quarterback who has had nineteen stellar seasons in the NFL, in a position with an average lifespan of three and a half years. Brady's TB12 brand incorporates a performance arm which preaches that 'cognitive conditioning is as important as physical conditioning'. It may have caused friction with head coach Bill Belichick, but it is backed up by a slickly marketed commercial programme, which 'targets brain speed and accuracy, so quicker and better split-second decisions become instinctual', and it claims to be supported by more than 100 peer-reviewed scientific papers.

One golfer, in particular, has been taking notes . . .

Chapter Four

SECRET SAUCE

The video, taken on the range at Carnoustie late on the first day of the 2018 Open Championship, inevitably went viral. It was golf's version of Basil Fawlty thrashing a parked car with twigs – a silent comedy starring Bryson James Aldrich DeChambeau, to give him his full name, which he did not realise he had until he enrolled in High School at the age of fourteen.

The mime was mesmeric. He stretched an errant driver across his back, just above his shoulder blades, and stared at the cloud-streaked sky, as if seeking solace from a higher being. He held his head in his hands and sank to his haunches, before walking four-teen paces with grim deliberation to an empty scoreboard, against which he leaned, face-first.

Tim Tucker, his long-suffering caddie, appeared to have acquired a sudden interest in ornithology. Three other members of DeChambeau's support team clicked into wise-monkey mode: hands thrust deep into pockets, they gave the impression of see-ing, hearing and saying precisely nothing. All that remained was for the breakout star of American golf to retrieve the clubs he had flung up to fifty yards, casually checking them for damage without breaking stride.

DeChambeau, who began his setpiece press conference at the Ryder Cup by thanking 'Mom and Dad for giving me the longest name in the world', was predictably called to account. 'Come on, guys,' he said, 'you've got to understand that's not anything out of the ordinary for me. People brought it up as a huge deal and a huge situation, but they just caught me at a vulnerable time.

'It's unfortunate. I do that all the time, because I'm trying to figure things out. When I get frustrated on the golf course, sometimes you don't see it because I'm trying to be professional, and I have to be professional, right? But there's a lot of fire in there. It motivates me in a very positive way, most of the time. It may look terrible, but it makes me who I am today.'

He gave an unwitting hint of his inner feelings by drumming his fingers against the base of the microphone stand, but at least we were spared the type of excruciating apology he delivered on US TV after suffering another meltdown, recognising winner Richard McEvoy with a curt split-second handshake when he lost the European Open in Hamburg by collapsing over the final four holes.

Enforced piety is rarely a good look, as Tiger Woods discovered during his infamous corporate mea culpa for infidelity, and it added to the sense of DeChambeau as a fairground attraction. Prod the bear with a sharp stick and watch it dance, folks. When he's invited to say something extraordinary, he usually obliges.

'Can you expand on what it means to be neurologically comfortable?'

'No. That's a secret.'

'Okay, that's the second time this week you've not given us the scoop. Give us a little insight.'

'You realise how important it is to me. I would say, just on a general basis, that it's something I've derived in my brain. It's like I have this black space and it's just my hands and arms and body. I see it and I just take it back, and have this neurological sensation or input that I have for applying force to the club. There is a track to it. I see it. Some people look and envision shots, do all that, but I just create it in my brain.'

He sounds like Victor Frankenstein, but, to add to the effect, looks like a character from *The Great Gatsby*. He has a habit of using his hands to amplify some weird and wonderful points, often closing his eyes simultaneously. His flat cap is a throwback to the sepia-print era of Ben Hogan, although, in a nod to modern Mammon, his kit sponsors have the commercial cuteness to charge £35 for a replica.

He leaves the pin in for chip shots close to the green, and for putts from the fringe, after judging 'the COR – the coefficient of restitution of the flagstick'. He uses a laser to detect the line of practice putts. He simulates the effect of early-morning dew by having an assistant scrub his clubface before every practice shot, for which he uses a brand-new ball coated in a fine spray of water. He regards the ability to control variables, such as the wind, as 'the Holy Grail'.

His sessions on the range are performance art, even without the histrionics. I watched him for more than an hour in Paris; he used two launch monitors to analyse the angle of flight and referred constantly to three assistants. One, in regulation khaki chinos, cradled his MacBook with the care more normally reserved for a sleeping child. DeChambeau should have been wearing a penitent's hair shirt, rather than a team uniform.

His unconventional swing, which according to range rats involves taking the club back on a single plane without 'breaking' the wrist, was developed from the age of fifteen, when his coach Mike Schy encouraged him to read *The Golfing Machine*, a physics-influenced instructional book by Homer Kelley. Published in 1969, it had taken twenty-nine years to write.

Kelley died aged seventy-six in 1983. He had a distinctive life, dictated by his beliefs as a Christian Scientist, a faith in which he found 'provable, definitive and demonstrable truth'. He drove across the United States in a Model T Ford in 1929, aiming to emigrate to Australia from Seattle, before the stock-market crash forced him to seek work as a cook in a billiards hall, whose owner taught him golf.

His problem-solving skills enabled him to become an instructor at Boeing, the aircraft manufacturer, in the Second World War, when he served in the US Navy. He subsequently lived in Hawaii, before returning to work in a precious-metals company in Washington, where he invented a method of separating mercury from silver.

Kelley's golf theory, formed on a local driving range, dictated that 'each human-shaped golfer' is a programmable machine whose swing is composed of twenty-four basic components. His 'power package' entails 'accumulating, loading, storing, delivering and releasing power' towards the ball through what he called 'the aiming point concept'. Needless to say, he stressed that 'golf was never meant to be a simple game'.

Two years of teenage experimentation by DeChambeau led to the geometrically inspired creation of a unique set of clubs. All his irons are 37½ inches in length, with the thickest grips commercially available. The heads weigh precisely 280 grams, and have specific names stamped on them. His sixty-degree lob wedge is 'The King' in homage to Arnold Palmer, and his six-iron is named 'Juniper', after the sixth hole at Augusta. Others are known as 'Azalea' and 'Gamma'.

Are you ready to mock? Many do. DeChambeau admits that the majority of US college recruitment teams stopped calling when they realised he was one of a kind. He 'butted heads' with his father, who surrendered and began using the single-length models in early 2017. His mother and his brother, Garrett, 'always encouraged me, though they thought I was crazy'.

He continues to argue that the clubs work 'from a physics and biomechanics perspective', but has little incentive to listen to the critics. He excelled at Southern Methodist University in Texas, joining Jack Nicklaus, Tiger Woods, Phil Mickelson and Ryan Moore in 2015 as one of only five players to win both the NCAA Division I championship and the US Amateur in the same year.

He is only twenty-five, and won four PGA titles in a twelve-tournament sequence in 2018; to place that in perspective, Rickie Fowler, the doe-eyed darling of corporate America, had only won four times in 214 starts on the PGA Tour up until that point. DeChambeau has yet to spawn a generation of anguished clones, but people are quietly starting to wonder.

What if . . .

For all the raised eyebrows and whispered scorn, there is a nagging suspicion that he might just be on to something. That's powerful juju in a profession containing driven individuals who would be prepared to play in a wizard's cloak and quote extensively from the Hogwarts *Book of Spells*, if it would guarantee the trimming of a stroke from their score.

If DeChambeau knows the answer to the equivalent of a Bat-Bogey Hex invented by Miranda Goshawk, he's not letting on: 'The ball is sitting right there and you're able to swing at it and hit it wherever you want to. You can take forty seconds or whatever to hit it. So that time allows us the opportunity to do some pretty cool things that I will not give away.

'About ninety per cent of the information that I have is proprietary and we will not let anybody know. I'm trying my best to keep it a secret as much as possible. That ten per cent I love throwing out there and giving everybody a little thought of something that's a little different. I've always been a guy that's been weird and unique, relative to everybody else.

'I've always gone about my business trying to do the absolute best I can. Let today's garbage be better than yesterday's. I don't view people's criticism as a negative thing. If anything, it's positive. I can be good at anything, if I love it and dedicate myself. I love history. I love science. I love music. I love golf. I love learning. I love life. I love trying to be the best at anything and everything.

'More power to everyone that does it their own way. Everybody is unique. I believe I found a way that works really, really well for me, and it allows me to be super-consistent, week in and week out. You know what? I hope down the road it'll keep happening. You never know, but so far it's proven itself quite a bit.'

Look a little deeper into his childhood in Clovis, California, and clues emerge. This movie is a cross between *Rocky* and *A Beautiful Mind*. DeChambeau embodies the diligence that underpins the American Dream, and although he admits, 'I wasn't great at reading and writing', he has made the most of his capacity to declutter mathematical challenges.

'I feel like I've always had to work twice as hard to be just as good as others. I was always a guy that would study for three hours and barely get an A on the test. You'd have another guy next to me who would study for maybe thirty minutes and ace it. That's been me my whole life. I've had to grind and work it out, and figure it out on my own.

'I've never been super-talented. I was a good junior golfer, but I always felt I wasn't the best, so I always had to find other ways to get a little bit better. I tried to find a little edge on the competition in other ways – understanding elevation changes, or whatever it was, back in the day. I thought outside the box, and tried to make my swing easier and simpler.

'I do like numbers. I'm more of a theoretical guy than a data/analytics guy, per se. I've got a great visual mind. For whatever reason, God has blessed me to see things in just a unique and different way, in regards to spatial awareness. It's nice. I'm just a little different cat. That's okay. I like that and appreciate that I'm able to stay true to myself.'

He played basketball, volleyball and soccer at school. His hand–eye coordination made him a very good goalkeeper, an exposed position that traditionally invites investigation into the occupant's sanity. Most typically, however, he practised Ping-Pong 'against this little robot' on every lunch break for 'a couple of years'.

He remembered: 'This thing would shoot out the ball, different velocities, and different spin rates. It was really cool. I got pretty good, needless to say.' Such excellence would help his integration, since one of the militating factors in the Ryder Cup revolt against US captain Tom Watson at Gleneagles in 2014 was deemed to be Watson's refusal to allow a table-tennis table in the team room.

DeChambeau dutifully packed 'a new rubber' (a table-tennis bat, for the benefit of the uninitiated) to compete in the internal competition staged at Le Golf National, where vice-captain Matt Kuchar took on all-comers. The resultant suggestion that DeChambeau is a perfectionist prompts theatrical incredulity: 'Really? Me? I definitely am, and it's something that I'll continue to try to perfect.'

His stated aim is to be able to practise less and get better. He admits, grudgingly, that human error is innate. A sequence of fourteen successive missed cuts early in his professional career proved pivotal, since he realised he had to change his game – 'to dig it out of the dirt', to use his graphic phrase. Only his faith in biomechanics proved constant:

'Biomechanics automatically translates to feel, for me. It is so important to have the proper response mechanism that says, "Hey, this is why I went ten yards right, or this is why I drew on spin axis of three degrees", or whatever. Once I have a better understanding of how my body is responding to each shot at hand, and how it is affecting the club dynamically, that will put me to another level.'

At times, when he attempts to explain the significance of spatial awareness, air tolerance, standard deviation and 'getting my proximities closer to the whole', it is like listening to the works of

Shakespeare, recited in Esperanto. Even the most basic understanding requires daunting study; DeChambeau is working 'to an
idea that is stuck in my brain so deep' it is inherently forbidding.

'It's a joy, a quest for me,' he argues, pre-empting debate. 'How
much better can I get? Oh, man, in short, layman's terms, yes,
absolutely, you can always get better. How much? I would say it
depends on what I can do in the restrictions of my biomechanics.
It's all about being less sensitive to air, so that when you do mess
up, it's not going to be that big of a mess-up. I hope that makes
sense.

'It's about having a higher level of stability in the golf swing,
so I know where the clubface is. It's a conscious thought you're
hopefully translating into a subconscious thought, but it doesn't
work out all the time. I felt like I had an S on my chest for a while,
and it just started to fall away a little bit and I've been trying to
get it back ever since. No matter what people say, I'm still going
to stick to this and try to figure out how to utilise it to my advantage. That's the best I can give you.

'There have literally been about thirty changes. Where am I,
on a scale of one to ten? Oh, my gosh, I'm not going to quantify
that, because I can't tell the future. I'm playing golf at the highest
level and winning, so there has to be some validity to it. Is everybody going to do it? No. But it works for me and I believe it's
going to benefit me.

'In physics I believe in momentum. But also in life I believe in
momentum. And it relates to the brain, absolutely, how the brain
is working, based on positive feedback from the environment. If
you get positive responses and you execute shots and make putts
and stuff like that, you're going to be positive in everything you
do, no matter if a bad shot happens.'

He has been working, since July 2018, with Neuropeak Pro,
which operates from a so-called Brain Performance Center in
Grand Rapids, Michigan. Neuroscientist Tim Royer, its founder,

describes his twelve-strong team as 'electricians of the brain body'. Clients include Minnesota Vikings quarterback Kirk Cousins and leading NBA teams such as Orlando Magic and the Portland Trail Blazers.

DeChambeau's most immediate benefit was generated by the use of a breathing belt, and respiratory analysis that reinforced the fact that 80 per cent of energy is created by oxygen. As Dr Royer told the Leaders Performance Institute: 'Everybody talks about nutrition and hydration, which are very important, but if you look at the overall scale of what provides you the most amount of energy, it's oxygen. It's probably the thing that most people are completely missing out on in sport.'

Travel schedules and cumulative sleep disruption – a common issue for professional athletes – can reduce the level of production of testosterone and DHEA, an endogenous steroid hormone produced in the adrenal glands, by at least 20 per cent. This can compromise conventional injury-prevention strategies, and is counteracted by study of electrical current in the brain and heart.

'The whole brain works off electricity,' Dr Royer explained. 'Your brain is working right now because neurons are firing and there's electrical activity in your brain; it's no different to a light bulb in your office. There are frequencies of electrical activity that cause your brain to work, while every organ in your body is working off electricity: your heart, your digestive system, the pores of your skin.

'It's understanding that if you don't regulate oxygen intake, you can have the greatest nutritional programme that you want, and have all those other things in place, but you're still going to fall short, because oxygen is so important for managing stress and creating electricity. Our autonomic nervous system is a regulator deciding, based on senses, what we need at any given moment in time.

'It has two extremes. A "sympathetic" state is fright and flight. That's when we use massive amounts of electrical current.

A "parasympathetic" state is rest, digest and renew. That's when recovery happens. The spectrum of electrical current defines how you're going to behave in a certain situation.

'If you step outside the office and see a lion, your senses send a signal to your autonomic nervous system. Your heart rate and breathing suddenly speed up and other systems, such as the digestive system, temporarily shut down. That's good in the short term, you'll have enough energy to evade danger, but you can't stay in that mode very long, as you'll become fatigued quickly.

'When you sleep, your body, hopefully, doesn't perceive any threats and it can go into a parasympathetic state, where neurons are able to rejuvenate and you're able to get the recovery you need. The key to excellent recovery is an autonomic nervous system that can downshift into parasympathetic as quickly as possible.

'The brain normally operates at sixteen cycles per second, but when it sees a lion, that jumps to thirty-two. The best athletes in the world are able to stay in the lower range regardless of the situation. For them, a five-foot putt is the same on their practice green as it is in the US Open; the free throw in the NBA finals is the same as in practice. Elite athletes have control of their autonomic nervous system.'

DeChambeau talks animatedly about 'a copper little thing that measures frequencies emitted from different parts of the brain', but in practical terms he gains most benefit from the breathing techniques he has been taught. He attempts to maximise effectiveness by exhaling when he looks at the target for the last time, relaxing the brain so that it can process the requisite information.

He praises Tim Tucker, who first caddied for him in junior golf a decade ago, since 'there's not another person that would put up with my crap'. He credits Greg and Steve Harrison for his ability 'to roll the rock' with a personalised SIK putter. They use a diagnostic tool known as the Quintic Ball Roll System to measure speed of club and ball on impact, launch angles and rates of revolution.

Chris Como, Tiger Woods's former 'swing consultant', joined the support team in the summer of 2018, when DeChambeau had a three-dimensional golf simulator installed in his new home in Dallas. He 'went through everything in my body' with Greg Roskopf, creator of MAT, Muscle Activation Techniques, at his headquarters in Denver.

Roskopf has worked in the NFL for twenty-five years, and describes his contribution as 'a neuromuscular overhaul' designed to highlight muscular imbalances that interfere with the path of the club on the way to impact. In essence, he focuses on stimulating and improving communication pathways from the brain, resulting in greater stability and strength and less pain and inflammation.

He has worked with lauded quarterbacks like Peyton Manning, but his most compelling case-study involves swimmer Amy Van Dyken-Rouen. He helped her recover from shoulder surgery to win the last two of her six Olympic gold medals in Sydney in 2000, and provided immediate support when she severed her spine in a quad-bike accident in 2014.

'I was dead,' she told espnW. 'I did see what some would [say] the light. I can tell you what it was for me. I was in a tunnel. It was green. It was light green, dark green, it was purple. It was orange. It was beautiful. It was warm. I felt so comfortable, I didn't see anyone there. I wanted to see my grandpa. I wanted to see my dog. But I got sent back. U-turn.'

Being paralysed from the waist down, it was assumed she would never walk again. Roskopf began by urging her to visualise lifting her leg. A light contraction triggered a two-year rehabilitation programme, during which she has stood independently, felt reflexive movement in her knees and ankles, and walked fifty paces with the aid of an exoskeleton attached to her legs and waist.

That sort of reality punctures even the bubble of professional golf, where deeply ingrained introspection becomes a defence mechanism. DeChambeau hopes 'people understand that I'm just a person, too. I'm human. I have the same faults and mess up every once in a while and do good things every once in a while, and I think we just do it in different ways.'

Ryan Lavner, a senior writer on the Golf Channel, posted on social media that he would 'never forget a college coach telling me in 2015 that "in five years, Bryson will either be No. 1 in the world or in a straitjacket".' Even his peers on the US Ryder Cup team, like Woods and Jordan Spieth, are not entirely sure how to take him.

Woods, a spent force when partnering DeChambeau to a 5&4 defeat in the Saturday-afternoon foursomes in Paris, reflected: 'I feel a lot of the things that he says, but we articulate it completely differently. It's a lot of fun to needle him and give him a hard time about it, but I definitely respect what he says because of the fact that he does a lot of research. I mean, he is very into what he's doing.'

Spieth says he understands DeChambeau 'to an extent'. They practise on the same course in Texas: 'Bryson phrases stuff differently than he needs to at times, but the belief in what he's doing is very important. This sport is all about the best miss. You're trying to fine-tune to the nth degree, and his fine-tuning within different parts of his swing is extreme.

'He likes his way. He's at what he likes to call an end-range of motion. If he really finds where it's at, this is a sustainable thing for him for a long time against other guys, including myself. I wouldn't look for anything to change soon. I feel like he's really figured out what he's doing.'

So, what's it all about? How much can we realistically read into the brain-fades, the whimsy of DeChambeau's much-professed love of pseudoscience and the simplicity of his fondness for eating popcorn on the couch? Is he playing to the gallery when he recycles a sixth-grade theory that 'gravity pushes outward, not inward', or when he mourns the fact that 'I can't control individual atoms'?

He smiles when asked to solve the mystery of his mechanics. 'This is something that I've worked my butt off for. I'll let it out eventually, but, you know, it's stuff that Dustin Johnson or Jordan Spieth have all figured out on some level as well. That's our secret sauce. I don't want to tell you everything. If I did, it wouldn't be fun any more, now would it?'

Meanwhile, in England, another man who dares to be different posts a photograph of his dog, Gus, taken on high ground above Didcot Power Station in Oxfordshire. It is accompanied by the following reflection on golf's vicissitudes: 'Shoulders back, look forward. A brighter future maybe, we'll wait and see. Head up, son. Missing putts and missing cuts, all feels like a kick in the nuts. Keep smiling. Enduring pain, lacking the gain, all the while going fucking insane.'

Chapter Five

CHAOS AND ORDER

If Bryson DeChambeau is golf's Spock, a precarious balance of Vulcan logic and human curiosity, then Eddie Pepperell is its Doctor Who, a deceptively driven, endearingly eccentric shapeshifter who is in closer touch with his feminine side than many realise. Their affinity is understandable, and their shared problem is that success sanitises, subtly and relentlessly.

Corporate instinct is to compartmentalise the Englishman as a token oddity, a whimsical, mischievous little chap whose personality can be massaged to millennial taste. That would be characteristically condescending, a familiar mistake. Pepperell has a serious game, even if his Twitter feed – acidic, provocative and insistently funny – is a politically incorrect diversion.

Look beyond archly delivered references to sex toys and luxury chocolates, to a body of work that acquired real substance in 2018. He experienced a strange serenity in winning for the first time, in Qatar, yet was visibly restless when we first met in Ireland, where the terse self-analysis quoted at the end of the previous chapter was prompted by his disappointment at narrowly missing the cut.

Stuck in traffic on the M40 the following Monday, Pepperell was two hours late for what turned out to be a pivotal two-hour consultation with putting coach Mike Kanski at Formby Hall in Southport, on the 410-mile drive from Oxfordshire to the Scottish Open. He was persuaded not to cancel the appointment en route by his partner, Jen, and emerged from the session mentally recharged, with renewed technical focus.

I found him on a plateaued practice green at Gullane, locked into a putting drill that used a black line and two tees as a gate. His posture was helped by the arcane ritual of foam rolling at his feet. He struck the ball well on the arid, undulating fairways, finished second, and questioned the suitability of the subsequent avalanche of nearly £2 million prize money into what had once been a barren bank account.

'It's a bonkers game, totally mental, but life can come at you fast,' he said. By the time he succumbed to a back injury in China, which precipitated subsequent retirement from the end-of-season World Tour Championship in Dubai, after twelve holes of the second round, he had morphed from curiosity to contender.

He famously confessed to playing hungover in the final round at the Open Championship, where his sixty-seven propelled him to sixth place, three shots adrift of Francesco Molinari. By mid-October 2018 he was celebrating another European Tour victory in the British Masters at Walton Heath, in weather that would have caused Robert Falcon Scott to pause and consider the merits of an afternoon in front of the clubhouse fire, with a schooner of sherry for company.

Feel-good headlines were fashioned by his mother, who lent him a pair of mittens halfway through the round. His misadventures three weeks previously as runner-up in Portugal, where he marked his breakthrough in the world's top fifty by hallucinating on a hospital drip, following severe dehydration, also fitted the unconventional narrative. As Pepperell reflected on social media: 'Imagine that. Four hundred and thirteen weeks it takes to achieve something pretty good, and all you have to show for it is psychosis and no hat sponsor.'

He admits to being 'almost addicted' to his weaknesses and, like many leading golfers, draws deeply from adversity. He remains 'haunted' by the experience of being unable to pay a hotel bill in France on the Challenge Tour in 2014 (he was bailed out by his friend and fellow pro, Laurie Canter) and lost his card on the main tour as recently as 2016.

Pepperell leans forward on his white faux-leather seat and makes eye contact: 'The line you tread between chaos and order is so fine that it's impossible to be in order for very long. The thing with golf, and this is where it is so tricky, like any sport at the top level, is you think you're in control and then something happens and you're not. How do you react? It becomes a real process of commitment and trust.

'I remember playing a practice round with Tommy Fleetwood on the Tuesday of the Scottish Open at Castle Stuart in 2016. He couldn't hit the driver on the planet. I've known Tommy since I was eleven, we're good friends, and he said to me on the third, "Ed, you go on." It was total resignation. He didn't want me to witness him struggling the way he was.

'Of course I felt sorry for him. I was shocked because I couldn't believe how bad he was, from how good he had been. Yet a year later he's winning the Race to Dubai. This is golf. If you have ability – which Tommy clearly has, which I have, and which lots of guys have – you can fall off the face of the Earth and come back. Your ability doesn't just go. You don't just turn crap overnight.

'Some people never come back. They may have lied to themselves, been much more jolly and tried to joke it off. You don't know how you're going to react until you're really in that struggle. Although I didn't find it that difficult, because I think my upbringing from my parents was pretty solid, I found myself trying even harder to be a really good person.

'I know that sounds really wishy-washy, but to say hello to people, to continue to act the way I was when things were going well, was important. You must not let the game change you, when you are down and out. It is almost inevitable that you will change on the way up, but when you are really struggling, you must try to be even more genuine and honest and happy, because that shows enormous resilience.

'In 2016 I was awful off the tee, and I knew it. I was standing there, dreading the worst, and the worst happened. I've been where Tommy was. I found a technical fix, and came back fairly quickly, because I didn't recognise the problem as being concrete and forever. I realised that if you can cascade into such despair, you can quite easily climb out of it.

'Even to this day I am not totally confident with my driver, especially on certain holes in certain wind conditions, but I've managed to work around it. I'm not of the opinion that anything is forever. I described chaos and order a minute ago, and in that sense I think it exists in everything we do, but particularly in golf.

'Since becoming a golfer, I've become a lot less judgemental of other sportsmen and other people, or at least I hope I have. You can look at a footballer on TV and draw many conclusions, if you want to, but because I'm a sportsman and I know people draw conclusions about me that are so far off the mark, then I'd be a fool to do the same to others.

'We're not unique. We're actually very similar, a lot of us, experiencing similar emotions, but the general public can fall into the trap of thinking we are somehow different. I love it when people fuck up, because I think we're designed to fuck up, and we're in the moment now where people can't accept it. For some reason, people expect us to be perfect. And I don't know where we've got that idea from.'

Pepperell had a volcanic temper as a child, crashing a pool cue through a bedroom door during an argument with elder brother

Joe over an online game of cricket. In his mid-teens he was banned for six months from his home club, Frilford Heath, for gouging a divot from the green after missing a putt. He has moved on from such adolescent excess, but is trenchant in his defence of individualism.

He told broadcaster Andrew Cotter: 'I don't feel a responsibility as a golfer to portray myself in a certain way. People may disagree with my views, and find them unpalatable. I don't care.' The point of his political incorrectness was reaffirmed by the following good-luck message, sent to finalists in autumn's European Tour Qualifying School: 'Just think, guys, two years ago I was there, and look at me now, tweeting about masturbation and anal beads.'

Golf's self-image removes the player's ubiquitous baseball cap and replaces it with a halo. Its ruddy-cheeked committee-room philosophers tend to be po-faced. The game demands integrity, yet it is not immune to such revealing examples of cynicism as Phil Mickelson's decision to deliberately prevent his ball rolling off the thirteenth green at the 2018 US Open in Shinnecock Hills.

Judging by the immediate furore, he might as well have been carrying out the orders of a modern Herod, to slaughter the firstborn of the good people of the nearby hamlet of Suffolk County, New York. Mickelson eventually apologised, after initially advising his critics to 'toughen up', but not before Nick Faldo sanctimoniously informed him that his behaviour was 'not cricket'.

Pepperell, by contrast, was highly amused: 'It was great. What Phil did, for me, showed an imperfection. People straight away jumped on the bandwagon and lamented him for it, as if they were no longer his fans. That's a crazy stance to take, when you consider all the good things he's done in the game of golf. It was only a slight lapse. It was nothing. I enjoyed the fact it was more calculated than many realised.

'He knew what was happening, saw the ball was going off the green, and just thought, "I'm going to take my two-shot penalty." There might have been an element of "Oh, this is going to show up the USGA", so there's a slight perniciousness to the action, which I love even more, because it shows there is a nasty side to Mickelson and most people think of him as pretty godly. Let's face it, none of us out here are perfect. None of us are really shit. We're somewhere in between.

'In terms of moral standards, I think golf is better than any other sport. But there is no question there are going to be guys who aren't whiter than white. They absolutely aren't. It's inevitable that somebody good at some point in history has taken drugs, as a golfer. I don't know who. But to think that nobody has is naïve, and history has got to have taught us different.'

An anonymous survey of fifty-nine PGA Tour players, including four major winners, taken at the PGA Championships and the Wyndham Championship in 2018, found that 44 per cent had witnessed cheating during a competitive round. This represented a 6 per cent increase from a similarly confidential poll in 2013.

A similar survey of 34 European Tour players, including six Ryder Cup players and four major champions, was taken at the Turkish Airlines Open in November 2018. 45 per cent had witnessed cheating, and 38 per cent had played hungover,

Sports administrators – a calculating, craven breed by nature – blanch at such frankness. Yet golf is different, in that the European Tour is run by the players. Though it might seem as unwise as King Louis XVI inviting Robespierre to oversee interior decoration at the Palace of Versailles, Pepperell is a member of the ruling committee, which has been overseen by Thomas Bjørn for a decade.

As such, Pepperell has 'gained an understanding of the game's politics' and accumulated insight into the Dane's definitive leadership qualities: 'Thomas, on the course, is flat-out miserable, but in that environment he is fantastic, very thoughtful, a great talker and willing to give of himself.' He was fascinated by details of Bjørn's personalised coping strategy.

'That's incredible. I didn't know that about Thomas, but it doesn't surprise me. Self-reflection, looking in the mirror – whether it's metaphorical or literal, as Thomas has described – is essential for anyone who is successful. I don't do that, because I'd probably punch the mirror if I was angry, so for me it's much more metaphorical, but I get that concept. It's a beautiful one and something you've got to be comfortable doing.

'I remember Nick Faldo saying he used to talk to himself. I think golf opens itself up to that. I often have a discussion with myself in my own head. There's a lot going on in there. I don't necessarily need someone to talk to. It would be great if I could find that person, but often my interests are so different I'm going to have a hard time doing so.

'There's constant dialogue. It's like I'm talking to an interviewer. I'm clarifying an answer, or a thought, to somebody who has asked me a particular question. When I'm alone in the car I'll talk out loud about all sorts of things, because I really enjoy doing that, but obviously on the golf course you're not going to do that because, well, you're just not . . .'

He laughs, as if abashed by the incongruity of the image. He insists that money is not a determining factor, preferring the 'enormous satisfaction of performing under difficult circumstances' or the more esoteric pleasure of 'flushing a six-iron, nailing it off a mat or the grass'. Pepperell is only twenty-eight, and resists sermons about materialism, but his representational role has been instructive.

'When people come up to me and go, "Oh, the players' lounge isn't very good" or "There's a courtesy car issue, can you bring this up with [Tour CEO] Keith Pelley?", I'm thinking to myself,

"There's no way I'm mentioning that, because the Tour has much bigger things to worry about. It's annoying when a courtesy car doesn't show up – I get that – but you've got to be able to see the bigger picture. Some don't, and can't. That's a direct result, I think, of an over-pampered culture. Go to America and it is even more marked.

'My interests outside golf are economics, the news, listening to podcasts about social issues. The beauty of playing in Morocco, for example, is we don't get free 4G, so you have to sit there idly on the bus for twenty minutes on the way to the course, as opposed to being on Twitter on your phone. It forces you to look out at the world around you, to observe the poverty that exists. Having that perspective is not hard, is it?'

It is harder when social life is reduced to room service, which Pepperell observes is 'surely an idea invented by loners for loners'. One of his most vivid experiences came at the start of his rookie year on the European Tour in Dubai in 2013, where he found himself washing down a fillet steak with a glass of Bailey's liqueur in a 'luxury hotel room with incredible furnishings and a bathroom worthy of Julius Caesar'.

It almost made him nostalgic for his first professional event, in Tuscany on the Challenge Tour twenty months earlier, where, 'with no book, no Wi-Fi and no friends', he spent six nights in unarmed combat with mosquitoes, ate at the local truck stop and was fleeced shamelessly by taxi drivers who knew he had no alternative for the thirty-minute journey to the course.

'Initially, being in that five-star room in Dubai, it was "Wow!" But what followed was the saddening reality that I had nobody there to share the experience with. That's when I realised that it's really not what you have. It's who you are with that is obviously going to determine how happy you are. Why do I play golf, then? I don't know, probably because it's all I've ever done, and I don't want to be poor.

'I mean, I've been there. I've had nothing, effectively. The irony, looking back, is that my performances picked up when I saw I had very little money in the bank, or when I lost my card. That suggests I have success by necessity, as opposed to motivation, desire or an actual goal. That's something I do struggle with. If I want a long and successful and happy career, I need to find something that honestly drives me.'

He suspects that increasing physical demands, in an era that rewards 'bomb-and-gouge' golf, will shorten playing careers. His career is in the ascendancy, but an alternative scenario suggests itself: he has the potential to develop into a generational version of David Feherty, the Irish former Ryder Cup player who has become one of golf's most idiosyncratic commentators in the United States.

Pepperell has a flair for communication and a natural intelligence that enable him to talk compellingly about the 'wilderness' of modern politics and the dubious morality of the merger-and-acquisition culture driving contemporary business. As his willingness to confront the subject of chemical assistance testifies, he possesses a highly marketable candour. His blog has a rare breadth of scope. I was struck by this excerpt, on his game's holistic potential:

Yoga, Mindfulness, Spiritualism and Meditation are all becoming more and more popular, along with Veganism and a general move towards holistic living. These are the signs to me that the balances of our lives want to shift back towards a centre point. Drug abuse, depression, obesity and stress related illnesses have been on the rise over the last two decades. This is another sure sign to me that we have pushed ourselves too far, in too short a period of time.

We are finding managing our health, and subsequently our lives, tricky. Now, there is the argument that things will keep moving in the same direction and that ultimately we will adapt because we have to. But dying isn't adapting, and there are too many people dying from chronic illnesses because they are unable to cope with modern day pressures.

I would therefore suggest golf doesn't need to change at all. I believe there is as much chance, if not more, that society rebalances and slows down, as there is that it continues to move at its current break neck speed. Golf has major therapeutic qualities. It's played outside, and so therefore it is effectively more in tune with nature. Yes, it is slow in its nature, unlike football, tennis and rugby, but this is a good thing as it can therefore be played by anybody. It is incredibly stimulating mentally, once you begin to grasp the movement of the golf swing.

The social aspects of golf can be fantastic, and help people remove themselves from screens and technology. All of these things I believe have huge potential in dealing with chronic illnesses, whether that be physical or mental. I would imagine golf as a form of healing from depression could be enormous due to what I've outlined above. Plus, why change a sport to simply 'conform' to what we believe society 'wants.' Conformity is boring, each sport is different in its nature and we should celebrate that, not the opposite.

That's infinitely more enlightening than Pepperell's thoughts on the tyranny of the time clock, or whatever manufactured thought for the day dominates conversation in the interview room at regular tournaments, although he admits that social golf 'wouldn't be very therapeutic personally, because it's my job and I couldn't ever detach myself from trying to be really good at it'.

The fragility of form, the capricious nature of fortune and the vagaries of character were reaffirmed in mid-May 2018 at the Sicilian Open, in the Verdura Resort complex on the southern coast of the island, where Pepperell and Bjørn shared an uncomfortable, yet ultimately illuminating opening two rounds with Thorbjørn Olesen.

'Thorbjørn missed the cut by a mile,' Pepperell remembered. 'His head had gone. I spoke to Thomas, he spoke to Thomas. I saw his frustration. He has everything, but had nothing to show for it. Three weeks later he goes and wins in Italy and walks away with a million euros. This is an impossible game, but there is always a rhyme and a reason. Success is so clearly down to details you sometimes wouldn't even consider.'

In Olesen's case, his career was reignited by the random opportunity of an hour-long rain delay at the Italian Open, in Brescia. He had played poorly on the front nine in the first round, and was flicking through a video library of swing sequences on his phone when he noticed a technical issue in his set-up. He walked, on his own, to a deserted range. Within half a bucket of balls, something had clicked. The clouds parted, literally and metaphorically.

'It's difficult to put into words,' he said, with the momentary reticence of someone who feared tempting fate into restoring the balance. 'I was thinking of what I had done in the past, when I found some small things. On the range I suddenly felt more stability in my legs. My shoulders were more on target because I kept my right hip from spinning, and I felt good.'

Olesen went on to beat Francesco Molinari by a stroke, and rode his momentum all the way to the Ryder Cup. Clinching automatic qualification for the European team in his home tournament in Denmark was a deeply personal achievement, since his relationship with Bjørn has an emotional profundity that is rarely found in the cloistered world of professional sport.

'Thorbjørn is on his second run, because he has been on his way once before and dropped off,' Bjørn reflected. 'He'll have learned a lot from not playing well and perhaps losing a little focus and belief. He'll know the answers. I think I know them, but

I don't like to make theories, because they may not be as he sees it, and then I'll be stepping on his toes.

'He has that God-given talent you can't teach. Once he gets his nose in, he's not scared. He will not back off. He will win a major championship, that boy, because of that. Is he good enough to get there consistently? Time will tell. Life, and all that. But when he first came on Tour, I saw so much of me, wanting to break down barriers and be better than people think you should be allowed to be.'

Those thoughts are echoed by Hugh Marr, Olesen's coach. They have worked together since late summer 2015, when Olesen 'was flat out losing his card', before technical changes allowed him to force his way into contention at the Dunhill Links Championship at St Andrews, traditionally the season's last-chance saloon. Once again, instinct kicked in.

'We had a clear task: earn enough money in a couple of weeks to guarantee playing next year. For a player of Thor's standard, that is a ludicrous position to be in, but he's not the first and won't be the last. What wasn't he doing? A little bit of everything, to be honest. While he is an incredibly self-sufficient young man, he is still growing up.

'You have to be comfortable spending time in your own company. You have to be quite robust to deal with all the stuff that's going on around you. It is a proper alpha-male environment. An awful lot of people are quick to judge, to criticise. They aren't afraid to put their point of view forward. Understanding who you are is such a big part of learning to manage that, because it ain't easy, at all.

'Technically, every golfer has their fingerprint, their DNA. Thor tends to move the club in a very specific way that requires managing. He got one sniff of victory in the Dunhill and he nailed it. That was when the penny dropped. This kid is a bit special. He has got the ability to do that. Give him that merest hint and he is on it. He's ruthless, but you'd never know it.'

That contradictory gentility underpins our conversation. Olesen deals with hard truth in soft tones. He is reflective, obviously relishes competition, yet admits he is at his happiest in isolation, practising at the exclusive Queenwood club in Surrey, where the joining fee required from aspiring members is said to be £200,000.

'I love the things no one sees, being on my own, trying to improve. When you get into contention, and see how that private stuff works, it is a massive buzz. When I get in those positions I try to appreciate the moment. I love the pressure, the voice in my head that says, "Don't be afraid of failing, but don't be afraid of winning, either."

'I have always loved that decisive moment. It energises me, brings something out in me. I love the goosebumps, the nervousness, because in this game you do not have those feelings every week. There are not that many opportunities to win. In three or four of my victories I didn't play that well, but my head was so good that I got myself in the right place, where concentration and focus just becomes better and better.'

Olesen has moved from Copenhagen to London, but spends at least thirty weeks a year on the road; 2018 was the first year he wondered about the balance of his life. As a twenty-eight-year-old single man he saw other players with their families in tow and felt lonely. Friendships began to acquire greater value. He told himself, 'Be sad, frustrated, angry, but get out of the prison of your hotel room. Try to laugh, see the whole world, and have a life.'

Bjørn's advice, when Olesen emerged, full-time, on tour in 2010, proved prescient: 'Keep doing your own thing, but have people around you that you can really trust, people you can say anything to.' The art of survival in golf is building the family – biological, surrogate or a mixture of both – to whom you never have to say sorry.

Chapter Six

SCENES FROM A LIFE

Scene One: Aronimink Golf Club, Newtown Square, Pennsylvania. Monday, 10 September 2018

'We did it, Dad . . .' With those four words, an expression of a son's unyielding love, Justin Rose placed the achievement of becoming the world's best golfer into a more meaningful, achingly personal perspective. His status was statistical, but his inspiration bordered on the mystical. It was the twelfth anniversary of Ken Rose's death.

Justin might have lost to Keegan Bradley in a play-off in the rain-delayed BMW Championship at Aronimink, after seeing a winning fifteen-foot putt lip out on the final hole of regulation play, but he became the twenty-second player, and the fourth Englishman (after Nick Faldo, Lee Westwood and Luke Donald), to reach the summit of his sport.

Paternal influence has been keenly felt in golf since Old and Young Tom Morris, godfather and gunslinger of St Andrews, won four Open belts apiece between 1861 and 1872. Ben Hogan was aged nine when his father, Chester, shot himself with a .38 revolver in an adjoining room, following an argument with his mother. Earl Woods turned his son Eldrick into a Frankenstein monster named Tiger, and was eventually buried in an unmarked grave.

Woods came to resent the manipulation, and still carries the burden of his father's narcissism and ruthlessness. Hogan, possessor of the game's smoothest swing, grew into a cold and forbidding champion. The legacy of Ken Rose, following his loss to leukaemia, is captured by his son's generosity of spirit and genuine warmth.

Appointing anyone as a paragon of virtue in professional sport is a hazardous business, but having seen him in a variety of social and sporting settings across a stellar year, Justin is worth the risk. He seems as attentive, responsive and empathetic to an autograph-seeking child as he is to a wealthy businessman living out his fantasy in the weekly chore of the pre-tournament pro-am.

He can be corporately correct, switching his baseball cap in the middle of a press conference to afford his sponsors optimal exposure. He was irritated when a guest posted a video of him drunkenly draining the Ryder Cup while dancing to Earth, Wind & Fire at the European victory party. Yet, in an indication of the double-edged nature of the social-media age, he used his mobile as a gauge of achievement.

'If you win a major, your phone blows up. You win a tournament, you get a nice bunch of messages. Getting to world number one, my phone blew up again. It's a moment we've worked hard for, but life goes on. The kids were happy for five minutes and then they're on to the next thing. My wife Kate gets caught up with her world, so nothing changes at home. I'm still number two or three there.

'I can say now I've been the best player in the world. I've been to the top of the game. That's an end-goal dream, for sure. It's a boyhood dream, something we've all thought about at some point in our lives. My advice to young kids, trying to make their way, is that it is a slow burn. I turned pro at eighteen, and it took me twenty-odd years to get to world number one. Just dedicate yourself to improving, to learning, to trying to get better.

'Winning tournaments obviously excites me, but the quest to get better gets me out of bed in the morning. Enjoy the moment, but the minute you start to reflect, it can soften you a little bit. I love the grind, playing under pressure. The reflection, the warm, fuzzy feeling we'll save for down the road. When you start thinking about your time, you're done, basically.'

The end-of-season stocktake was still seriously impressive. Rose had chiselled out twenty-four top-ten finishes in his previous thirty-one events on the European Tour. His PGA Tour scoring average was a fraction over 68.9, a personal best. The little matter of a $10 million bonus from the FedEx Cup series ensured his career earnings exceeded $80 million.

The respect of his peers was reflected by Ryder Cup colleague Jon Rahm: 'I'll simplify it. He's a world-class driver of the ball, a world-class iron player. He has a world-class short game, a world-class putting game. The best thing is that he knows what he is good at. He always has a plan and he executes that plan. He makes very, very few mistakes. He's always going to be in with a chance on Sunday. It feels like he's there every single week.'

At thirty-eight, there are worlds left to conquer. Global golf is condensing, becoming more elitist. Rose's New Year resolution in 2019 was to win more majors, since they 'are very important in how you are perceived in the history of the game'. He spoke quietly about diligence and sacrifice, 'doing fifty things each day just to be able to play my best'.

Look closely and you saw the boy, rather than the man.

Scene Two: Royal Birkdale Golf Club, Southport. Sunday, 19 July 1998

With his freshly scrubbed features, wide-eyed smile and shapeless, billowing red jumper, Justin Rose could have passed for a member of Brother Beyond, the boy band that was about to enjoy fifteen seconds of fame on *Top of the Pops*. Out of position in the rough on the seventy-second hole of the 127th Open Championship, he passed the audition to become the housewives' favourite.

His chip with a pitching wedge landed softly; the ball bounced three times before it rolled unerringly into the cup. 'Way to go kid,' screamed Curtis Strange, ABC's analyst, as the camera panned to Ken Rose, applauding ecstatically from a narrow walkway beside the green. Justin felt numb. Cap off, arms aloft and head tipped back, he allowed the adulation to soak him like a soft summer rainstorm.

His family posed for photographs with the silver medal, presented to the Open's leading amateur. His mother, now known as 'Grannie Annie' by the Rose entourage, but then referred to as 'Mother Goose', held him proudly by the left elbow. Her husband leaned forward, as if to confirm the joy in his son's face. Margi, their daughter, who subsequently forged a successful career in interior design, was a self-conscious presence on Justin's right shoulder.

Parenting skills can splinter under pressure applied by professional sport, but this nuclear family proved bombproof. 'Annie and I decided when our children were born that whatever it took, we would do all we could to give them the best,' Ken once explained, in an article by Humphrey Ellis, a pseudonym used by John Hopkins, the distinguished golf writer, in honour of his maternal grandfather. 'We did not want them to go through life wondering about what might have happened. We treated them both the same.'

A seven-handicapper, Ken was a better squash and tennis player than a golfer, but had the placidity and persistence of a natural teacher. Justin was aged one when he thrashed around with a plastic club in the garden of their Johannesburg home; within four years the family had returned to England, and he was playing nine holes daily at Hartley Wintney, in the verdant countryside of north-east Hampshire.

It was a time of parental devotion and understated life lessons. Ken shared driving duties with his wife, as the amateur circuit expanded from local to national, and took care to inculcate timeless values. His son was taught to respect golf's fundamental decency. Shortcuts were tempting, in sport and in life, but were ultimately self-defeating.

Justin broke seventy at the age of eleven and within a year had solidified his ambition to play professionally. He lowered his handicap to plus four at the age of fourteen, was English Boys' champion at fifteen, and became the youngest Walker Cup player, at seventeen years and ten days, in 1997, when he contributed two of GB & Ireland's six points in a heavy defeat at Quaker Ridge in Scarsdale, New York.

Before Birkdale, he was working towards a three-year plan, in which he would 'sneak in through the back door' by accepting occasional sponsors' invitations, quietly attending European Tour qualifying school and playing a season on the Challenge Tour. Tabloid acclaim for the prodigy they christened 'Baby Spice' had barely begun before 'all that went out of the window'.

Caught in the rip tide of sudden celebrity, Rose turned professional immediately. Pursued by major TV networks and half of what used to be called Fleet Street, he followed a first-round seventy-seven in the Dutch Open the following Thursday with a redemptive sixty-five, but, after a six-hour wait, missed the cut by a single shot. It was a sliding-doors moment with long-term consequences.

'My expectations changed, and so did those of everyone around me,' he admitted, twenty years later, as he patiently retraced his steps for the umpteenth time. 'My game wasn't ready to deal with all that. For a long time – five, six, seven years – I was trying to live up to that boy, who finished fourth in the Open.'

Scene Three: Golf du Médoc, Blanquefort, Bordeaux. Friday, 7 May 1999

The players' bus purred contentedly with stories of the previous evening's wine-tasting at Château Margaux. Justin, compressed into the back seat, stared disconsolately out of the window. Ken had taken the last available place beside a veteran pro, who took it upon himself to offer unsolicited advice, in a surreal stream of consciousness.

'Golf is an art form, not a sport,' he intoned. 'You communicate the ball from one place to another. The problem is that when your boy is over the ball, he is living in his past and in his future. He has a wonderful swing, but he is destroying himself on a daily basis. Trust me, I've been there. I had sixteen years before I saw the light. Just give me an hour with him and I'll sort him out.'

As a compassionate, decent man, Ken Rose nodded sagely and agreed to set up a lunch the following Tuesday, in Oxfordshire. 'Justin has to sort out his nerves,' he confided. 'He's as tight as a drum.' With the benefit of hindsight, I was culpable in rushing to the conclusion that Ken's paternal pride and protectiveness complicated an already complex situation.

As a national newspaper columnist, seeking a fresh angle on a familiarly poignant story, I was part of the problem of exaggerated expectation. We had walked the near-deserted fairways of the Golf du Médoc complex on the outskirts of Bordeaux, where Justin, partnered by Henrik Bjørnstad – a Norwegian in a porkpie hat, who carried his own clubs – missed the cut by four strokes.

It was the eighteenth such setback in succession. The sequence of missed cuts would extend to twenty-one before he made the weekend at the European Open at Slaley Hall, in Hexham, Northumberland, where he tied seventy-fourth, following a third-round eighty-two, and earned his first cheque, for €1,340. Rose had gone into the tournament with the Tour's worst stroke average, 76.58.

Ken, courteous to a fault, had walked quietly, recording the statistics of his son's round in a black notebook. Justin's growing pains were literal; he had added two and a half inches in height during the previous ten months. His father caddied for him occasionally; Ken's protective instincts led him to offer to spirit Justin away from the scorers' tent, so that he did not have to indulge in recurrent inquests.

'When he makes a cut, he'll burst from the vortex and never look back,' Ken insisted, prophetically. Seve Ballesteros, who scored only one stroke better in France and was struggling badly with a back injury that was to force him off the Tour for six years, sought out Justin and assured him: 'I know there are big things ahead for you. Don't get low.'

On this particular Friday evening, before we shared an early flight back to Heathrow the next morning, Justin owned his failure with impressive maturity. He was eloquent, unsparing and ready to confront the truth, without resorting to cliché or self-pity. 'Let's just say I don't believe in fairy tales any more,' he said with a thin smile. 'This is a cruel game.

'It is a game of millimetres, which are magnified into miles, if your mind is not working right. On the course it is lonely, but in a way the lonelier I feel, the better it is. If I notice my dad around the place, it means I am playing terribly because I am not concentrating solely on my game. I don't care what other people think, but at times I have been embarrassed for myself.

'I want to do better, for my own sense of self-worth. I desperately want to get the business of making a cut out of the way. The only

way I am going to do that is by not letting it get to me, by not thinking about it. It's a catch-22 situation. The more I want to get it out
of the way, the harder it is going to be, because I am trying too hard.

'It's crazy. I know I am much better than turning up every
week and ripping my guts out. I still believe I am the best around.
I have grown up in my own way. What I've been through has been
hard, depressing, but deep down I know I have what it takes.'

Fast-forward nineteen years, to the Bahamas-based father of
two who is comfortable with being one of the Scottish Open's star
attractions. Justin is at ease in the media tent and on the range,
where he lingers, shooting the breeze with a series of players and
coaches, before examining the feel of a new driver with the sensitivity of a jeweller studying a diamond for flaws.

'I got ahead of myself,' he reflected. 'I put too much importance on making the cut, instead of looking at my skill set. I was
asking, "Who are you? What are you?" Rather than beating
myself into the ground, I should have been concentrating on
small improvements. I guess the game came easy to me as a kid.
Although I worked hard, winning was easy, golf was easy.

'Turning pro and missing those twenty-one cuts has kept me
honest, kept me working hard and never taking it for granted. I
don't mind expectation. You've got to be a big boy. You've got to
be able to handle self-inflicted pressure at the top level. There
were some dark moments, but Dad taught me to be my own man.
One of the greatest things a parent can give a child is the independence to live their own life.'

Ken Rose passed away on a Monday night, 9 September 2002,
after going through an arduous cycle of recovery, remission and
regression. Justin had six days' grace with him, after pulling out
of a tournament in Germany. He had won four times in the previous nine months, in South Africa, Japan and England, and
consoled himself that he had given his father 'a bit of peace'.

Ken told his son: 'You have to be the strong one now.'

Scene Four: East Course, Merion Golf Club, Ardmore, Pennsylvania. Sunday, 16 June 2013

Happy Father's Day. Justin Rose retrieved the ball from the hole on Merion's eighteenth green and kissed it, before pointing at the sky with the index finger on his right hand. He knew he had won his first major title, the US Open, in a manner in which Ken would have approved. His priority was to share the moment in a tearful transatlantic telephone call with his mother.

Their loss was renewed and their emotions were raw on a day of spiritual intensity that evoked the power of memory. Justin had awoken in fifth place, two shots behind overnight leader Phil Mickelson. He received a deeply affecting text that morning from Sean Foley, his coach: 'Go out there and be the man that your dad taught you to be and that your kids can look up to.'

There are instants, in all of our lives, when we gaze into the mirror and see the shimmering reflection of a parent. Justin experienced just such an episode on the way to the course, when he caught himself in the rear-view mirror of his courtesy car. There was something in his eyes, something in the way he held himself, that reminded him of Ken and told him he was not alone.

The final round had hints of history. Rose effectively clinched a two-shot win over Jason Day and Mickelson, with a crisply struck four-iron from the eighteenth fairway. He was barely ten feet from where Ben Hogan hit an iconic one-iron to set up 'the miracle at Merion' – his win in the 1950 US Open – sixteen months after a head-on crash with a Greyhound bus left doctors doubting if he would walk again.

Golf fetishises its past, yet there is contemporary relevance to the photograph that immortalises that one-iron shot. It is golf's equivalent of Nureyev being captured, mid-leap. Hogan is frozen, perfectly balanced in his follow-through. His left foot is planted, his right heel is extended, and the club, which would be stolen before resurfacing thirty years later in a set sold to a dealer for $150 by a nameless old man, is parallel to the ground above his head.

Ken admired mental strength; association with Hogan's definitive achievement somehow felt right. When his father died, Justin hailed him as 'my guide, my mentor, my best friend'. Now, as the jigsaw puzzle of perspective began to be assembled, he remembered his father's assurance to his mother, just before he passed away. 'Don't worry,' Ken said. 'Justin will be okay. He'll know what to do.'

The stars aligned at Merion. Justin told *The Guardian*'s Ewan Murray: 'I guess everybody was emotional. I sensed people who had known me for a long time felt for me as well, in a good way. I had been full circle. My dad had seen me struggle, but fortunately he had also seen me win on tour as a pro. What I'm most grateful for, about winning the US Open, is just how connected I felt to my dad.'

Rose has a long-standing, tightly knit support team that includes caddie Mark Fulcher and London-based strength and conditioning coach Justin Buckthorp, who oversees diet and pre-round preparatory work, 'based on a pyramid of mobility, stability, strength and power'. Jason Goldsmith addresses the psychology of putting, while Phil Kenyon acts as technical putting coach.

Brendan McLoughlin, a physiotherapist and chiropractor, works with Rose in the United States. Alejandro Elorriaga provides up to 100 hours of acupuncture a year. Foley, an engaging Canadian with a disconcerting habit of spitting what I took to be tobacco juice, understands the delicate process of underpinning Rose's success.

'When you look at success in sports, it is almost the ability to endure pain, handle disappointment and get up the next day to go again. The one thing about Justin that has always fascinated me is that he has accomplished so much, but most days he shows up like he's late on his mortgage and his kids aren't eating. In amongst all the fame, the money, the victories, I still just see the twelve-year-old kid at North Hants Golf Club who is not happy with where he is at.

'He's grateful, but knows he can be better. That is why the run of missed cuts is such a reference point. An interesting thing that we haven't looked at, as human beings, is the idea of original trauma. I had a player I worked with who hit the ball left. Even if the shot still found the green, he would freak out. But if he hit it right in the trees, he was okay with it.

'As time went on, I came to find out he had lost a junior tournament at twelve by hitting a key shot left, into trouble. That was the first time his father had ever screamed at him. So what happens is the more we react to an emotion, the deeper we reinforce it.

'We've built a blueprint together with Justin. We've been working on it for nine years. Some weeks we have it, some weeks we don't. None of these players really understand the overall effect of what they originally learned. That's deep in there, in their subconscious.'

Scene Five: Walton Heath Golf Club, Surrey. Friday, 12 October 2018

Wherever he looked, Justin Rose was confronted by scenes from his life, emblazoned at least ten feet high. The most serene but striking image of his torso – arms folded and set against a backcloth of a gigantic Union Flag – overlooked the final green at Walton Heath. It was strangely reminiscent of Gulliver reviewing the army of Lilliput.

Sixteen years after winning the British Masters in front of his father at Woburn, Rose was hosting the event on one of his favourite heathland courses, where heather and gorse envelop errant golf balls and drive even the best golfers to distraction. Though initially feeling weak and nauseous, run down by the ferocity of the Ryder Cup, he did his professional duty.

He would reclaim world number-one status by successfully defending his Turkish Open title the following month, but this was an appropriate time to reset, and review. Winning the FedEx Cup had provided faintly obscene financial reward for his consistency, but the principles and processes of performance, rather than the outcome, offered insight into a champion's mindset.

'I probably don't take stock often enough,' Rose said, with that measured inflection that had become so familiar. 'It's sometimes hard to stand back and look at what you've achieved. 2018 will certainly go down as a special year. You always want to summarise your career in a couple of sentences, and I think I've added a couple of lines this year.

'As a kid, I would have said being a major champion was the most important to me. The Olympic gold medal has become as important, based upon people's reaction to it and how special it felt. Being number one and becoming FedEx champion is right up there. It's going to be very important for me, going into next year and the year after, that I continue to push for improvement, but also understand what I am doing well.

'I have a good team of people around me, for sure, and I lean on them heavily. It's like ten-pin bowling with the bumpers up. If I start to veer off, there's somebody in place to keep me on the straight and narrow. I think that we've made some good choices in the last couple of years. We've found areas of my game, we've made good decisions.

'Talking about not leaving any stone unturned is a dangerous mentality, too. You start changing things, you start searching too hard, you can upset the apple cart. You need to know what works

'The moment where you recognise that whatever you have done, it is the best you can do, is when you begin to discover who and what you are. That is the basis of your story.'

THOMAS BJØRN

'I try to make sense out of many things, but I've also learned that some things are not meant to be understood. I keep having to remind myself to just go with the flow.'

MARTIN KAYMER

'We are right there on the edge every week, trying our best. Everyone who goes out on the first tee is exposing themselves, almost like they are on stage at a rock concert. You are playing with your heart and your soul. In normal life you can get by not exposing yourself fully, but if we are going to do any good, we'd better be fully committed.'

ROBERT KARLSSON

'There aren't many more complicated games, but I tell young players that resiliency is very, very important. It is not all going to be plain sailing out here, so you have to build your brain to deal with the tough days, learn from them.'

GRAEME McDOWELL

'You must not let the game change you when you are down and out.
It is almost inevitable that you will change on the way up, but when you
are really struggling you must try to be even more genuine and honest
and happy, because that shows enormous resilience.'

EDDIE PEPPERELL

'Talking about not leaving any stone unturned is a dangerous mentality, too. You start changing things, you start searching too hard. You can upset the apple cart. You need to know what works for you. To win a tournament you want to stay as free, as loose as possible. That's when your best golf tends to come out.'

JUSTIN ROSE

'In physics I believe in momentum. But also in life I believe in momentum. And it relates to the brain, absolutely, how the brain is working based on positive feedback from the environment. If you get positive responses and you execute shots and make putts and stuff like that, you're going to be positive in everything you do, no matter if a bad shot happens.'

BRYSON DeCHAMBEAU

'Thomas is very principled. He always tries to do the right thing. For being quite a big and intimidating sort of character, he's actually quite sensitive. He's a big softy.'

RORY McILROY

for you. To win a tournament you want to stay as free, as loose, as possible. That's when your best golf tends to come out.

'Keep it simple Thursday to halfway through Sunday. Then you have to click into the mindset of "Right, now's the time, now's the opportunity." Then it's about finishing it off. I think I've done a good job of that, the last couple of years. I've really identified the couple of areas that I can improve, and worked hard within that. Now I'm seeing the results.

'Though I won the gold in '16, I had a pretty bad back injury that wasn't that well documented. I knew I needed to make a change in my putting. I made a recommitment to my short game and my fitness. I'm always trying to adapt. That's the key. You have to adapt in order to keep with the pace of everyone else's improvement.'

Mark Fulcher, his caddie, believes 'There is no give-up in Rosey.' Typically, Sean Foley is more verbose: 'The game doesn't know who Justin Rose is. When we started out, Rosey was seventy-fifth in the world, so to get to number one was so cool. But you also have to understand that before he was seventy-fifth, he had been fifth. So it was in there. There was a lot more talent than understanding. In this world, knowledge plus wisdom equals understanding.'

No one knew that better than Thomas Bjørn. 'Justin and the Open was one of the great Cinderella stories,' he said. 'But, by his own admission, he got thrown into something he wasn't ready for. Everybody has these intentions and thinks, "Oh, I can go with this", but one result doesn't make anything, ever.

'Justin, for me, is one of the most complete golfers in the world game today. He has all the aspects, and he's learned the hard way. That gives him an admiration for the people that struggle, even though they work hard. So, that keeps him in a very good place. There are more than two hundred players out here, and you've got to remember the guy who is struggling to get through life.

'Justin doesn't want to betray that person. He doesn't get in people's faces, because he knows what hardship is in the sport. We're all different. Some players respond emotionally, negatively and positively. Justin is a guy who has a lot of time for what has happened in his life. He knows how fragile it can be, so he's not going to get too excited about it.'

My final image of Rose was one of the most abiding. He was putting in fine rain on the practice green in front of the Walton Heath clubhouse, as twilight took hold. He lined up every attempt as if a major title depended on it. Beside him, Leo, his nine-year-old son, was trying to hole out with a straight-faced iron.

Father and son, in harmony, forming the invisible bond that lasts a lifetime.

Chapter Seven

FRIENDS

They were just out of school, sent to Australia for a month by their management company. By day, they played golf, wove dreams and plotted a way through life's maze. By night, inadequately armed with provisional driving licences, they acted as chauffeurs for their fathers, reprieved from the respective mundanity of tending a bar and driving a fruit-and-vegetable van to act as their caddies.

A little less than thirteen years later, a week before the 2018 Ryder Cup, they were linked by the universality of social media. Oli Fisher had become the first man to shoot fifty-nine on the European Tour, at the Portugal Masters in Vilamoura. Since it had taken 690,000 previous rounds, over forty-six years, to reach that milestone, golf's glitterati lined up to pay their respects.

Rory McIlroy addressed a camera phone, with the mock-Tudor clubhouse at East Lake in Atlanta in the background. The wind that rippled his blue shirt sounded like a gathering gale, force eight on the Beaufort scale. 'Oli,' he said, through the din, 'many congrats. Unbelievable. Watched the last few holes this morning. So happy for you. What an achievement.'

His European teammates, Tommy Fleetwood, Ian Poulter, Henrik Stenson and Alex Norén, followed suit. Justin Rose was beamed in from his courtesy car: 'History made. Serious stones down the stretch, bud.' All identified with Fisher's reward for persistence over more than a decade, without having McIlroy's insight into the deeper meaning of the achievement.

Close friends, Fisher and McIlroy were once the princes of the amateur game. Fisher, the youngest Walker Cup player at sixteen years and 334 days, had won Sir Nick Faldo's Junior Series, a reliable barometer of latent potential, in three successive years. He was nine months older than McIlroy, a generational talent in incubation, and turned pro at eighteen.

McIlroy did likewise and was transcendent in his twenties. He won four major titles, earned more money than he could ever spend, and survived the assault course of instant global celebrity. Fisher, his partner in the Junior Ryder Cup, won once on the European Tour, at the Czech Masters in 2011, two years after he had lost his card.

Fisher has been successful, winning more than €4,500,00 in prize money on the main tour, but his name is more generally clustered in small print, lower down the leader board; his friend's is invariably garlanded in headlines. When McIlroy described the European Tour as 'a stepping stone' in 2019, the golfing world inhaled sharply. The two men embody the difference, in professional sport, between being very good and exceptional.

Why the disparity in progress? Why did Fisher, in 100th place on the first tee and more concerned with making the sixty-seven he calculated he needed to make the cut in Portugal, walk off the course to a champagne shower from Matt Wallace, having accumulated ten birdies and an eagle in the round of his life? It was an M&M experience, a fusion of momentum and memory.

He played the first twelve holes in ten under par, and noticed he had attracted an ever-expanding caravan of cameramen and curious spectators. His mind went back two years to a smaller version of the same phenomenon; then he shot sixty-four, birdieing the last two holes to save his Tour card. Here he turned to his caddie Guy Tilston, after holing a pivotal twenty-five-foot par putt on the sixteenth, and said, 'Let's just enjoy this.'

Fisher could have shot fifty-eight, shaving the hole with a forty-foot birdie putt at the last, but ultimately his performance under pressure at Vilamoura in 2016 was more satisfying, because of the ramifications of failure. His greatest lesson from finishing tied for seventh place, following predictably anticlimactic weekend rounds of sixty-nine and seventy, was confirmed by a group of Olympic rowers.

They were working with Chris Shambrook, Fisher's sports psychologist: 'These guys were smart, had all sorts of degrees, but Chris talked about getting them to row dumb. It doesn't matter how intelligent you are, get in that bit of carbon fibre on the water and row. That's it. It sounds so basic, but it simplified my thoughts.

'The game has not been how I envisaged it, growing up. It throws things at you when you least expect it. I once played a practice round with Rory in Holland and lost nine balls on the front nine. I shot seventy-nine, seventy-eight in my first Open, at Turnberry in 2009. No way I saw that sort of stuff coming when I was a kid. I ask myself all the time, "How can I stay in my head and not lose it?"

'You've got to be able to hole that putt, feel you can take a tournament by the scruff of the neck and turn it into a two- or three-shot lead. That comes down to ability, self-control, managing your body and emotions. Don't get me wrong, but the best players, when they are under pressure, make it the most basic game.

'Hit it where you want to hit it. It's the simplest thing. All you've got to do is find fairways and greens. The best guys turn up at the biggest tournaments and go, "What's my default here?" They have the self-belief to tell themselves that they will be in contention, coming down the stretch on Sunday, if they do their things properly. The rest of us over-complicate it.

'Say you've got a one o'clock tee time on a Thursday. You stand there on the first tee, and the big leader board beside you says so-and-so has shot minus eight in the morning. You think, "Fucking hell, this course was really hard when I played a practice round on Tuesday. The rough's up, the greens are quick. Jesus Christ, how's he shot that?"

'The next thing you know, you've bogeyed the first and you're nine back. You are at panic stations. It's important to get a grip and say, "You know what, everyone else doesn't matter." I can honestly say the biggest thing I have learned is to be myself. I'm not looking to be, or play, like anyone else. The biggest guys get out of their own way.'

We were having breakfast at Bearwood Lakes, an exclusive club near Wokingham in Berkshire. Fisher was instantly engaged, talking football over avocado on toast, but suddenly exclaimed, 'Look at that.' Out of the picture window he had glimpsed a deer, nervously steeling itself for a dash across a sloping fairway on the parkland course. It was tempting to draw parallels with the fight-or-flight instinct that so often prevails in professional sport.

Instead, we returned to the theme of simplicity, a lack of pretension. Fisher spoke of reducing his internal conversation to three words: 'back, hit, stop'. That is the golf swing, boiled dry. Its starkness is a convenient distraction from the physiological and psychological challenges of reproducing it in stressful circumstances.

'You've got your brain and you've got your body. I can hit the ball well, but it's matching the two up, you know? How am I connecting with what my mind and body are doing? Is my unconscious mind in control? It's like driving a racing car. You can't do it properly if it's got too much under-steer or over-steer. You need to know where you are at. You don't need to rush, or be amazing.

'There are so many aspects of the game – the putting stroke, the long wide arc of a driver, the short arc of a chip shot – but really you've just got to go out there and play. Play as a kid, play unconsciously. It's funny, some of my best rounds have been when I'm a little angry, but in general, you need the feels. You need to find the state of mind to be at your best.'

That had been a topic of discussion a couple of weeks previously when McIlroy visited him for a barbecue. Fisher sees the private side of the superstar, the human being recoiling from constant scrutiny and the conventions of celebrity. Each is as consumed by the game as they were in Australia, 'where we took our dads out for a ride like they were our wives'. The difference, of course, is one of scale.

'We're good pals and go back a long way. Rory has always struck the ball really, really well. He had a lovely flowing swing, still does. But the funny thing is when we played with each other as kids, I played a bit more down the middle, fifteen foot left or right of the pin, middle of the green, give myself a chance, on to the next hole. I'm a little more erratic now, but I remember vividly that he would hit the flag once a round.

'He's done that three or four times from around a hundred and seventy yards while I've been with him. He would be quite aggressive and make bogeys, but in full flow he's "Boom, boom, boom!" When he's got his eye in, he's like Ronnie O'Sullivan in snooker, just a natural. He's got a rare eye for seeing a shot and being able to hit the ball straight down that line.

'Everyone wants a bit of his time. It's hard to know how that would affect you or me or anyone else in that position, but Rory is smart enough, and knows himself well enough, to be able to take control of what he wants to do. He obviously wants to go out and win every week, like we all do, but it is a very hard game. He doesn't win for, say, eight events and he has to deal with people saying, "Oh, what's happening to him?"

'Let's have a bit of perspective. He's won four majors, won however many tournaments around the world. He has the most worldwide ranking points of anyone, and people are wondering if he is done. I could see from his mindset the other day that he is really, really close to doing something special. Golf's a funny game like that, isn't it?'

The arc of McIlroy's professional life, from prodigy to power broker, is difficult to align with personal growth. Only Jack Nicklaus and Tiger Woods have matched his feat in winning four majors by the age of twenty-six, but his search for the fifth – given emphasis by the proximity of his thirtieth birthday in May 2019 – has involved following a parallel path.

Weight of money, from clothing and club contracts worth in excess of $300 million over a decade from 2013, lightens the load. The glare of silverware loses its capacity to dazzle. Whenever he turns up at a tournament, McIlroy faces a barrage of questions about instincts and intentions, but the most pertinent line of enquiry is increasingly internal: 'Is that it?'

The Beatles went to India to seek spiritual compensation for overwhelming success. Michael Jordan deflected his greatness as a basketball player by pursuing an unlikely dream, of making it in Major League baseball. Muhammad Ali sought succour in his faith. Golf doesn't encourage experimentation, since its legends are expected to evolve into august museum pieces, but McIlroy is different.

Marriage to Erica Stoll, who, in her role with the PGA of America helped him make his tee time at the 2012 Ryder Cup in Medinah, following his infamous failure to align time zones, confirmed a change in emphasis. He found a divergent, deeper outlet for his obsessiveness. He meditated, read widely and learned to juggle, as a means of relieving stress and maintaining mental acuity.

He used a *New York Times* profile in the build-up to the Ryder Cup to stress that he didn't want golf 'to define who I am'.

The book *Essentialism: The Disciplined Pursuit of Less* by Greg McKeown, a prominent blogger for the *Harvard Business Review* and LinkedIn's Influencer group, 'helped me learn to say "No"'.

McIlroy argued, 'There's a reason I try to keep my private life private. I guess for me, my thing is: what is my goal in my career? My goal is to be a master of my craft.' To use a journalistic colloquialism, he gives good quote. His press conferences can initially be terse, but when freed intellectually by the strength of the subject, he is expansive, earnest and entertaining.

Typically, he was asked at the 2018 Open Championship whether he had established harmony in his life. 'Depends which day you ask me,' he answered with an impish grin. 'Golfers are touchy at the best of times. I've become more balanced, I guess. I try to see the bigger picture, and I try to have some perspective in my life. It isn't all about trying to win golf tournaments and chase titles. There are other things that give me fulfilment.

'I've always had other interests. But getting married, thinking about the future and what that entails, that's huge. As you get older and as you evolve as a person, you change. It's not just the golf nowadays. There's a lot more that goes into it. It's still my career and I feel I have a lot of time left to make my mark, but it doesn't keep me up at night thinking, "If I never win another major, I can't live with myself."'

Those are dangerous words, because the sentiment is so seductive. They also contain an element of self-deception. His failure to convert a chance to win the 2018 Masters led to revealing reflection, when he returned home: 'It was just the quiet moments when you're staring off into the distance and you're thinking about a certain shot or a certain putt,' he recalled. 'It got to the point where I needed to see a bit of daylight and get outside and go for walks and start to do my usual thing.'

The standards he set himself, in winning four majors in four years, are absurd. Golf's talent pool is deeper than it has ever been. A new generation, blessed with brutal strength and biomechanical purity, is already announcing itself. As McIlroy seeks balance, entering the fourth decade of life, the questions almost begin to pose themselves:

'Do you put the pressure on yourself, or does everyone else do that for you?' he said, without supplying an immediate answer. 'Is that a recent phenomenon, since Tiger started winning at a young age, and they expected him to keep winning and winning? Maybe people are judging everyone by Tiger's past standards.

'I've always said my performance in majors up to 2014 wasn't the norm. That was above my normal level. You go back down, build yourself back up, and everything finds its balance. There are going to be times you struggle with this or that. There's only been one guy who sustained his peak over ten years or so, and that's Tiger. He won fourteen major championships in eleven years. I mean, that's pretty ridiculous, in anyone's book.'

Victory in the Players Championship at Sawgrass in March 2019 seemed redemptive: 'I desperately wanted the win today, but it's just another day. It's just another step on the journey. I've been preaching perspective, and I feel like I've got a pretty good handle on that perspective. My career is hopefully going to last another fifteen or twenty years, so one tournament or one day or one month in those twenty years is nothing. It's just a glimpse, so it doesn't change anything. It doesn't change who I am.'

Pádraig Harrington is a source of much-needed perspective on McIlroy's status: 'Clearly, his career is now solely based on how he does in the majors. There seems to be no other yardstick for Rory, and that's probably the yardstick he uses himself. Back in 2011 he had stolen a march on the field when it came to driving the golf ball, which brought tremendous confidence all the way through his game.

'I think at this stage players have caught up. There are many who drive the ball comparably and have certainly eaten into that advantage. In 2011 he was competing against himself, similar to how Tiger has been for most of his career. Now it's just a tougher ask. The beauty for Rory is he's still very young, he's still very capable, and with patience those majors will come.

'I'm just trying to word this correctly. If we look at history, when you start in the modern era, it took twenty years for Jack Nicklaus to get eighteen majors. It took Gary Player twenty years too, for his nine. And you're judging Rory over seven years. Give him another seven years and see if he's got eight majors in the bag. Are we disappointed with that, then?'

At a certain level, professional golf becomes a self-help group, a web of informally associated friends who understand each other's needs and neuroses. Two underpinning factors in Thomas Bjørn's successful captaincy were the respect he commanded and the quiet, occasionally unsentimental advice he offered. It was unsurprising to learn of his relationship with both McIlroy and Fisher.

'When you're around the best people in the world, yeah, they are good guys, and they are nice, but they have also got that switch where they can be fierce,' Fisher reasoned. 'You talk to people about Thomas: he can be fierce, really fierce. But he has always been there for me, since I came out on Tour. He's always chatted to me, spoken to my dad. I've listened, taken notice.

'The older I get and look back at what I've done, I'm quite disappointed in how my career's gone, in terms of results, but there is still a lot to learn. When you're out there, you need people you can trust, someone who can offer sound advice – someone you can just sit down with and they'll go, "Listen, don't panic here."'

McIlroy is surrounded by people who want something from him: his time, endorsement or patronage. Bjørn needs nothing; by contrast, he is willing to share his expertise and experience on a technical or human level. He understands the perversity of golf and, in McIlroy's case, passed on his perspective as one of the best wedge players in the world.

'Thomas and I got off to a bit of a rocky start,' McIlroy remembered. 'I first played with him in the 2007 Madrid Masters. I was a cocky eighteen-year-old, he was a veteran. I might have shown a couple of bits of bad etiquette from time to time, and Thomas let me know about it. I thought this guy was a . . . whatever.

'We sort of hugged it out the next week on the range in Portugal, and we've been really good friends ever since. Thomas is very principled. He always tries to do the right thing. For being quite a big and intimidating sort of character, he's actually quite sensitive. He's a big softy. I had a really good chat with him about my wedge play in Scotland.

'Basically, what makes me so good with the driver is sometimes what makes me inconsistent with the wedges. It's to do with hand-speed and body-speed and rotation, and the fact that sometimes you need a lot of separation in your upper and lower body with the driver in your hand. You don't need that separation with a wedge.

'Thomas said it was the opposite with him: what made him such a good wedge player also made him not a very good driver of the ball. It's just about trying to find that blend. I've definitely become a little more rotational in my swing over the past couple of years; some of that is through bad habit, and some is through injury. I'm trying to get back to the way I swung the club the last time I won a major, in 2014 at Valhalla.'

Fisher's horizons are slightly more indistinct and inevitably narrower, but he identifies with the principle of pursuit: 'We're all looking,' he said, wistfully. 'Golf is a game that really beats the life out of you. When you're out there, and you think to yourself, "I don't know whether I'm going eighty yards left or forty yards right here", you're on your own.

'We all have our points of crisis, whether that's being on the cut line or coming down to the last couple of tournaments of the year with your card under threat. You can do all the right things and still play terrible. When you are hovering around the bottom, it is an entirely different feeling to being at the top, and trying to win tournaments. I'm ticking away. My career has been a bit rickety, up and down, no fireworks. I'd like to think my time is still coming, you know? I'm thirty and I've played three hundred-odd tournaments as a pro. There won't be many of my age on Tour who've done that.

'It's funny. It is so easy to get on the treadmill as a pro. You fly out Monday night or Tuesday morning. You play eighteen holes Tuesday afternoon. You're practising Wednesday. Thursday tee time, what is it? Friday, have I made it to the weekend? Right, Sunday. What can I get done? Next week, where are we going?

'You play thirty tournaments a year. You practise sixteen, seventeen of the weeks you're at home. You're thinking all the time. How am I managing my time off? What am I doing? How fresh is my mind? My body might be a bit stiff, but I know if my mind is fresh, I'll be able to make decent decisions at important times.

'The hole is four and a half inches wide, and there is always an element of luck involved, but you have to take ownership of what you do. Lose that, get too far ahead of yourself, and whoa, it throws you. You can never go through the motions. It's not like football, where if you are feeling a bit sluggish, you can tuck in, not see the ball and hide for a bit.

'It's so easy to fritter away a shot. When you play people like Tommy or Rory, they are so much more consistent off the tee. They can take a course on and knock it down there, three hundred and ten every time. We're playing with one hand tied behind our backs. You've got to be the eternal optimist, as a golfer. If you're not, the game is going to drag you down.'

His friendship with McIlroy cuts across golf's class divide. Fisher lives in an executive new-build in Berkshire and seeks more than a fifteen-minute introduction to global fame. McIlroy has just sold his waterfront mansion in Palm Beach, Florida, for $11.5 million and craves the reassurance of another major title. The game that seized them as schoolboys continues to hold them in thrall.

And that is a blessing, even if it is well disguised.

Chapter Eight

TRUST YOUR HEART

Of all the bars in all the world, Sam Torrance had to run into Eddie Pepperell and Jordan Smith in the clubhouse at The Dutch, an inland course in Spijk, near Groningen. The emerging stars of European golf were winding down after finishing in the top ten at the Dutch Open. The former Ryder Cup captain had been commentating for the international television feed.

Perhaps it was because Torrance had celebrated his sixty-fifth birthday three weeks earlier. Perhaps it was because his pride no longer permitted him to play, since he had lost the swing and touch that enabled him to win thirty-two tournaments, world-wide. Or perhaps it was simply because he had a sudden, understandably melancholic vision of what once was.

He had an urge to reach out across the generations.

He had spoken to Pepperell on the range that Sunday morning, and was touched by the younger player's subsequent gesture, in sending the commentary team a large box of chocolates. Torrance understood and admired his idiosyncratic approach, since he shared Pepperell's love of good red wine and had, in his heyday, been known to dance on tables, stripped to the waist.

'They're sitting there, in their tracksuits and trainers, having a glass of wine. They could be the stars of the future. I looked at them and I was so envious. You know, forty years ago that was me. I just thought, "Awesome." I wanted to go over to speak to them, but I didn't want them to think, "Who's this old fucker?"

'The chocolates gave me the opportunity to thank Eddie, and to introduce myself to Jordan. I had a priceless clip on Whats-App, really funny, to show them. We had a good laugh and I had to say what I've just said to you, that forty years ago I was them. I just said to them, "Boys, just love it. Enjoy it. You've got the best life coming ahead of you."

'Anyway, I've said my piece and I'm heading back to my table when Eddie called out to me. He said, "Did you say *forty* years?" And I came back at him. "Actually, it is forty-six. I just didn't want to tell you that." Everyone started laughing. That was a lovely wee moment. What a life. What a great life . . . It doesn't last for ever.'

A life has to be lived, before it can be fully appreciated. Professional sport moves too fast, too randomly, to allow reflection on the run. At heart, Torrance remains the ten-year-old boy who played the last hole at the Routenburn club, overlooking the Firth of Clyde, for a shilling (that's five pence, kids.) Those money matches, against Brother Nicholas and the priests known as the 'holy fourball', ingrained his fondness for a bet.

Torrance's love for the game was in his genes, since his father, Bob, was one of a generation of golf teachers whose influence spread, like ice dropped into his favourite dram. He was a disciple of Ben Hogan, helped Pádraig Harrington to win Open Championships in successive years, and was given golf's equivalent of a state funeral at Greenock Crematorium when he died in 2014, aged eighty-two.

Sam played 685 tournaments on the European Tour between 1971 and 2003, walking an estimated 15,000 miles in the process, but the Ryder Cup has given his life symmetry. The image of him, arms aloft and putter held ramrod-straight towards the heavens, after holing the winning putt in 1985, is iconic. Seventeen years later, after a Ryder Cup campaign interrupted by the obscenity of 9/11, he was celebrating wildly on that same eighteenth green, at the Belfry.

Traditional golf clubs tend to have the feel of lovingly tended local museums. Certain members, it must be said, are fossils. Yet there is something about the mahogany-lined walls, and the unabashed genuflection to the past, that overcomes scepticism. These places smell of old men's reverie, rather than teen spirit, but deserve to be taken on their own terms, as an expression of devotion.

Torrance's social circle revolves around the Sunningdale club, his close friend Michael 'Queenie' King – the former Ryder Cup player who was forced to retire, due to a severe form of arthritis in the spine – and games of backgammon featuring a cast of characters who, down the years, have answered to such soubriquets as Huge Bum, Dodge and Cashmere.

We meet nearby, on the terrace at Wentworth, over a cheeky pre-lunch glass or two of Merlot, to discuss the intrinsic attraction of golf. Torrance is gently spoken, animated by opinion and subdued by reminiscence. He may occasionally be profane, but the game that frames his life is sacred.

'It's fucking awesome. It's a great game, a very honest game. There have been cheats over the years, but they are very few and far between. It's one of the hardest games to play, one of the most rewarding games to play. You spend your life as a loser. You don't win every week, you lose every week, virtually, but you build to win. Wins come infrequently, sometimes frequently.

'It's about the love of the game. Anyone who plays golf loves golf. The game is trying to change with the times, to sell itself to the masses, but you can't beat the Open Championship, the Masters – that thrill of coming down the last nine, six and three. Needing something to win on the final hole is just fantastic.

'You've got the other side of the coin, the guys trying to keep their card, or make the cut for the weekend. In snooker, people used to say safety games were boring. I loved them, because you saw the intricacies of the sport; what the players can actually do. It's the same in golf, but with different scenarios. Three ahead this week: how does he handle it? Five behind: hello, how does he handle that? I think it's a fabulous sport to watch. Yes, it takes time, but that's never really hurt.'

In today's content-rich, time-poor, click-happy culture, how can golf expect to explain to the uninitiated the maddening, elusive quality of a perfect swing, or the skill required to make a small dimpled ball be an obedient servant through the unseen eddies of a freshening breeze? How can something that percolates for four days, gathering depth and flavour, be consumed by a generation that has the attention span of a goldfish?

'There are so many fragments to a golf swing. Everything has to work together for it to be perfect. I don't really know enough to class golf as a science, but I know it's an art form. Look back at TV footage of Seve. There's an art form right there in front of you. It's like watching Messi. It is not black and white; it's this, it's that, it's a body and brain functioning.

'If anything, you play better when you're not in control. Sometimes you can't help yourself, because what happens on the range before the round comes out onto the course with you. If you've been nailing it, floating the wedge beautifully and just ripping every practice shot, you walk out onto the first tee saying, "Oh, yeah. I'm going to fucking kill this game."

'You're fucked, because you are complacent. You're a millisecond out of focus. Before you know it, you've knocked it out of bounds and there's no comeback. You're now three off the tee. But if you've been conscious of your frailties on the range, you rely on focus and concentration. There is a commitment to what you are doing.

'So when I get over a ball and I've got one hundred and eighty yards to hit, I know it's a six-iron job. I'm not going to go in there thinking, "Is it an easy five, or a hard seven? Or is it a chippy six, a high six, or a cut six?" My mind is made up. I see the shot in the distance, and commit to it. No other thoughts should come into your head. It ultimately doesn't matter if it goes wrong, because you've done what you thought was right.'

As we are discovering – to quote that famous newspaper masthead – all human life is there. There may be rigid conformity in certain technical drills, but personality traits are kaleidoscopic. Quirks and qualities vary from individual to individual, but what, in Torrance's view, is the optimal profile of a consistently successful professional golfer?

'Somebody who is very comfortable with himself. Happy with himself, happy at home. Very competent. No frailties, no negatives. Everything is on the up. Someone who can contend with bad conditions. I used to revel in that. Everyone is pissed off, the greens are shit, and I'm fucking loving it. That's the kind of attitude you need.

'Be kind. You know, it's a tough life out there and you really need friends. You don't want to be a loner. Look at tennis, for instance. The pros never talk to each other, because every week it's in or out. And some poor bastard on Monday morning has got Federer, or Djokovic or Murray. It's completely nuts. Sunday is a bit different in golf, but there's no animosity.

'You're aware of everyone else's failings, and they're aware of yours. You can't hide it. It's a very descriptive game. It's right there, in front of you. It's not like tennis or snooker, where you're in a wee arena. Golf is on such a big scale that your frailties show up very easily. If someone hits a bad shot, you're reading his body language and assessing his action.

'If that action is a bit quicker than normal, and they're in contention, it is a sign they're not comfortable. Many of the top players have frailties. I don't want to name them, but some aren't good chippers; some aren't great putters, but they get there. A strong mind, I think, is one of the keys.

'When Poulter was asked why he didn't use a sports psychologist, he said, "Why would I pay someone to tell me how good I am, when I know how good I am?" And I think that's fantastic. Half of today's players have about six people around them. Fine, if that works for them. I found it much more rewarding to sort my own problems out. After all, you're out there on your own.

'The work ethic is different now, and whether it's right or wrong is arguable to me. My father was one of the best teachers of all time and he changed his plan, he changed his frigging tune eventually. What he said to me, growing up, was, "If you don't take it with you, you won't find it there." That meant that when I was at home I did all my work, I practised hard.

'And so when I went to the tournament, I went to play. I'd hit maybe twenty shots before my round, come off the last green and leave the course. I'd go to the movies, go back to my room and read. Reading was wonderful, because you've got so much spare time on your hands. If you're slogging balls away on the range all afternoon, it's just a waste of time.

'If you've got a fault in your swing, you're only endorsing it. If you're dependent on a coach, how on earth can you play under pressure when you are out there, all alone? That's not to disrespect coaches, by the way. My dad was one. In his day there wasn't enough money on Tour. They had club jobs. They were teachers of the game, who helped it grow.'

Such traditions were established around the advent of the twentieth century by the original 'Great Triumvirate' of Harry Vardon, J.H. Taylor and James Braid, who won sixteen of the twenty-one Open Championships held between 1894 and 1914. They were faithful retainers, club professionals; Braid, for instance, was attached to Walton Heath from 1904 until his death in 1950. He beat or matched his age in a ceremonial birthday round until he was eighty; he shot eighty-one and passed away nine months later.

Vardon gave his name to the now-traditional method of gripping the club, in which the little finger of his right hand overlapped the index finger of the left. But for tuberculosis, which debilitated him for a decade, he would have added to his record six Open titles, won over eighteen years until 1914. Taylor won five times, playing in all thirty Championships staged between 1893 and 1927.

No one has a better grasp of golf's lineage than Ken Schofield. When he took over from John Jacobs as head of the European Tour in 1975, it consisted of seventeen tournaments and offered total prize money of £500,000. No professional golf was played east of Berlin, since the Communist Bloc viewed the game as decadent and unworthy of an allocation of land.

The founding fathers of the game would be astonished by the ubiquity and prosperity of the modern European Tour, which warps time and stretches geographic logic. The 2019 season began on 22 November 2018 in Hong Kong. It girdles the globe, encompassing forty-eight tournaments in thirty-one countries spanning five continents. Total prize money is in the region of $140 million.

Yet even in a game that cherishes its heritage, politics pervade. The drive for the strategic revision of the international calendar, involving the creation of an elitist World Tour in conjunction with the PGA Tour, seems irresistible. Golf's distinctive ethos, in being run by the players for the good of the majority of players, is under strain.

Thomas Bjørn's determination to protect the independence of the European Tour was a significant source of friction during his captaincy. Schofield, who was the Tour's executive director for twenty-nine years until 2004, acknowledges his detachment from day-to-day affairs, but supports the current model, which requires a 75 per cent vote to trigger change, because 'there are no barriers, no middle men'.

Crucially, he had the foresight in the late Seventies to recognise the importance to television of sport on Sundays. Until he intervened, leading players had appeared in independent Sunday pro-ams, which offered as much money as, if not more than, tournaments. Priorities quickly changed. The BBC was unamused in 1980 when live coverage of a breathless finish to the Martini International at Wentworth, featuring Seve Ballesteros, Greg Norman and Brian Barnes, delayed the 6 p.m. news, but golf was at a pivotal point in its evolution.

Schofield attended his first Ryder Cup at Laurel Valley, sixty miles north of Pittsburgh, in 1975. Its inertia and inequality were summarised by the formality of the United States's 21–11 win over Great Britain & Ireland. There were very few spectators, and American media interest was minimal. Jack Nicklaus, whose reverence for tradition was embedded by another great golf teacher, Jack Grout, recognised the existential threat.

'I'd grown up with grainy pictures of Jack and Arnold Palmer,' Schofield recalled. 'They were down-to-earth men, but giants who bestrode the game. Jack told Lord John Derby, of the PGA, that "Our challenge in the US is to make our team. We know we are probably going to win. We should do something."' By the time the Cup returned to North America in 1979, opposition was provided by an extended European team.

International sport operates cyclically and is occasionally boosted biologically. Europe's emergence was eased by the so-called Famous Five: Ballesteros, Nick Faldo, Sandy Lyle, Bernhard Langer and Ian Woosnam. Born within eleven months of one another, from April 1957 to March 1958, they formed the nucleus of the team that won the Cup for the first time in twenty-seven years in 1985.

Torrance was its poster boy. He holed a twenty-two-foot putt across the final green to secure overall victory after his opponent, Andy North, had driven into the water, but is prouder profession-ally of the eight-foot putt he had converted to level his match on the seventeenth. 'Everything was shaking on that one,' he said. 'The club, my hands – the lot.

'That was the one that really counted. The eighteenth was nothing. I had three putts to win. My mother could have done that. But that moment, and the aftermath, will never leave me. People still come up to me, because it was an unbelievable moment. They ask for your autograph and ask if it fucks you off. God, no. It's when they stop asking me that it's going to piss me off. It doesn't take much to make someone's day.

'You can't really describe the Ryder Cup. David Feherty, one of my best mates on Tour, made the team in 1991. "Come on, you can tell me now," he said to me. "What's it like?" He had three kids, the same as me, and the only analogy I could come up with was it's like having a kid. You just can't explain the bond that's there with your children. It just blows your mind. The Cup is the same.'

Europe's victory under Torrance's captaincy in 2002, which even made Tony Blair's speech at the Labour Party Conference, had been postponed for a year, following the 11 September attacks. It was an event that had slipped into a time warp, since all on-course branding referred to it as 'the 2001 Ryder Cup'. Both teams remained unchanged, despite the hiatus.

'It was unique. God forbid there's another one like it. Because it was the same team a year later, half of them were playing shite. I had some broken men come into my team, but I didn't care. The Americans were in the same boat. Half of them also wouldn't have made it, had teams been picked on current form. It's irrelevant. This is my team. That's it. Let's go.

'You can mould a team. I love Sir Alex Ferguson. I think he's one of the greatest managers of all time. I had a lot of time with him on the phone when I was captain. The best thing he said to me was, "There are no superstars in your team. Every man is an equal. Every man is doing a job." And that was just such a key. Remember, this was a first for me as well.

'You have to make your special players feel special, because they are special, but without making it obvious. Your lesser players will know you're looking after the others, but you're also looking after them more than normal. It's a difficult one to get absolutely right, but it's there to be done. The more you put in, the more you get out.

'It was almost incomprehensible to me that I would be so relaxed. I don't know if it was because I didn't have to play. I think it was more down to the preparation that I'd done; I was ready for anything that came at me. Anything. The only thing that terrified me was the speeches at the opening and closing ceremonies. I always thought I could never pull that off in a million years.'

He was helped to do so by Professor David Purdie, a globally renowned specialist in the treatment of osteoporosis, the brittle-bone disease, who is an acclaimed after-dinner speaker. They worked on the speech for more than a year; in the final week they arranged for the ceremonial podium to be installed in Torrance's garage, so that he could spend three hours a day reciting from it. The power of memory and repetition overcame his stage fright.

Formalities fade over time, yet memories of spontaneous joy endure. An unbidden smile breaks over Torrance's face as he recalls the post-victory party, and such surreal moments as being given a standing ovation the following afternoon when he took the Cup into Kentucky Fried Chicken at a motorway service station on his return journey to his Surrey home from the Belfry.

'So many stories. After we'd won, Lee Westwood found me and my wife Suzanne, wherever we were, and said, "Come on, we've got to go down to the bar." The bar at the Belfry is enormous, it's huge. You couldn't move. Westwood had rounded up the team. He's up on the sofa, announcing the players to the assembled fans, as if it was WWF wrestling.

'It was brilliant, they were going absolutely mad. So I get up and they go mad, Suzanne gets up and they go mad. Then they find Phillip Price, who had beaten Phil Mickelson in the singles that day. Probably the best victory of his life – a day he will never forget as long as he lives. As he's climbing up onto the sofa, he's whacking Westwood on the arms and saying, "Tell them who I beat! Tell them who I beat!" It's just a moment that you'd never forget. It's the first thing I say, whenever we meet.'

Tendrils of brotherhood entwine players and rivals. In another example of the Cup's synchronicity, two future captains featured in what was to be the decisive singles match on that storied day in 2002, when Europe's victory was sealed by Paul McGinley's half-point against Jim Furyk. Bjørn, another future captain, defeated Stewart Cink.

'Thomas was awesome. A huge talent. You just had to harness it, and let him go do his thing. I'm not saying he was a difficult person, because he's not, but he has a very strong mindset. I like that. His positivity, his strong mind, makes him a formidable figure, and a captain is a kind of headmaster. Even though he may be your mate, and you've known him all your life, it's daunting to go to him with what you think is a problem. You might just let that problem fester, because you're intimidated by disrupting his job. '

These were the themes they discussed on a promotional visit to New York, a month or so before the 2018 event. Their conversation was effortless and intimate. Men from different cultures and successive generations had a rare form of solidarity because of the burdens of responsibility. One had survived and thrived under the ultimate pressure; the other awaited his appointment with fate.

'It's your team and you have to do what you feel is right, deep down inside,' Torrance told Bjørn. 'That's not always easy, but that's why you are there. You're not going to glean the information from anywhere else. Think of what you've learned so far, what you've seen, all the players you've looked at, the five rookies you've got around you. Have faith in yourself.

'Trust your heart.'

Chapter Nine

THOMAS BJØRN: CAPTAIN'S LOG

It doesn't take a rocket scientist to understand the Ryder Cup. It's black and white, win or lose, sadness or euphoria. The more people care, the greater the contrast. Every single person I have met in golf – players, caddies, fans, even journalists and broadcasters, who normally protect their professional objectivity – is emotionally attached to what it represents.

I bumped into Michael Calvin in the natural bowl behind the ninth green at Le Golf National on the Saturday morning. He was following the pivotal fourball featuring Rory McIlroy and Sergio García, whose lead over Tony Finau and Brooks Koepka had just been trimmed to three holes. We stood together for a couple of minutes, while the players drove from the tenth tee.

Having taken my earpiece out, briefly, I was struck by the intensity of the crowd's chant: 'Rory . . . Rory . . . Rory.' The hills, packed with people dressed as superheroes or in a variety of national costumes, were alive. 'This is great, isn't it?' Michael said. I must have been locked in PR-mode, since I replied, 'We keep pushing. There's work to be done.' Yet I managed to pause, the hardest thing for a captain to do in such circumstances. 'Told you,' I said, when he suggested casually that such days make the Ryder Cup the greatest sports event in the world. Michael was obviously locked in journo-mode, since he shot back: 'You enjoying it, then?' It certainly made me think 'Yes . . . Noooooo . . .'

Sergio was first on the range before seven o'clock that cold morning, when the moon was still visible in the salmon-pink streaked sky. He was wired. When their TV interviews had been done, after victory had been assured on the seventeenth green, Rory ran downhill, ducking low and shooting at imaginary targets in a gunfighter pose.

High on adrenaline, yet still swigging their energy drinks, they climbed onto a buggy and were taken around the eighteenth green on their way back to the team room. They saluted the crowd like conquering emperors; it was the stuff of boyhood fantasy, another reminder that sport is, in essence, about people.

The flaws and fragility of players are as compelling as their fortitude and ferocity under pressure. The Ryder Cup is golf's greatest team event, but identification with the individual is never stronger. TV viewers can read every twitch, share every emotion. Spectators provide the soundtrack. Everyone lives in the moment. Boom . . . something happens right there, right now. Deal with it.

The flipside of this is the intensity of the inquest. It is human nature to not quite see the whole picture when you analyse emotionally. It is much easier to pick out one aspect and leap to general conclusions. It is not as simple as saying, 'Well, this was right, and this was wrong.' It is also far too easy to load the blame on one man.

The captain is the lightning conductor, the cat that gets kicked. If you don't understand that, it is not the job for you. I know, to my cost, that the Cup unleashes emotions that can ruin relationships. Things were said and done that were not right when I attacked Ian Woosnam's leadership qualities, after learning on TV that I had failed to earn one of his wild-card picks in 2006.

I apologised, but the damage was irreparable. The saddest thing is that I lost the friendship of a man who meant a lot to me.

Woosie helped me, as a young player. I played my first Ryder Cup match with him, a win over Justin Leonard and Brad Faxon in the Saturday-morning fourball in 1997. In other circumstances, he would have been a valued confidant in Paris. As it is, we are civil, but distant.

The most recent, and certainly most poignant, example of volatility was at Gleneagles in 2014, when Tom Watson's captaincy of the US team was challenged by Phil Mickelson, in what became a notorious post-match press conference. It is difficult for me to comment, since I wasn't in their team room, but I was surprised, while being sympathetic to both men.

Tom is one of the legends of the game. Phil has suffered more hurt in the Ryder Cup than any other player. He'd obviously had enough of hurting. Whoever was captain was going to get it. I understand that, to a degree, because I experienced losing for the first time when I was one of Darren Clarke's vice-captains at Hazeltine, Minnesota, two years later. As experiences go, it's pretty awful.

A losing locker room is deathly quiet. Everyone takes time to sit and reflect. When they have a few beers in them, the mood begins to change. It doesn't become a party room, but gallows humour takes over. Fuck it! Let's just enjoy ourselves. Everyone in the outside world thinks we are useless and we're not very good at what we do, but we might as well enjoy being here. Eventually, you filter out into what passes as the real world, and discover that things are not quite as dark as they seem.

People criticise the losing captain, on both sides. I felt bad for Darren. I knew how much it meant to him. He is such a close friend, and had done such a good job, putting so much time and effort in, but it all turned a little sour. When any team gets it right, as the Americans did in Hazeltine and we did in Paris, it is a huge force to contend with.

It irked me when people looked for fault and said, 'Why did Darren do this?' Darren didn't 'do this'. Sure, he stood up in front of everyone to take the heat for certain decisions, but they were not reached in isolation or on a whim. He had a conversation with his vice-captains. When you've got individuals of the calibre of Ian Poulter, Sam Torrance, Paul Lawrie and Pádraig Harrington contributing, most rational people would respect the validity of collective opinion.

Nothing gets past people of that quality and experience. Decisions don't come out of thin air. We know these players as friends, as well as golfers. We know their characters, their weaknesses and their strengths. We know how they are playing, whether they are happy or unhappy at home, if there's a problem with a sick child or a parent who is not there, as usual.

Nothing is left to chance before we choose which way to go. That doesn't necessarily lead to success. Consciously leaving no stone unturned can, strangely, lead to self-doubt, because you over-think things. You can do the job perfectly, getting players fired up and creating an environment in which they can play at their best, but lose because the team on the other side is very, very good.

It can come down to one putt. Whatever environment you have created doesn't make someone hole or miss that eight-foot putt on the last green. All it does is enhance the possibility of them being in a position to make or miss that putt. As a captain, I'm not there to test myself. I'm not paid by a federation or a club to manage a team, a profile or an expectation. I'm there to use everything I've seen down the years to make it a great week for twelve guys.

They are not my players. They are their own men. I'm there to help them, as individuals, achieve something together. I'm well aware that they base their careers on individual achievement, because I've done the same. It's not a case of turning up on the Monday morning and magically affecting how they are going to play. The approach is fine-tuned by weeks and months of quiet conversations.

The Ryder Cup appears gradually on a player's radar. I had a bit of a moan about Frankie Molinari's schedule, but when he won the Open he texted me on the Sunday night: 'We all right now?' About six weeks before Paris, at the PGA Championship at Bellerive, Missouri, I could sense the likes of Rory, Justin Rose and Tommy Fleetwood beginning to get their brains in gear. They were more insistent in asking about the course, my thoughts on pairings and personalities.

Selection was a mosquito, buzzing in my ear for months on end. There were so many factors to consider, from the juncture of a candidate's career to specific qualities, suited to course and distance. Although most pieces of the puzzle had fitted together in the final month, it was still a very stressful process.

It's not like being a football manager, where the nature of authority lends distance. This involved people I knew very well. I am a golfer, first and foremost. I play with and against these guys. I am still out on Tour. I am very much an equal. All of sudden I had to make this 'thanks, but no thanks' call to someone I knew as a colleague as well as an opponent.

I was not brought up to do that type of thing. I am not educated in those ways. I don't have a method of dealing with it. I knew how hard and how long they had worked, so I sat down and said to myself, 'Okay, how would I want this to happen?' I would want someone just to be honest with me. Of the ten phone calls I made, informing players they had not received a wild card, two were very difficult.

The one to Rafa Cabrera-Bello was by far the hardest. This was not business, but something deeply personal. I felt physically ill, because I knew the magnitude of the blow I was inflicting on someone I liked, admired and respected. He was the only European not to suffer a loss at Hazeltine, and came terribly close to clinching an automatic place.

Matt Wallace came from a different place. He obviously hadn't played a Ryder Cup before. I'd watched him win the final qualifying tournament in Denmark with remarkable nerve, resilience and competitive drive. He has a stellar future. Both he and Rafa were very good with me, although I could hear the hurt I had caused in the tone of their voices.

The team wasn't a mates' club, as some insinuated when it was announced. Poulter is a force of nature. I told Henrik Stenson he was sure of a pick at the Open, because I knew he would gear the rest of his season to peaking in Paris. His focus, calmness and wisdom would prevail. Paul Casey impressed me as a team player at the Eurasia Cup in Malaysia, early in the year. His maturity and desperation to make up for a lost decade were persuasive.

Sergio García is more complex than he may appear to the casual observer. There are aspects of his personality that he allows few people to see, but in private he gives everything of himself. When I referred to him as the heartbeat of the team, I was not referencing public expressions of passion to which fans relate, but deeper qualities, such as his ability consciously to energise those around him.

Pressure is a privilege. I know it is easy to mythologise that first tee shot at the Ryder Cup, but it forms part of the ultimate test of a professional sportsman. When the best players walk through the avenue of fans and stand there, facing their destiny, they prepare for a unique sense of peace to descend. They tell themselves, 'Everything is okay. I was made for this.'

You are tested to the full throughout the week. There's nervousness, second-guessing and self-doubt, which always creeps into any high-pressure situation, but there's also a blossoming of belief. You go with the flow, wonder why you were getting so wound up about something so central to your nature. You discover you belong.

There was a great feeling of the group never taking anything for granted. It was nobody's divine right to be in that team. They had earned that right. I didn't have to talk to them about golf for our conversations to have value, because I picked up little bits about them in their attitudes towards life. I didn't tell them what they should do, because they would have switched off. I made them aware of what they *could* do.

It's relationship-building. My job was to affect them through their own thinking, not my thinking. Confidence is critical: go out there and grab greatness. Believe you can achieve. When you sit with Poulter, for instance, he can't help himself. When we met in the parking lot at Augusta in 2018, he told me with complete certainty that he was going to make the team.

I tried to explain his importance to one of the caddies in the build-up to the event. There are people who are happy to qualify because of the prestige it brings. There are people who are happy to be there because it is an awesome experience. You have to find the rare ones, the people who are desperate to be out there on the golf course, savouring the scene and winning points. Poulter is one.

No one type of person becomes a great golfer. A great team needs a mix of different personalities. There are moments in Ryder Cup week when things are not going your way. You need people who are calm, have natural stature and can dig you out of a hole. When things are going great, you fire off the guys at the front, who are so excited they are almost out of control.

I trust all of them, but trust some more than others. Certain individuals are my eyes and ears. Some players will be honest with me, some won't. Not everyone will admit to playing poorly. It is a sportsman's instinct to tell you he is playing fantastically well, and that he can't wait to get back out there. Sometimes you have to say, 'That's not what I'm seeing, mate.'

Poulter doesn't shy away from how important the Ryder Cup is to him. He manages his time, his whole world, around that week. He loves every little second of it, and drives himself so hard. There is no other player who does that. That is his moment. I don't know what it is, but it starts way before the event. Even when he was not assured of a place in Paris, he couldn't stop talking about it.

I imagine he must sit at home sometimes and think, 'Why can't I transfer that to my individual game?' He has it intermittently on Tour, but he always has it at the Ryder Cup. It's freaky. He just shoves his problems aside. Why can't he pick that up and deliver it, week in, week out? Well, that's the nature of the game – the different challenge of me against 155 others.

Without knocking him too much, Poulter's one of those guys you would find really annoying, if he wasn't great at laughing at himself. He has a terrific, sharp sense of humour and is brilliant at realising when he is making a fool of himself in all his silliness. He is a perfect spoilt sportsman; there is a side to him that is so human That's why people who know him really well love him.

Poulter realises when he goes too far and makes a joke of it. In private he is a genuinely good guy. Look at where he has come from. Everybody told him he was never going to be any good, so he's always had a point to prove: 'I'm not going to stand in a pro shop and sell golf tees. I'm going to show them that I can make it as a golfer. Everybody's laughing at me, but in the end, I'll be the one laughing.'

If he doesn't achieve greatness as an individual player by the traditional gauge of becoming a major champion, he has achieved greatness as a Ryder Cup player. Some people will take that. I look at him as the perfect team sportsman, playing an individual sport. A little like Sergio, there's a lot of footballer in Poulter. Once every two years he gets to live as the team player he never got to be.

The expectations of the outside world can seem so unfair. Rory, for instance, is inured to the inconsistencies. I can't say he finds it difficult to deal with, because he understands the dynamics, but it is jarring. I can relate to how, when he feels as if he is in a good place and all he can hear is constant criticism, he wonders, 'What are they on about?'

Golf is not a straight-line sport. You can finish second greatly, and you can finish second disastrously, but no matter what, you still finish second. What the outsider, peeping through the keyhole of limited experience, and the player, at the sharp end of competition, feel about an identical situation can be so different, and wearing.

Rory often refers to the joy he got from the game as a kid. That's interesting, since that joy you had – playing with a mate, going out on your own or even standing there on the range, hitting balls – doesn't exist on the circuit. You can try to find it, but it is always going to be elusive. As much as it can be fun, and you still enjoy it, golf becomes a job. As soon as it does that, you have a responsibility both to yourself and to the game.

There are thousands of people working hard, hitting balls and trying to become better. No matter how much talent you have, that is never going to be enough. You've got to drive yourself. You'll struggle to reconnect with that ten- or eleven-year-old boy who just loved playing golf, because he lived in a world without restrictions.

The better you are, the brighter the spotlight you are under. Everything that Rory does is always over-analysed. Nobody has been through that phenomenon more than Tiger. He shows up in the parking lot and they are all there with their cameras. Every single thing he does is a point of discussion: Is this right? Is that wrong? Why's he doing that?

Rory is trying to put into words what it feels like to be that child. He's such a natural talent, so gifted. When he freewheels and lets his talent flow, he almost enters a time warp. The years fall away, to reveal the boy taken to Holywood Golf Club in Belfast, by his dad, Gerry. Rory thinks he is the best player in the world because that's what he is, but he must operate with restrictions, opinion and unwanted analysis.

So much swirls around him. He must weigh his words, because they carry political weight. He knows his scheduling decisions will be magnified, as they send a strategic signal. He must ration his time, concentrate his energies, since celebrity and commercial success can never dilute an eternal truth: if the greatest player fails to stay in the present, and loses sight of what it takes to excel, he will disappear.

Rory remains the only guy I would pay to watch. He was a huge source of personal support, since he used his stature for the common good in the team room in Paris. He got under the skin of some of the younger players by sharing ideas and showing unforced affinity with their ambition. They visibly responded to him, obviously wanted to learn from him. They fed off his energy.

He knows what others say about him. The sadness is that there is nothing better than seeing him playing, almost without thought. It's a lot more complicated than that, of course, but that's how it looks to the naked eye. The nature of the game makes people prone to over-complication. By and large, idealism doesn't work in professional sport.

I started out as captain, in 2016, thinking I had so much time. I had an idealistic notion that my captaincy was going to make a difference, beyond the result. I was going to break down barriers. I have been involved in the Tour for so many years, and have seen the Cup from so many perspectives, that I saw an opportunity to really change the face of it.

It is the one event in the game that goes beyond the golf enthusiast. It enables the sport to absorb a wider audience. I wanted it to be more fan-engaging. I wanted it to be more modern. I wanted to lower the veil, attract a generation that has grown up in a world of transparency, through social media. I wanted to bring everyone forward, as one.

Golf will eventually have to go there, through social and commercial necessity, but when I put my ideas on the table, they just didn't fly. I suppose it is normal for people who protect the brand to say, 'No, no, we've always done it this way.' I understand the 'what's in it for me?' mentality of professional sport, but it all became too complicated.

Eventually I recognised the danger of allowing myself to become frustrated. I had to refocus, concentrate on my sphere of influence. An opportunity had been missed, but my basic philosophy – of building everything around, and about, twelve players – was renewed. It became all about them. I wanted them to be themselves, not try to be something they are not.

Some players make a Cup team and are suddenly seized by the idea that they are somehow unworthy, that they need to be better. No. There's a reason why they are there. They have proved themselves as an individual. It's my job, with the people I have around me, to comprehend how a diverse set of characters can work together.

I took a conscious decision to surround myself with the best practitioners. I picked the brains of sports psychologists like Tom Young, to get a sense of the cerebral aspects of the week, and was in constant contact with Duncan Carey, who headed up our analytical team, to get a balanced view of potential partnerships and strategies.

Billy Foster oversaw intelligence-gathering from the caddies. I stressed, through him, the paramount importance of honesty over understandable loyalty. I didn't want flannel about how well their guy was playing, when he was struggling. I needed the truth, however bitter, though I recognised the bonds between them and their employer.

Billy has seen pretty much everything over the past thirty years. As if I needed reminding, he still describes carrying my bag, during the 2003 Open, as his most painful experience in golf. He was an alternative captain, advising the younger, less-experienced caddies about the unique nature of the week. He eased their nerves, took their temperature.

All you can do is attempt to predict, with a degree of confidence, what is likely to happen in any given circumstance. We're not dealing with androids; even Francesco Molinari can miss a fairway. Much depends on character and confidence, how players relate to one another as people. World-class golfers don't tend to conform to cultural norms, because their workplace is global.

They don't sit in their birthplaces for 103 weeks out of 104 and suddenly turn up at the Ryder Cup. Their lives are baggage carousels. I knew many observers would miss the point when I spoke at the opening ceremony about how we related to playing for the European flag. Some, predictably and perhaps deliberately, leaped to the mistaken conclusion that I was making a tangential reference to Brexit.

As a team, we related to the concept of Europe as an indication of humanity, rather than as a political framework. It drew us closer together as a group, gave us a distinctive identity. It was about how we saw ourselves, how we channelled our passion and celebrated our differences. We were one, formed from millions.

I designed the team room to reflect that reality. It was a sanctuary, a place of refuge. I invited Michael in, as an outsider, to share the experience and make his own judgement about its authenticity . . .

Chapter Ten

WHERE MAGIC HAPPENS

'Hello, love.'

Lee Westwood, a forty-five-year-old teenager, is changing into his golf shoes on the right-hand edge of a horseshoe-shaped locker room. His ceremonial bag leans against a pillar on which the mantra 'One Goal' is written vertically. Thomas Bjørn grins indulgently at the impertinence of the greeting. His ego, like that of everyone around him, has been left at the frosted double-doors.

The converted pro shop at Le Golf National, white-walled, high-ceilinged and open-plan, may lack the splendour of the alternative team room at the offsite hotel – a salon in which, on 7 May 1919, French Prime Minister Georges Clemenceau dictated the conditions of the Treaty of Versailles – but it contains holy relics.

The spirit of Seve Ballesteros is omnipresent. His golf bag from the 1997 Ryder Cup match in Valderrama, in a glass container on a dais, is centrally positioned so that it is in the eyeline of players who change, alphabetically and in pairs, from left to right. An inscribed message from Bjørn, in white capital letters, reads: 'He is why we are here today. Go out and make him proud.'

The message is in braced brackets { }, which commonly signify hugging in electronic communication. For the purposes of the European team, they are an allegory for unity, tightness. 'Seve will always be in our world,' Bjørn reflects, as an iconic blown-up photograph from '97, which captures the Spaniard's urgency and vivacity, makes the point for him.

The walkway is designed as living history. Portraits on the wall range from Sam Torrance's winning putt in 1985 to Darren Clarke's triumphant tears in 2006, and on to Jamie Donaldson, the understated hero of 2014, whose face, tilted upwards and picked out from a media scrum by an ethereal shaft of sunlight, is taut with joy and self-justification.

Nothing is for ever. Donaldson was at Le Golf National as an on-course radio commentator. He had fallen to 174 on the European Tour, and 544 in the world rankings, by the time he underwent wrist surgery in November 2018. It seems cruel to dwell on the symbolism of that stirring image being hung next to what usually operates as an emergency exit.

This is where players leave, to meet their fate. They turn right, along a narrow privet-lined pathway, and into a courtyard that leads to the practice green, which is dwarfed by the monolithic grandstand behind the first tee. On this Wednesday morning, less than forty-eight hours before the match begins, Aretha Franklin is immortally demanding respect over the public address system.

The last thing players see, on the lintel above that exit door, is a direct challenge: 'Now it's your time.' It is equally impossible to miss a timeless reflection from the late Arsenal footballer David Rocastle, a player of grace and a man of substance: 'Remember who you are, what you are, and what you represent.' Bjørn, a Liverpool fan, admits, 'We borrowed that because it is very relevant.'

The feng shui of performance sport favours short, pungent slogans. One-word entreaties, inscribed in brackets on yet more glass cabinets featuring golf bags from former captains, such as Tony Jacklin {win} and Clarke {believe}, are accompanied by more lyrical observations, such as the one from Paul McGinley {be the rock when the storm comes}, poet laureate of the win at Gleneagles in 2014.

In the wrong hands, and expressed in the wrong way, this could have the artificiality of a sales conference for middle managers in Maidenhead. The language of modern motivation can be florid and faintly risible. Yet although the sentiments are earnest, the mood is light. Sergio García is whistling as he walks by, and taps his captain playfully on the hip as we lean against the wall in conversation.

Bjørn set the tone on the Monday evening by disguising the levity of a ten-minute video, in which impressionist Conor Moore staged a series of mock press conferences that poked gentle fun at such foibles as Justin Rose's Olympic gold-medal obsession, Tommy Fleetwood's luxuriant hair, Ian Poulter's breast-beating and Francesco Molinari's deadpan manner.

The captain did not escape. He was lampooned by Moore, who wore a shower cap to emphasise Bjørn's baldness, and a pair of eyebrows that resembled hedgerows. 'What do I think of, when someone mentions Thomas?' asked Rose, who would assume greater internal influence as the week progressed. 'Eyebrows. And I don't need to explain why.'

The two greatest table-tennis players of modern times, Jan-Ove Waldner, the so-called Mozart of the game, and seven-times Olympian Jörgen Persson, provided additional light relief by playing the players and their caddies. Bjørn had considered enlisting other motivational figures, such as Roger Federer, and even had an exploratory conversation with Zinedine Zidane, before deciding to narrow his focus.

'It is just us now,' he said. 'This is their place, where they come in from long days, where they can simply be. They know they are not going to run into anything here. Nothing faces them. No media, no requirements. There are a lot of things on their mind. There is a time to be serious, but you can't just bombard them.'

We lingered in a corridor brightened by a montage of team members with their parents, wives and children. 'One Family,' proclaimed another slogan, above a door leading to a dining area dominated by a huge replica Ryder Cup trophy, made from golden Lego. 'This is for the people who revolve around them, who mean something to them,' Bjørn said, quietly. 'It is a reminder we are not just twelve players.'

I was struck by the intimacy of a portrait of Rory McIlroy, with his parents and the Claret Jug. He exuded the pride of a dutiful son; that pride was mirrored by their demeanour when they followed him inside the ropes. Without the selflessness of his father Gerry, a trim figure in a black Masters bomber jacket, and mother Rosie, a small, shy lady, a rare talent could have withered.

In order to fund their only son's golf development, Gerry worked from 8 a.m. to midnight as a cleaner at a sports club and as a barman at Holywood Golf Club. Rosie worked night shifts at the 3M factory in Bangor. When drudgery threatened to overwhelm them, she would tell her husband, 'One day this could all be worthwhile.'

I noticed Bjørn was extending his vowels as he spoke, a sign of tiredness and distraction. He admitted that he had slept for little more than three hours a night since arriving in Paris the previous Friday, when he climbed to the top of the grandstand behind the first tee, looked out on the deserted course and allowed his imagination to soar.

'Amazing,' he recalled. 'For some reason, I thought of meeting Pep Guardiola in 2012. He just said, "Wow, this is the best thing ever." Coming from someone in his world, that made me think. You don't sleep a lot, to be honest with you. That's the part you can't really prepare for, because that is not the way you live your life as a sportsman.

'There's just no time. You are doing all the big-picture stuff when you are with the team. You deal with the little stuff when they are sleeping. You are making hundreds of decisions a day, from what's in the bloody sandwiches to sorting the pairings. Once you put yourself in a leadership role, everything goes through you.

'Man-management means dealing with specifics of personality, nitty-gritty details. It's much more stressful than you think. Right now, there's a weird lull. We're still in the process, still being focused. When we get to tomorrow, and put down on a piece of paper, "This is what we are doing, this is what we are going with", then the nervousness of what is coming will hit home.'

Robert Karlsson was in the dining area, poring over the latest statistical printouts. The impending ordeal of the opening tee shot was influencing the media agenda and intruding into the thoughts of the five rookies, in particular. Such moments of fantastic theatre are eased by an emotive inheritance, passed down from player to player.

'My first one was at the K Club in '06,' Karlsson remembered. 'I was with Paul Casey in the second group. The first was Pádraig and Monty against Tiger and Furyk. I'm following my plan, get to the course, do my own thing, don't worry what's going on around you. I'm warming up and hear this commotion. I'm staying where I am, hitting balls, but my caddie Gareth, who works for Henrik now, comes up and says, "You'll want to see this."

'I say no, but he's saying, "You have to watch this." I look up, and there, on a giant screen, I see Tiger almost miss the ball on the first tee. On the first hole at the K Club you have the fairway, a bit of rough, the ropes, ten yards of people, more rough and then the lake. We've played the European Open there probably ten times, and I've never seen anyone hit it in that lake. Tiger's ball comfortably pitched ten yards into the water.

'And I thought, "Yeah, I really wanted to see that." When I walked onto the first tee, even the starter was so nervous he pronounced our names wrong. Gareth told me later he'd never seen my face turn completely white. I got it down there somehow, but the pressure is so different to anything you face. My biggest help was from Monty and Darren, who took me aside the previous night.

'They told me, "We know it's your first one. We know you're a good player, but just so that you know, tomorrow is going to be something you've never experienced before. It's different. It doesn't really matter how experienced you are, we all feel it, and everybody else is feeling it. You will beat it. It's a different type of nervousness." And it was.

'The big difference with the Ryder Cup is that it's the only time we have the crowd for or against us. We don't ever have that on Tour. If I'm playing tournament golf in Ireland, they want Rory to win, but some still like me, or some of the other guys. It's never polarised. Here, they either love you or they hate you. There is nothing in between. And that is a very, very different atmosphere.'

The intelligence operation was instinctive, rather than intrusive. Bjørn liaised with the players' personal coaches, who operated from a first-floor room, together with a six-strong statistical team. He coordinated personality profiles with Karlsson and sports psychologist Tom Young. His vice-captains were assigned in rotation to each of the four players who underwent daily inquisition in the media centre.

Bjørn explained: 'We are taking note of what we see, not just where they are golf-wise, but in their personalities and actions. We are watching every little move, watching their conversations with each other, sensing their mood. You try and learn everything that's going on. I haven't seen any warning signs.

'If they're not playing particularly well, they are frustrated when they come in. We see that every week. We're looking out for the player who is playing great and comes in unhappy about something. You flag it up and go, "What's going on there?" If there's an issue, I'll assign someone to deal with it, based on an historical fit.

'Usually it either comes from tiredness, being under time pressure, or from maybe not playing the best the day before. They're straight off the plane, most of them. I know what I was like myself. You can put me through hell and I'll still go out on the golf course and absorb myself in my game. If things go wrong, and I don't understand why, I will be extremely frustrated. Eventually, that wears off.'

Bjørn's analytical personality was emphasised by his pre-event profiling. He delegated well, and was particularly close to Karlsson, who had a ninety-minute FaceTime conversation with Young to impart practical strategies, if he felt the captain was ever under undue stress. The vice-captaincy team was well balanced, from the slightly reserved, creative Luke Donald to the decisive Lee Westwood. The psychologist's work was designed to help the leadership team 'understand how to push the players' buttons'.

I had watched Alex Norén, comfortably the best table-tennis player, but one of the quieter members of the team, in the twilight the previous evening. Last on the range and lost in concentration, he worked methodically, yet intensely. His calloused hands testified to his dedication to practice, but was there a danger of over-elaboration, due to the magnitude of the occasion?

'Alex always does that,' Bjørn rationalised. 'They are all different, but all work extremely hard. That's where some of them get their comfort from. It is about a mental attitude, about being on top of their game. It's not like they come here as strangers. We are aware of what we are looking at because we see them on tour.

We know what they are like, what they go through and how they prepare.'

The group dynamic was initially driven by the resident extroverts, Poulter and García – so-called 'sunshine yellows' in psychological terms. McIlroy took Thorbjørn Olesen under his wing, and Tommy Fleetwood's dry wit settled the human chemistry. Henrik Stenson's humour was sharp, but his wider impact was subtle. The faith of his friend and captain had not been wasted.

'Henrik is not the type of guy who takes up a lot of space,' Bjørn reflected. 'He's not in the middle of the room, swinging his arms around. He's the one in the corner, quietly having great conversations with people. He's so good to have around. He's in a different place when he is building for something like this. There was never any doubt in my mind that I wanted him here. When you look at his stats, he is bubbling under, looking like he is about to play great.'

Senior players came to the fore the night before the match started, when, sprawled across seats and a large sofa in a junior suite at the hotel, the team watched a motivational video organised by freelance TV producer Grace Barber, Bjørn's partner. It featured three former Ryder Cup captains: Brian Huggett, Sam Torrance and José María Olazábal.

Bjørn had played the video ten times in deciding how to maximise its raw emotional power, and was determined to share it in an intimate setting. It encapsulated his beliefs, struck the right tone. Months later the memory would still summon a tear; on the eve of competition it was greeted by an eloquent silence.

The video, 143 seconds in length, was underscored by the swirling strings of a suitably emotive soundtrack. It was beautifully shot, perfectly paced. Every word was an emotional depth charge. It began with Huggett, the 1977 captain, making himself a cup of coffee, before sitting down at a pine kitchen table and studying a photograph album.

He addressed the camera, and a captive audience: 'You know, as you get older, things get taken away from you, and that's part of life. You learn to treasure the opportunities you've had, and reflect on those moments that have defined you, both good and bad.'

Torrance was depicted walking through a glade as the sun broke through the trees, before he, too, made eye contact through the lens: 'This is more than just a game. You live it. You breathe it. And you've worked hard to be here. It's not just about taking part. It's about winning. Nothing else.'

Olazábal was filmed at his home club in the Basque Country: 'Seve showed me there are times when you need to reach into the depths of your soul to get you through,' he said, before his voice broke, his face screwed up and he shielded tearful eyes with extended fingers. 'Sorry about that,' he said, when he had composed himself. 'Honesty is everything. You only get out what you put in, but you never give up.'

Huggett returns: 'So outdo what they can do.'

Torrance follows up: 'You outdrive them.'

Olazábal intones: 'You outperform them.'

Then Huggett delivers the line that was to galvanise Rose, in particular: 'You wear them down with excellence.'

Torrance is stern, but soft: 'You beat them. You give it absolutely everything. So come Sunday night, you can honestly say to yourself: I had no more to give.'

Olazábal adds: 'Somebody said, "All men die, but not all men live." Well, this is the time to feel alive.'

The three bring the film to a climax by speaking seamlessly.

Huggett: 'And when you stand there on your final round, remember . . .'

Torrance: 'There is a tomorrow as a Ryder Cup winner.'

Olazábal: 'Or there is a tomorrow where you are not . . .'

The last word is left to Huggett, the old man on the tee: 'Don't leave with any regrets.'

Bjørn's eyes had flicked regularly from the giant TV screen to the faces of those around him. He saw some swallow hard. Others surreptitiously swept away a tear. He allowed the silence to settle, and his players to collect their thoughts, before he addressed them with disarming simplicity: 'If that doesn't inspire you, I can't give you anything else.'

Bjørn felt the Ryder Cup's lifelong impact had been placed in its proper context. His endlessly rehearsed speech at the opening ceremony earlier that day had also found its mark, because 'I could see them thinking, "Oh, he means business."' He radiated pride and projected passion, where Jim Furyk, his opposite number, tried hard to sound presidential in a typically overblown setting.

Despite the focus on captaincy, successful teams self-manage to a degree. Huggett's concentration on excellence concentrated minds. Rose, McIlroy, García and Stenson circulated with a common message: 'You can only focus on yourself, and what you are doing. Try to be an individual.'

Bjørn had been consensual in deciding his pairings. Four rookies, Jon Rahm, Tyrrell Hatton, Olesen and Fleetwood, would make their debuts in the morning. His strategy involved enticing the Americans into naming an unbalanced line-up by flipping the traditional format and kick-starting the event with fourball matches.

There was a sense, within the team room, that the biggest American names would be their biggest weaknesses. Mickelson, 192nd out of 193 in driving accuracy on the PGA Tour, was having difficulty locating France from the tee, let alone the fairways on the Albatros course. Woods's appearance at the gala dinner in the Palace of Versailles on Wednesday was noted. In the words of one European official: 'He looked seventy-five years old.'

The scene that awaited before dawn on Friday was surreal. Indistinct figures shuffled in the shadows, and marshals began

turning fans away from the 6,500-capacity grandstand behind the
first tee, ninety minutes before the first ball was struck, at 8.10 a.m.
A crass cheerleader, whose announcements collided and coalesced
into a barely intelligible howl, screamed, 'Make some noise.'

Poulter, who had been up among the spectators at first light,
taking selfies that showed crowds snaking around the 419-yard,
par-four opening hole, mercifully took over as master of ceremonies. He stood on the tee, turned to face the grandstand and
opened his arms wide. The crowd hushed momentarily, syn-
chronising the Thunderclap made famous by the Iceland football
team.

Rahm followed suit. García, sipping coffee, giggled. Yet when
it came to business, it was possible to hear the clubhead hit the
ball. Tony Finau, partnering Brooks Koepka against Rose and
Rahm, exclaimed, 'Wow!' when his opening tee shot rolled three
inches from the water that came into play, around eighty yards
from the green.

Olesen found the water, and received little support from his
senior partner, who subsequently apologised for his fallability.
McIlroy, normally so reliable in the fourball format, was working
through persistent problems with ball flight and direction.
Though narrowly ahead at the turn, their loss to Dustin Johnson
and Rickie Fowler was confirmed by four American birdies in five
holes from the tenth.

Rose was, statistically, Europe's best bet. He was rated first
overall, being 2.63 shots better than the field, adjusted for course
on course. He had the best short game, was ranked second in
approach play, fourth on driving and fifth in putting. He and
Rahm did not trail until they walked off the eighteenth green; his
second shot found the water, and the Spaniard was out of position from the tee.

When Casey and Hatton also lost on the last, to Jordan Spieth
and Justin Thomas, the WhatsApp group, through which Bjørn,

his vice-captains and analysts communicated, was in ferment. Europe would, at best, trail 3–1. Under time pressure to name pairings for the afternoon foursomes, Bjørn assessed the real-time data dashboard and considered changing long-set plans.

McIlroy was playing poorly, but remained talismanic; resting him would have sent out the wrong signal to the Americans. Bjørn considered temporarily breaking up the partnership of Fleetwood and Molinari, who were in the process of grinding out a draining victory against Woods and Patrick Reed. They had been the most visibly tired of the players to have flown directly to Paris from the US Tour Championship.

The leadership team even went as far as referring to the personality profiles, on how best to impart bad news to them, before Bjørn decided to stick, rather than twist. It was a sliding-doors moment, in which trust and respect, established over the previous year, proved decisive. A new team motto – 'Stick to the plan' – was forged, and was emphasised most strongly by Westwood.

Blake Wooster, who headed up the analytical support team, foresaw fatal American flaws, but needed the courage of his convictions. 'I didn't want to speak out of turn too much, but people were panicking a little bit. There was almost too much to think about. Thomas was a brilliant captain, because his leadership style naturally created an environment for rigorous and open discussion.

'Our biggest role that lunchtime had nothing to do with statistics. It was to do with influencing people, saying, "Let's all calm down and stick to the plan." Without building relationships, it's almost impossible to have the respect and platform to challenge people in a constructive way. When we saw the American pairings for the afternoon, we were ecstatic.'

Mickelson was a predictable liability in the alternate shot format, in which he gave Bryson DeChambeau a harrowing baptism. He took an iron off the tee for safety at the par-five third hole, but still hit into the water on the right. García, by contrast, was the perfect babysitter for Norén; seven up at the turn, he threw his arms around the rookie's shoulder and savoured redemption. Norén wept through sheer relief when victory was confirmed, a bewildering experience because, as he remarked, "I never cry."

Rose, urged by McIlroy to 'give us something to chase' during his thirty-one-minute break between matches, justified the decision to save Stenson for a session that demanded greater interdependence. They never trailed against Johnson and Fowler. When Rose reflected afterwards that 'My back is okay, but my legs and butt are feeling it', the Swede shot back, tartly, 'It's carrying that wallet that does that.'

McIlroy was rebooted by Poulter's emotional energy, and helped to trounce Bubba Watson and Webb Simpson. 'Great players, when they don't perform to the standards they want to achieve, have an ability to just go and prove to themselves they can put it right,' reflected Bjørn in his post-play press conference. 'If I start doubting Rory, I probably shouldn't be in this job.'

By that time the Dane had given Fleetwood, whose partnership with Molinari was edging towards legend, permission to leave early to be with his son Franklin on his first birthday. Before being excused, Fleetwood waited, along with his teammates and caddies, in the locker room for Bjørn to return, with his vice-captains, from confirming the Saturday-morning pairings.

Bjørn cancelled a team meeting, planned for later that evening, and spoke from the heart about a sweep of seismic proportions: 'Right. I just want to say: that was unbelievable. That was history. It is what everybody in this team is all about. You looked at each other and said, "We have a job to do" and then you went out and executed it to perfection. You've brought it all to life.'

Even Furyk admitted the Europeans had 'unbelievable momentum'. He was downbeat, almost forlorn. 'Absolutely, one hundred per cent, you see a change in body language. The Europeans significantly changed to all smiles, boisterous hugs and high-fives. I'm sure the looks on some of my players were not quite the happiest. We're making a game plan. We'll figure it out.'

The media-room dais is a Ryder Cup captain's Calvary. Bjørn was preoccupied when he returned there on Saturday evening. Europe had won the first three of the morning fourballs, and shared the afternoon session to lead 10–6 going into the Sunday singles. Instinct told him that he had to return to his players as soon as possible; he hinted at inner turmoil by idly twirling his watch and massaging his forehead.

'When moments strike to make a point, you have to take them,' he explained later. He stood up in the team room when his players were eating, having instinctively abandoned arrangements to take them into a separate area for a debrief. 'I thought, "Let's do it here and now, get it done." They were great at being focused and paying attention to what was going on around them.'

Again, less was more. This was not the time – and, on reflection, probably not the politically correct country – for a re-creation of Henry V's Agincourt speech. 'They are going to come hard at you tomorrow, you know that,' he told the team. 'He [Furyk] has to stack it. You can pretty much see in their draw where he thinks everybody is with their game. Just stay focused. Win your point, win your point, win your point. That's all you can do. Tomorrow is a long, hard day.'

Victory, confirmed on Singles Sunday, was followed by a long, hard night. Once the media duties had been completed, Bjørn triggered a floodlit champagne fight in the gathering gloom. He soaked Karlsson and McIlroy, before being doused, in turn, by Olesen. McIlroy then pursued Hatton, who was being double-teamed by Poulter, across the practice green, before coming across Fleetwood.

The latter half of Moliwood had smeared his hair behind his ears. Barefoot and apparently oblivious to the chill, he wore a soaked fleece and a baggy pair of shorts. 'I've never seen you looking so good,' laughed McIlroy, as Rose handed a half-empty magnum of champagne to some Swedish fans, who had appeared out of the darkness. It was a moment of release, and a moment of realisation.

It is possible to rediscover that ten-year-old boy who innocently fell in love with a diabolical game. You just have to win the Ryder Cup to do so.

Chapter Eleven

FAMILY

It was the third time Thomas Bjørn had cried on a golf course. He saw two of his three children, Filippa and Oliver, snaking through the celebratory scrum at the back of the fifteenth green at Le Golf National and succumbed to the moment. 'Sometimes,' he said, 'you forget they live all your pride and your pain. I live theirs, as they live mine.'

Golf is a game that can never be beaten, just as mountains or oceans cannot be conquered – only passed safely, with nature's blessing. Everywhere he looked, Bjørn was ambushed by memory and humanity. Each of the players breathlessly recounting their experiences had harsh elements to their backstory. Although, as Justin Rose said, 'These are the days of our lives', the scars are more than skin-deep.

The first occasion Bjørn shed tears in such a setting was in 2013 when Adam Scott, whose wife Marie had worked as a nanny for the Bjørn family, won the Masters. He explained: 'Adam was like a younger brother to me, and I knew how much it meant to him.' Bjørn did so again at Royal Troon three years later, when Henrik Stenson won the Open Championship.

That was an indication of a deeper bond, a form of friendship forged painfully and privately. Stenson was a matter of feet away from Bjørn on this sun-dappled Sunday evening in France, corralling his own children, Lisa, Karl and Alice, and coming to terms with what he acknowledged to be one of the highlights of a career of dizzying contrasts. In spirit, he and his captain were together on a deserted driving range in Dubai.

'Henrik has had some really low moments in his career,' Bjørn remembered. 'There were times I didn't think he was going to get back. We were once in Dubai practising before the season, and he literally couldn't hit the ball. I cried at Troon because I thought of all those moments when he stood on the range with tears in his eyes, because he didn't want to put himself through it any more.

'I sat there and encouraged him. His wife, Emma, was there for him. It says everything about Henrik that he worked through that and became, when he is on it, the finest golfer I have seen, apart from Tiger. He might be not on it as often as other players, but when he is, he is amazing. To see him with his family shows that, for all the negative things it can do to people, sport can be so special, so positive.'

Stenson probably did not expect to be confronted with such an intimate recollection, when only the formalities of the trophy presentation prevented the night-long party from getting started. He could so easily have brushed away my line of questioning with platitudes or empty humour, but he is a man of substance. His mouth stretched into a tight, thin smile before he gave it his full attention.

'If you don't know Thomas, and you've only seen him out on the course with his competitive fighting-man head on, you won't realise that there's a big softie in there, with a big, big heart. We have been alongside one another for so many years. He has been just brilliant with this team, and he has trusted me to go out with the mindset that "this is made for me".

'Nothing in life follows a straight line, and he has always been there for me. We are so attached emotionally, because we have been through the highs and the lows together. My highs have been big, but the lows have been bigger. This is one of my proudest moments and I am happy to call him my friend.'

Stenson was brought up in Ytterby, a hamlet on the Swedish island of Resarö in the Stockholm archipelago, known principally for the seven elements discovered in the local quartz mine. He has been mainlining golf since he struck a surprisingly straight five-iron at the age of eleven, after being invited to a driving range at the Gullbringa club by a friend, Pontus Eriksson.

No one in the family had played golf, but Henrik's father, Ingemar, bought him a set of clubs and fulfilled the traditional domestic role of taxi driver. He tired of waiting in the car park, tried the game himself with little immediate success, but saw his son flourish so swiftly that Henrik had reduced his handicap to nine, from the men's tees, within a year.

He moved to Skåne, in southern Sweden, at the age of fifteen so that he could develop his game at the Barsebäck club. He made the national team, met Torsten Hansson, a former Navy diver who became his sports psychologist, and gained an enduring reputation as a practical joker. His speciality, releasing water-filled balloons from high-rise hotels, was established during the world amateur championship in Chile.

Stenson turned pro in the autumn of 1998 and grew up fast. He finished fourteenth in his debut, in Argentina, and had to queue outside the tournament office to receive his winnings, nearly $2,000, in cash. He failed to qualify for the European Tour in 1999, but earned his card by winning the Challenge Tour Order of Merit the following year.

He had already experienced the malign power of the mind, losing a tournament in Córdoba when he could not handle the adrenaline rush of a local caddie making the fundamental mistake of telling him that he led by four strokes with seven holes to play, but seemed set fair when he quickly won the first of his eleven European Tour titles, the Benson & Hedges International at the Belfry.

Within two months, on 5 July 2001, he walked off the course in the second round of the European Open at the K Club, because he was scared he was going to hurt a spectator. He needed three tee shots at his opening hole before he could put a ball in play, and had no idea where he was hitting it. Another sliced drive, three holes later, landed 400 yards from where it had come to rest the previous day.

He had succumbed, with savage speed, to full-swing yips, which had effectively curtailed the careers of Seve Ballesteros, David Duval and Ian Baker-Finch. In the argot of the trade, he was a 'manipulator' – a player who relied on exceptional reflexes to adjust the clubface during a shot. Brilliant in patches, he was fatally flawed under pressure. Constant repetition of the correct movements, on the range, was his only hope of redemption.

Stenson kept his card narrowly in 2003, falling to 621 in the world after effectively writing off the previous year; and it was not until 2005, when he broke into the European top ten, that coach Pete Cowen felt he had fully rebuilt his swing. Hansson dealt with signs of mental burnout, an illogical sense of guilt and shame. He told espnW: 'He could understand the process intellectually, but it was more difficult emotionally.'

The Swede became statistically the best driver on Tour. He won twice in 2006, and holed the winning putt on his Ryder Cup debut, yet fate had not finished with him. His form slumped from 2009 when he lost an estimated $8 million in a 'Ponzi scheme' organised by Allen Stanford, the fraudster who also infamously deceived the great and the gullible of world cricket.

Stenson's recovery, complicated by viral pneumonia and the contraction of a waterborne parasite, took him from 230 in the world to second. In 2013 he became the first man to win both the

FedEx Cup and the Race to Dubai. It was on his way home to Orlando, from winning $11 million in the season-ending US Tour Championship in Atlanta, that he enjoyed the karmic satisfaction of flying over the federal penitentiary in which Stanford is serving a 110-year sentence.

Justin Rose, with whom Stenson has won seven out of nine Ryder Cup points, spoke in awestruck tones in Paris about his 'balls of steel'. The Swede's capacity to compartmentalise problems allowed him to overcome a long-standing elbow injury through sheer force of will. Rose may say that 'grey hairs count for a lot', but the intensity of Stenson's two-hour pre-round preparation, at the age of forty-two, is revealing.

He starts with a series of assisted exercises designed to increase spinal mobility and flexibility. He then enters an active warm-up phase, which varies from classic yoga moves, such as a Cat–Cow stretch, to a so-called Fire Hydrant, in which he extends and raises each leg, while on all fours, to strengthen the gluteus medius, a muscle that provides stability to the hip.

Only then, having fired up key muscles, does he emerge onto the course. He begins by putting for between twenty and twenty-five minutes, before going on the range. In psychological terms, like many of his Ryder Cup teammates, he is known as an impatient perfectionist. Analytical, demanding and driven by detail, he has acquired natural resilience.

So why does he persevere? What hold does the game have on him? Again, there is that thin smile of recognition: 'It's hard to explain. Golf is not something you do for money or fame. You know the game is never going to be finished with you. You can only deal with it as a lifelong journey. It is a long process. You have to keep working, practising.

'I suppose I use golf to satisfy my competitive nature. There is something about standing there for hour after hour trying to hit a particular shot. It is about not giving up when things don't work, and not walking away when you want to. You know how to hit it, but you have to live it. You must never be satisfied.'

Bjørn's wild-card picks, informed by psychology, analytics and the intangible benefit of personal experience, garnered a record nine and a half points in Paris. The personality profiles of the three other selections – Ian Poulter, Paul Casey and Sergio García – were distinctive and, ultimately, complementary.

Poulter's maverick nature made him an outlier in the group, though he visibly relished the team context. His motivation, deeply set and highly personal, was filtered through the presence of his fourteen-year-old son Luke, whose life spanned his father's Ryder Cup experiences as a player and vice-captain. A photograph of the pair embracing, once victory had been secured, proved emblematic.

The image of Poulter holding his son's tightly creased, tearful face in his hands symbolised the precious nature of parenthood and acted as a bookend to another photograph, taken on the return flight from the 2004 Ryder Cup in Oakland Hills, when Luke, as a baby, slept with the trophy, before being disturbed by García, who clumsily displaced the lid.

Poulter directly addressed his son on social media: 'As a parent, these moments we get to spend with one another sometimes are few and far between, Luke, but when moments like this come around, I was not letting you down today. You lived every shot with us this week. Love you, buddy. Dreams do come true.'

It symbolised a rite of passage, since little more than a year earlier Ian had survived a slump in form that left him 'swimming at the bottom of an empty pool'. He recognised its broader importance, in allowing his son to 'understand golf as a young man at fourteen. He's an excitable character, because the apple doesn't fall far from the tree.'

He leaned over the dais after the celebratory European team press conference to confess to Oliver Holt, the co-writer of his autobiography, that he was 'emotionally wiped out'. Singles Sunday is his stage, his release. "It's a lovely day, a selfish day" he told Sky Sports. "Don't get engaged by 'what if' scenarios. Be ruthless enough to get your point ." Poulter had been unsparingly honest from the outset: 'When you are at the low of lows, and that wasn't that long ago, there's a little voice in your head that says, "You might not get back."'

Casey, the other figure in that airborne snapshot in 2004, was familiar with such an internal conversation, yet sanguine about its impact: 'When you're playing bad golf, you can never see how to play good golf again; and when you're playing good golf, you can never understand how you play bad golf.'

Casey was, by reputation, difficult and self-defensive. Culturally more of a product of the US Tour, he seemed, to the casual observer, to be more comfortable with superficialities and soundbites than authentic self-expression. Yet realignment of his personal and professional lives released latent potential. He emerged as a key lubricant in the team, a hugely positive presence.

His second marriage, to TV presenter Pollyanna Woodward in 2015, and the birth of their children, Lex and Astaria, signalled a shift in perspective. Casey consciously valued the simple pleasures of family life, and threw himself into an ambassadorial role for UNICEF. His decision to re-join the European Tour at the start of the 2018 season, in an attempt to make Bjørn's team, repaired battered bridges.

The purity of his ball-striking and his nerve on and around the greens makes him formidable in match play. He restated his competitive mettle in March 2018, when he won his first PGA Tour title for nine years, holding off Tiger Woods and Patrick Reed with a final-round sixty-five at the Valspar Championship in Tampa, Florida.

In his valedictory press conference Casey spoke of being at peace and 'content with the life I have built'. Victory filled 'a void', but he insisted his family took priority over golf. Such reflection was understandable, since he immediately flew to London for the funeral of Mary Colclough, the wife of Ian, a close friend. They had taken him under his wing as a youngster, and drove nine hours from Weybridge in Surrey to Gleneagles to see his first professional win, in the 2001 Scottish PGA Championship .

Technically, Casey had made a small but effective adjustment, 'opening the putter face on the way back and allowing it to close and rotate'. He admitted that 'trying to be perfect wasn't getting anywhere. I was getting in my own way.' Temperamentally, he responded to Bjørn's early indication that, all things being equal, he would make his first Ryder Cup team for a decade. He kept a personal diary in Paris because 'at forty-one, I just want to make sure I remember this'.

Moved to tears by winning his first point in twelve years in the Saturday-morning fourballs, when he and Tyrrell Hatton were nine under par in beating Dustin Johnson and Rickie Fowler 3&2, he had already proved his point in losing on the final hole the previous morning. Data showed that he had been the team's best performer in that session, gaining +5.83 strokes on the field.

Casey responded to another act of faith on Sunday, when Bjørn sent him out second in the singles, behind Rory McIlroy. He halved with Brooks Koepka, the US Tour's Player of the Year, and spoke starkly of 'not being scared'. He promised, 'I'm not going to be as teary as yesterday, but, yeah, it still gets me. I'm not embarrassed to care.'

Revealingly, he was the European player whom American journalists sought out afterwards, in an attempt to prise out the secrets of Bjørn's bonding techniques. Asked 'What is the meaning of team?' as he signed a souvenir flag for a child suffering from leukaemia, Casey replied: 'It's a difficult one to describe. It is something you can't measure.'

The untrammelled joy of García, who had entered the media room with a whooped 'Yeah, baby', offered another clue. This was his ninth Ryder Cup, but his first as a major champion, and his first as a father. Both life-changing events contributed to the historic achievement of his confirmation as the event's most successful player, with 25.5 points.

He had missed eight cuts in thirteen tournaments, failing to make the weekend in the Masters, US Open and Open Championship, before playing himself into form in Portugal the week before Paris. He wasn't there on mates' rates. Bjørn's due diligence involved data analysis; in terms of the key 'strokes gained' metric, the Spaniard was not playing as poorly as the results implied.

Like many extroverts, García is prone to private introspection. He valued Bjørn's public praise, and had worked assiduously at his home club in Castellón with his father, Victor, a club pro who began teaching him the game at the age of three, to repay his faith. 'I didn't feel I was that far off,' he said, during a retrospective look at a difficult year. 'I missed some of those cuts by one, and I just couldn't find a rhythm. The Ryder Cup kind of got my juices flowing again.'

The Cup had already been won when he secured his singles victory over Rickie Fowler, but he broke down in tears, kissing an index finger and pointing towards the heavens. It was another genuflection towards the legend of Ballesteros, a recurrent reference point since a shot off a tree root with his eyes closed signalled García's emergence as a future star at the 1999 PGA Championship at Medinah.

The Green Jacket, won at Rose's expense in a play-off in 2017, removed a monkey from his back. The birth of his daughter Azalea, named after Augusta's thirteenth hole, on 14 March 2018, kept him grounded during his struggles. His motivation, a familiar theme, is for her 'to be able to grow up and see the TV clips, the trophies I won after she was born, so she can be proud of her dad'.

García rarely grants individual interviews, but he expressed his love in a blog entry on the European Tour website: 'Becoming a father earlier this year definitely brought about something of a change in focus and meant that golf was just one of many different things to concentrate on,' it read. 'She is amazing, though. We're so lucky.

'As anyone who is a parent will tell you, it's hard work. Not just changing diapers, or waking up in the middle of the night. Don't get me wrong, that is tough, but what has been harder for me is the deep, emotional feelings. It takes so much out of you because you are so focused on that little baby. People told me I would understand this feeling when I became a father, and they were right.

'I realised it straight away. It's hard to believe how you can love someone so much that you've never met in your life. Just instantly, as soon as that baby comes into the world. It's like, at a click of a finger, everything changes. You love them so much. Your attention just switches completely. Coming home and seeing her makes you laugh, and puts things in perspective.'

He is a complex, multi-layered character. Soon after Azalea's birth, at a press conference to mark what was to be a humbling defence of the Masters, involving rounds of eighty-one and seventy-eight, García was asked if he regretted his candour when he once wondered aloud whether he 'would ever have the stuff' to become a major champion. The defiant tone of his answer was intriguing.

'I don't regret it because, for good or for bad, you guys – the media – are always asking for people to be truthful, and I'm not sure there's many more out there more truthful than myself,' he said. 'Unfortunately, sometimes when I'm truthful, you guys don't like it. So at the end of the day I'm just trying to say what I feel.

It's as simple as that. I'm just trying to make you guys realise what I'm feeling, what I'm going through. Then it's a matter of how you guys take it.'

Bjørn never had any doubts that he would be vindicated: 'Sergio is very much the centre of what we do, and I've been saying this all the time. He walks into the room, and he is right in the middle of everything. You've got to have great people that look at the team from the outside, but you've also got to have great people from the inside, and he's one of them. These people understand one another.'

Respect from his teammates, expressed by a standing ovation during the final media conference at Le Golf National, clearly meant a lot. He might have pretended to cry when Jon Rahm paid homage to him, as an inspiration in the manner in which Ballesteros had stirred García through his televised exploits, but the clown's mask is occasionally insecure.

The night before the singles matches, García sought out his fellow Spaniard. They had played together in practice, and he recognised Rahm's desperation to prove himself, after defeats in his two fourball matches. 'You are the present and the future of golf in Spain,' García told him, with appropriate gravitas. 'You are a wonderful player. Believe. Go out and show them what you can do.'

Rahm, the boy from Barrika in the Basque Country, who became a man playing collegiate golf for the Arizona State Sun Devils in the United States, needed no further invitation. He would live up to his heritage on the greatest day of his young life.

Chapter Twelve

LIFE LESSONS

Jon Rahm dared not look at Tiger Woods, golf's Medusa, lest he turn to stone. He isolated himself in a bubble of anxiety, determination and unrelenting concentration for nearly four hours before he sealed the most important victory of his life, on the seventeenth green at Le Golf National. This is the story of that match against his hero, its immediate emotions and its lingering significance.

2 p.m., Friday, 28 September 2018

Rahm was having a buffet lunch in the European team room with José María Olazábal. He had taken that morning's defeat, in partnership with Justin Rose, badly. Addressing the former captain respectfully but urgently by his nickname, Chema, Rahm confessed: 'I can't help to think that I let Rosey down, I let the team down and I let Thomas down.' He was 'very mad because I didn't play good on the back nine', and was evidently unprepared for the ferocity of the response.

'Don't ever think like that again,' Olazábal ordered him, launching into a ten-minute tirade about the futility of adding unnecessary emotional burdens in an already-overwrought environment.

Rahm learned English at college in the United States by memorising rap songs, which helped with pronunciation and allowed him to be able to talk faster and more lucidly, but they were speaking, loudly, in Spanish. It was the sporting equivalent of a domestic disagreement between father and son, across the dinner table.

'He was yelling and I'm like, "Okay",' Rahm remembered. 'Basically the one thing he made me realise – win or lose – is you're not letting anybody down. It's golf; you win points, you lose points. He started sharing stories about him and Seve until he calmed me down, then I learned my role for the afternoon was basically to get the crowds going, make them energetic.'

7.00–8.30 p.m., Saturday, 29 September

Rahm was brooding on another defeat, this time alongside Ian Poulter. They lost 2&1 to Jordan Spieth and Justin Thomas, who reeled off four birdies in seven closing holes. Thomas Bjørn thought him unfortunate, because of the complexities of selection. He felt Rose needed a rest before reuniting with Henrik Stenson in the afternoon; he considered sending Rahm out with Rory McIlroy, before deciding the chemistry between the Irishman and Sergio García was more potent.

Graeme McDowell had been on lunch duty with Rahm in the team room. 'Win the singles and you will feel a thousand times better,' he told him. 'That's where your singularity will come out.' At the close of play Lee Westwood, another of the vice-captains, had lived up to his new nickname, 'Concrete' (he's hard and sets fast). He pointed to a large-screen television and told the rookie: 'Look at the top corner. 10–6. That's the only thing that matters.' Bjørn came in and handed Rahm the singles pairings.

'I know I was fourth out. I start looking from the top down and I see Rory, Justin Thomas; Paul Casey, Brooks Koepka; Rosie against Webb Simpson. And me. I see a "T" and a "W". I was like, "Great. I'm playing the guy who just won his eightieth PGA Tour event. He's 0–3, he really wants to win." I'm not playing my best golf and he's also my idol. Never played with him, never played against him.

'This course, his entire history, the way he hits the ball, should fit him. He doesn't have to hit drivers. All he needs to do is keep it in the fairway. He's the best iron player there is and he's a great putter. I like to hit driver, but holes are narrow, so I don't hit many. I'm not as good a putter as he is, and I'm going to have to do something very well to beat him. Yeah, that was the first twenty thoughts within a minute and a half. I'm like, "This is going to be fun."'

Bjørn sensed the simmering anger and read the body language. He told Rahm: 'This is your greatest opportunity. The Ryder Cup is about opportunities; it is not about what has happened, but what lies before you. Win tomorrow and you'll never ever think about the first two days. It will be with you for the rest of your life.'

12.38 p.m., Sunday, 30 September

Bjørn approached Rahm on the first tee, three minutes before the start of his singles match against Woods. He had been surprised on the opening morning by the Spaniard's self-confidence in leading the grandstand in a Thunderclap before undertaking what, by common consent, is the most terrifying shot in golf, but was reassured by the intensity of Rahm's focus.

'There was so much going through my mind,' Rahm said. 'I can't explain it, but the number-one thing I thought was, "This has happened for a reason." I'm playing against arguably the scariest player in history, the best player in history, on a course that suits him pretty well. It's not like the odds are in my favour. I had to play Jon Rahm golf and keep my emotions in check.

'Thomas said it best. "Tiger just does not make mistakes. He's going to try to capitalise on your mistakes, and he's going to hole a ton of putts, so don't be surprised." So I kind of went with the mindset of "I'm going to have to beat this guy at his own game."'

12.41 p.m.

In Woods's world, the volume is always turned up to eleven. He acknowledged the howl of expectation, and drove the ball with the assurance of a man who had been beaten only once in seven Ryder Cup singles, by Costantino Rocca, a rookie twice his age, at Valderrama twenty-one years previously.

Rahm is built like a defensive end, but could his mind match his physicality? He had spent the previous night picking the brains of Tommy Fleetwood and Francesco Molinari, and formulated his psychological strategy on Sunday morning with Joseba Del Carmen, a former bomb-disposal technician who has worked with him for four years as a self-styled 'emotional trainer'.

He would attempt to imagine he was playing on his own – an immediate challenge, given the roar in response to his opening shot, boomed thirty yards past that of Woods, into a welcoming swale on the left-hand side of the fairway. It was a sign of maturity; Rahm had resisted the first temptation, to use his power to propel the ball in a dangerous trajectory over the humps on the right.

12.47 p.m.

Advantage Rahm. His shadow fell fractionally behind the ball on address, but he struck his second shot, across the edge of the water, perfectly. He held his pose as it bounced gently below the hole and rolled to within three feet. Cue bedlam, and a clamorous chant of 'Olé, Olé, Olé' from fans in the natural amphitheatre around the green.

12.52 p.m.

The silence as Rahm surveyed what seemed a straightforward putt was broken by the strains of 'Let's go, Tommy' from the tee, where Tommy Fleetwood was setting out in his match against Tony Finau. His stroke was smooth, his aim was true and he had an early lead. Rahm was not to know it, as he impassively picked his ball from the bottom of the cup, but he would never be headed.

1.04 p.m.

Woods complained to Joe LaCava, his caddie, about discomfort in his feet as they walked across a wooden bridge towards the third tee. Rahm had passed another early test of nerve, judging the pace of a recovery shot from the back bunker so that it rolled, sharply downhill, close to the second hole. He conceded Tiger's tiny return putt to halve.

1.10 p.m.

Woods drove into the left-hand rough, where globules of water in the lush grass refracted the strong sunlight. Rahm, who had 228 yards to the flag from the centre of the fairway, hit a three-iron to forty feet, but missed the eagle putt. The hole was halved in birdie fours, but Woods refused to concede his opponent's return putt, from little more than two feet. The mind games were under way.

1.32 p.m.

Both men struggled on the fourth. Woods highlighted what would be a fatal flaw by once again driving deep into the left-hand rough, that had been strategically fertilised, hand-raked and watered, on Bjørn's insistence, in the six weeks leading up to the event. Rahm three-putted on the steeply sloping green, but the American missed what would have been a winning attempt for par from ten feet. Tiger radiated self-loathing and ignored the fan who bizarrely urged him to 'shoot to kill, Bro'.

1.45 p.m.

Woods once again missed from ten feet, when presented with an opportunity to level the match. Rahm was keeping to the game plan: not to pay Woods overt attention. He kept his temper in check, resisted the urge to be influenced by his rival's tension-infused personality, and permitted himself an instinctive fist-pump when he holed from a similar distance to protect his lead.

2.16 p.m.

The lanyard army emerged from hospitality tents along the right-hand side of the seventh fairway towards a wire fence, behind which they paid homage to a superhero who suddenly seemed all too human. Woods once again drove wildly into cloying rough on the left, and he was unresponsive to their sympathy when he missed a long par putt. Rahm, who had struck a seven-iron from 180 yards to twelve feet, ushered his ball to within eighteen inches and had the hole conceded. Two up.

2.28 p.m.

By way of variety, Woods went right from the tee on the eighth, which was halved in par threes. The strain of the week was beginning to tell. Normally so self-contained, he allowed a snippet of a toxic internal conversation to slip as he walked off the elevated ninth tee. 'Yay,' he said, to no one in particular, 'I hit a fairway.'

2.40 p.m.

He made the most of such unaccustomed efficiency on the dogleg
par five, firing his second shot high, over a guarding bunker to
fifteen feet on a narrow, double-tiered green. Rahm's birdie was
answered by an eagle putt that prompted Woods to flinch with
relief and flail at the air with a right-handed roundhouse punch.
'Go, big dog,' shouted a disembodied voice in the gallery.

3.21 p.m.

The boxercise class continued when Woods drew level on the
twelfth with a birdie putt that prompted another fist-pump. An
American fightback was under way; a crimson tide began to lap
against the scoreboards. The giant screens were magnetic; on the
previous hole, I couldn't help but notice the reaction of Justin
Thomas, when he missed a short putt in the lead match against
McIlroy. 'My God,' he exclaimed, before covering his mouth with
his free hand.

3.32 p.m.

Rahm refocused and reminded himself, 'He's not going to go
easy.' It was an admirable act of self-control, but not an entirely
accurate prediction. The Spaniard two-putted from twenty feet;
Woods, once again out of position on a hole where precision driving was at a premium, could only make a bogey five. Rahm had
a lead he would never lose.

3.50 p.m.

Tiger was no longer burning brightly. He missed, left, from no
more than four feet, for another bogey that doubled Rahm's

advantage. Thousands of European supporters listening to on-course radios were hearing Thomas, the most admirable of the American players, talk breathlessly about the 'heavyweight pillow fight' that ended with McIlory's concession on the final hole.

4.14 p.m.

'I think I was pretty balanced all day,' Rahm would later say. He didn't look it on the par-three sixteenth, after three-putting to hand Woods a lifeline. These are the manic mood swings of match play; the American's stare suddenly hardened, so that it carried the threat of a Taser. He walked imperceptibly faster to the next tee.

4.18 p.m.

Perhaps Woods should have taken his time. Yet another ruinous drive into the left rough gave him no viable second shot to the green. Rahm, meanwhile, channelled his frustration into a monstrous 369-yard drive, which came to rest on the fringe of the first cut on the left side of the fairway. History beckoned, invitingly.

4.24 p.m.

Woods, inevitably, was short with his second shot. Bjørn, in a hollow to the left of the green, watched impassively as Rahm's three-quarter sixty-three-degree wedge shot from 126 yards, aimed at a TV Tower, proscribed a textbook arc and ended seven feet from the hole. Microphones, which picked up a French-accented entreaty to 'get in da hole' in the early stages of the ball's flight, were detonated by a wall of noise. Rahm, strangely, couldn't hear a thing.

4.26 p.m.

Finally, a moment destined for endless instant replay. Rahm dropped his putter a fraction of a second before the winning putt, across the slope, dropped into the hole. Shoulders shoved forward and, eyes wide, he screamed, 'Come on!' as he walked in a seven-pace horseshoe, before hugging his caddie, Adam Hayes.

It was a heartbeat before he noticed Woods waiting, with his red cap and redundant putter tucked under his left arm, to offer his congratulations. Rahm removed his white cap, in a semi-conscious reflex action born of the game's courtesies, and gabbled a few words that he would struggle to remember, beyond their intended respectfulness. He would seek out Woods later that night, to stress what an honour it had been to compete against him.

In tears, he exhaled hugely as McIlroy ran towards him. If nothing else, the resultant tangle of legs and limbs, in which McIlroy spoke into Rahm's right ear, proved that golf is a game for all shapes and sizes. Bjørn beamed, because all twelve players had now contributed at least a point to what was developing into a comfortable victory. Eight minutes earlier Thorbjørn Olesen had confirmed an equally redemptive win, 5&4 against Justin Spieth.

4.30 p.m. onwards

An emotional dam had burst. Rahm dedicated the win to the memory of Seve Ballesteros, and to his late grandfather, who had passed away seven weeks earlier while he played in the US PGA Championship. He told Sky Sports: 'To beat Tiger Woods, who is one of the greatest of all time – if not the greatest – on a Sunday, is the best feeling of my life. I mean, I grew up watching that guy. The pride I feel right now is indescribable.'

No one had doubted the magnitude of his talent, expressed initially when Rahm became the first player to win twice the Ben

Hogan Award, given to the top US college golfer. Now destiny's man-child had proved, conclusively, that he had the character of a champion. Bjørn had juggled the hand grenade without dislodging the pin.

'Robert [Karlsson] was very good with him, but to be honest I felt Rahm needed the captain, the direct route to know what was going on. I wasn't going to put him in the situation where he felt like he wasn't receiving information, straight up. He has strong opinions about himself as a golfer. He believes he is going to be the best player in the world.

'He was disappointed, angry that the Ryder Cup was not giving him what he thought it would give him. Then he goes out there and plays like he did, and he thinks it is the greatest thing in the world. That will live with him for ever. It will stand him in good stead, because he will be the backbone of the European team for many years to come.'

Valderrama, 17 October, 2018

Bjørn was playing in the Andalucía Masters as a gesture of support for Sergio García's charitable foundation. He would tie for fifty-eighth place in the depressurisation chamber of a course he cherished, as the scene of his Ryder Cup debut, in 1997. He was inevitably prevailed upon to place Rahm in the pantheon of Spanish heroes in the competition.

'1997 was a unique week. It was a transition in European golf, in the sense of Seve and the way the week unfolded. There was a group of guys in that team, Darren [Clarke], Lee [Westwood] and myself, who were determined to make the Ryder Cup special. When I walked into that team room for the first time, and saw Faldo and Monty, Langer and Woosie, Ollie and Seve, I realised my career was going pretty fast towards a place I'd never thought I'd be.

'That moment is big for any young player. It is sometimes difficult to make the transition from individual to team player, but Jon now understands what it is all about. That will make him one of the Spanish players who have meant so much in the Ryder Cup over the years. He is standing in line, to take over from Sergio.'

Dubai, 14 November, 2018

Rahm would finish fourth at the season-ending World Tour Championship on the Earth Course at Jumeirah Golf Estates, securing eighth place in the world rankings. It was only his second event since the Ryder Cup, so a degree of reminiscence was unavoidable. Inexorably, the conversation veered towards *that* putt.

'At end of the day I let nothing affect anything within me,' he said. 'Knowing me and how passionate I am about the game of golf, and how up and down that day was – with the magnitude of things, and how much bigger everything was – I am so proud of the way I acted and the way I worked it, to be able to turn it around in twelve hours.

'If I have to say the most special memory, it was right before I stood up to the putt, walking towards it. Somebody in the crowd thought it was a great moment to yell, just at the top of their lungs, 'Do it for Seve.' So, you know, it's not that I did it for him, but to hear that in the middle of the process and within three seconds to be ready . . .'

Nassau, Bahamas, December 2, 2018.

Rahm won Woods's tournament, the Hero World Challenge at the Albany Club, with a final-round sixty-five. The story is seamless . . .

'On the Sunday of the PGA, my grandpa passed as soon as I finished. When they yelled about Seve, in my mind I'm like, "I know he's up there with my grandpa. I know my grandpa's telling him everything about golf, even though Seve knows a little bit about it." I kind of got calm and thought, "I'm just going to make it for them. There's no way them two are going to allow me to miss this putt."

'And when I hit it and it went in, it's all feeling, right? Making the putt to beat Tiger, my all-time hero, man . . . I had to apologise because I didn't see him coming towards me. He came to me with a smile and said, "Man, don't worry. You played great." I just started crying. There's not many things in golf that are going to be better than that for me.'

Enough said.

Rejection is the base metal of professional sport, unattractive, desperately common and deceptively valuable. Jon Rahm's response to it was widely admired, yet he had suffered less than Thorbjørn Olesen, who had taken out his anger on Jordan Spieth in a stunning singles victory that was somehow lost in the mix.

This was, in some ways, a reflection of personality. Rahm might be slightly awkward socially, but someone of his size is difficult to ignore. Olesen, smaller, softly spoken and more finely featured, had the air of a twelve-year-old invited to a brother's sixteenth birthday party. Teammates rallied round and involved him in everything, but he seemed somehow on the fringe.

At its heart was a hint of personal betrayal. By taking the decision to exclude his close friend and protégé from three sessions, following a solitary appearance in a fourball defeat with Rory McIlroy, Thomas Bjørn exposed himself to a crisis of conscience. Victory offered validation, but it did not entirely soothe the soul.

He had not spoken to Olesen, who was walking in with Alex Norén in the final match, when we met immediately after the trophy had been secured. Bjørn insisted, 'I am not scared of hard decisions', but was understandably emotional. 'Thorbjørnis one of my greatest friends,' he said. 'He was so upset, and hurting so much, that it went through my mind: "Is this the end of our friendship?"'

A couple of minutes later, Bjørn headed up the eighteenth fairway to find his fellow Dane. When he did so, as Norén was setting up a tumultuously received victory over Bryson DeChambeau on the last green with a second shot, over the water, to fifty feet, he swamped him in a bear hug and spoke from the heart.

'You are everything we are,' he told Olesen. 'To stand up and do what you have done today is everything a captain can ask for. You are what we represent, and who we are. Golf is about fronting up, and you have the respect of everyone for how you did that. I am so proud of you. You have been phenomenal.'

Olesen initially kept his own counsel, restricting himself to a two-paragraph summary of his joy on the official newswire. He was one of the few European players not to speak at a triumphant press conference. He was still dripping from the mass champagne fight, and unconsciously smoothing down the sodden Danish flag hanging across his slim shoulders, when he finally unburdened himself.

'That was very special,' he said, when I asked about Bjørn's embrace. 'I was frustrated I didn't get to play more, and felt like I wanted to prove something. I was proud of the way I won, because Jordan is one of the great competitors, and I was so fired up. Yesterday was a long, tough day, and I had to do what was best for me.

'It was a long time to sit out, and it put pressure on me. I felt a little bit like an outsider, though the whole team knew how tough it was for me and did what they could to make things easier. This has been an unbelievable experience. This has also been one of the hardest things in Thomas's career. It was a very tough decision for him. I respect him one hundred per cent for it.'

This was the harsh edge to the fairy tale. Olesen had vague memories of watching the 'Battle of Brookline' in 1999, when he was ten, but Europe's win at the K Club in 2006, sanctified by the tears of the recently bereaved Darren Clarke, seized his imagination. Becoming an automatic Ryder Cup pick was a rite of passage.

To then find himself practising alone on that sad Saturday in Paris was a debilitating shock. He attempted to purge himself in the gym, and forced himself through the surreal experience of playing half a dozen practice holes when the afternoon four-somes were building to a crescendo on the far side of the course. The roars of the crowd merely emphasised his isolation.

Graeme McDowell was among the vice-captains who kept watch. 'Thor was definitely one of the most difficult guys to han-dle,' he said, without reproach. 'Rightly so, because he had played well and found himself at the raw end of the deal. That was the biggest and toughest decision Thomas made all weekend. We were delighted how it turned out for Thor.'

Olesen's plight inadvertently highlighted one of golf's eternal truths: that there is no place to hide in adversity. The acidity of the game strips a man to the bone. Perhaps the best perspective, in its broadest sense, was provided by Olesen's coach, Hugh Marr, who stood, steadfast, alongside him when it mattered most.

'I coach six guys on the Tour, and each one of them is funda-mentally different,' he said. 'All of them require handling in a very different way. How long does it take to build that relation-ship? How long is a piece of string. There are guys you take a long, long time to understand. It is not as simple as "Do this, this and this and you'll be okay."

'How things are off the course is generally reflected by how things are on the course. If you are unsure about yourself, it is very easy to ask yourself questions and come up with the wrong answer. It is interesting spending time with these guys. There is a group who appear to be rock-solid, confidence-wise. That is their mask. They are not going to let you break that down.

'Deep down they might know they're not quite on top of everything, but they will never, ever let you see that. Then, on the other side of the equation, you have guys who don't even understand the value of creating that robustness. They just get up there and hit it. Basically, everyone fits in on that scale.

'Look at golf as a sport. There cannot be many sports where you are surrounded by failure on a daily basis. Not just one failure. You could hit a hundred balls and eighty of them could be failures, or perceived failures. Tiger, who is arguably the greatest that ever lived, has just won his eightieth tournament. How many has he played? Six hundred-plus? So the win rate is pretty miserable.

'If you don't have that deep emotional intelligence – I call it Golf IQ – that deep understanding of the game of golf and what it can do to you, it does get you. You look at the journeyman pros, who have been out there for fifteen, twenty years. It has fundamentally affected who they are. It takes something out of them.

'That's why I am so in awe of all those players who have been at the top of the game for so long. Their ability to deal with those little failures – on a daily, weekly, monthly, annual basis – is staggering. It does take a special human being and someone who really knows himself. Everything is public. Everyone understands weakness.

'Golf is getting the variables right, getting the fact that in certain instances your failure might not be down to you. It could involve misjudging the effect of wind, misjudging the effect of temperature. There could be flag positions that don't suit your ball flight. There are just so many factors, and the consequence of making the wrong decision can make you look a complete idiot.

'It is still the one sport where the very best in the world have days where they are incompetent. You don't see that in tennis. You don't see that in football, where the best can hide a bad day within the team context. Generally the very best footballers' bad days aren't that bad, but you have seen, this week, players hitting shots that are appalling? What other sport provides that challenge?'

A fundamental question – one that we are on the way to answering.

Chapter Thirteen

TOMMY: A ROCK OPERA

With his lustrous hair, loose limbs, beach-bum beard and blissed-out demeanour, Tommy Fleetwood resembled a rhythm guitarist in a West Coast soft-rock band. He had experienced a footballer's adulation when the galleries chanted his name across the golf course, but now, for the first time in his life, he felt like a rock star.

Some players threw their shoes, or themselves, into the crowd on a triumphal march from the European team room, down through a funnel of humanity and across a bridge to the eighteenth green at Le Golf National. Fleetwood was surveying the scene with a sense of wonder when his face flashed onto the giant screen and triggered a familiar refrain.

'Tommy. Tommy, Tommy. Tommy, Tommy . . . Tommy. Tommy Fleetwood . . .'

He was cradling his infant son, Frankie, because he wanted to use the experience as a mental bookmark: 'Any time you get to cuddle your son is amazing, but to have him in my arms, to carry and hold him at that sort of moment, with everything going on around us, was so, so special. I will tell him this story. These times will pass, and he is my ultimate motivation.'

The 'Moliwood' fable, created by four wins and two complementary personalities, would be confirmed just before midnight when, in golf's *Harry Met Sally* moment, he and Francesco Molinari giggled their way drunkenly through a mock post-coital video sending up the supposed intimacy of their relationship. It duly went viral, as an indication of their ability to laugh at themselves.

Another largely unseen image, immediately after the trophy presentation, was infinitely more personal. Fleetwood made a point of posing with those who knew the magnitude of a struggle that had been masked, over the previous two years, by his victory in the European Order of Merit and his development into a blue-collar fan favourite in the United States.

They meant more to him than a throwaway characterisation as 'Team Tommy' could convey. The photograph featured his wife, Clare, and his father, Pete, who sneaked onto Royal Birkdale with him as a child and carried his bag, before his knees succumbed to their daily battering on a succession of building sites. Ian Finnis, his friend, caddie and fellow Everton fan, was a focal point in the back row.

Alan Thompson was Fleetwood's coach from the age of thirteen. Phil Kenyon first worked on his putting when Tommy was fourteen. Graham Walker finesses his short game. Kevin Duffy oversees his strength and conditioning programme. Performance psychologist Tom Young provides perspective. All coalesced around him at his lowest point.

Fleetwood had a successful amateur career, secured a maiden professional win on the Challenge Tour in Kazakhstan in 2011, and won on the European Tour for the first time at Gleneagles in 2013, before consolidating over two years in which he admits he felt, naïvely, that he could move on from his mentors.

Ambushed by a flawed swing in 2016, he was consumed with such fear and uncertainty that he had continually to fight an instinct to walk off the course. One opening tee shot, at the symbolic home of European golf, Wentworth, crystallised his frazzled mind.

'I didn't want to tee off, because I didn't know if I was going to get the ball off the tee. Somehow I made contact and sprayed it miles right into the trees, but I was happy, because I could deal with that. When I had a driver in my hand, I had a sort of twitch in my shoulder and I would spray it all over the place. I couldn't stop it, and it was terrifying.

'I thought, "You could be done, here." I remember all those feelings. There is a sense of helplessness. You have to hit the ball, but you have no idea what is going to happen. You watch people doing things that suddenly you can't do. You try and you try, but you just can't do it, even when you are at home with no one watching.'

Fleetwood reconnected with Thompson, who analysed the problem on the range at the Heswall club, situated on the Wirral between Chester and Liverpool, before moving on to the adjoining tenth hole to confirm its extent. When Fleetwood hit six successive drives over the trees and into a lake, Thompson understandably feared that his returning pupil was beyond salvation.

Technical issues invariably have a mental dimension and, with his mind in turmoil, Fleetwood asked to work again with Young. The pair had initially met at a barbecue at the golfer's house, bonding over a shared love of football and rugby league, before agreeing to work through a basic model of cognitive behavioural psychology.

In layman's terms, this involves focusing on how thoughts, underlying beliefs and attitudes affect feelings and behaviour. Fleetwood, an avid reader with an inquisitive mind and strongly held personal principles, was responsive to the coping skills taught by Young, and unafraid to incorporate them into his game.

'I've worked in other sports, and so appreciate there is an undercurrent of scepticism about psychology,' Young admitted. 'It is less pronounced in golf, because of its individual nature, but it still helps that you can provide an element of proof that, for instance, visualisation works in the learning of a skill.

'The science is now much more accessible. You can go on You-Tube and show a player what a thought looks like. You can visually track electrical impulses, so a player realises, "Oh, this is not just about thinking positively then." It's a part of it, and helps with motivation, but it's not everything. Psychology can be misrepresented as a magic pill, but for Tommy, at that time, it was very educational.'

They worked together for eighteen months before Fleetwood decided to move on. Young was hurt, since he was still learning to maintain a sense of professional distance, but was hugely impressed by Fleetwood's integrity in choosing to tell him to his face, rather than hiding behind the impersonality of an email or the expedience of an agent's telephone call.

'I think maybe he felt it had got a bit stale. It was tough at the time, and the conversation will have been hard for him, but he could so easily have done something cold. That's a great indication of his character. He said he wanted to go in his own direction, but was sure we would work together again. When we did so, the second time around, he was a clean sheet of paper.

'The talent has been unquestionable, since he was a kid. When you meet Tommy he is always friendly, and can hide the hurt quite well, but he was pretty low. When he speaks about the experience of struggling, he doesn't embellish it. During our first sessions back together, he would write things down later and text me. He obviously didn't want to talk.

'You can understand that. He is known to most people as Tommy the golfer, so he's suddenly like a footballer who gets injured at twenty-five and can't play any more. Where has his identity gone? You feel you become the role you are playing, the job you are doing. Suddenly you perceive that has been taken away. Identity is stripped, confidence drops, and you are left with almost a sense of personal shame.

'The nature of the sport means you have nowhere to hide. You are pursuing it. You'll always be pursuing it, even if you win the Ryder Cup or reach great personal heights. And that's where you have that fascinating internal dialogue, that little voice saying, "Yeah, you've had your time now. You'll be back down there soon." The doubts will creep in.'

That's why, in golf, they say the scorecard paints few pictures. Fleetwood worked through his technical issues with those he trusted, but ultimately had to draw something from within. He comes from a distinctive family – according to mother Sue, her grandfather kept the milkman's horse in his kitchen – with clearly defined values.

Fleetwood speaks softly, maintains eye contact and impresses with his authenticity: 'There are hundreds and hundreds of balls being struck, loads and loads of rounds being played, and you don't seem to be getting anything out of it. The mind is a massive thing, in life and in sport, and things start to come together in your head. You have to let the game, and your confidence, come to you.

'I never lost my desire to get where I want to be. Some people don't have the work ethic. They don't want to get out of bed to graft, to get out there and do it. Whatever mood I was in, I would have got up at five in the morning, and still been there on the range at seven in the evening, if I thought that was what was needed. My struggle gave me freedom, within myself.

'When things started coming round, I had people I was familiar with all around me. It's the best journey you can go on. When you struggle you learn about yourself, and people learn about you. The number-one thing my dad always said to me was, "You are a person first and a golfer second." Whether I was brilliant at golf or terrible, he always wanted me to be a nice person.

'Fortunately I kept that perspective when things went wrong. You see so many people who can't do that. The ego gets involved. This is your life. Everything goes into it. Your friends, your family, your coaches – all live and breathe your golf. It doesn't matter whether you want them to think like that, but that's just the way it happens.

'It's about self-worth. Players define themselves by their golf careers. Your dreams lie in your life. That's why people struggle when they can't hit it how they want. I don't want to use the word "depression", because that is a big word, but I can see how people suffer from it. They get into a habit of thinking negatively about themselves.

'The journey means something. One hundred per cent, when I stood on that first tee at the Ryder Cup, the place where people get more nervous than anywhere else, I was nowhere near as nervous as I was on that first tee at Wentworth. I'll always have that. It's fuel that I use. It's not something to avoid; it's something to embrace. You feel miles better, having come through the fire.'

That broader context, of sport's place in everyday life, is an indication of Young's influence. Fleetwood explains, 'We do a lot of life psychology, a lot of perspective, goal-setting, and outside-the-box stuff', but Young is more professionally precise.

'Our first area is around direction. Do you know why you play golf? What are your goals? What's the biggest thing you can achieve? What are the attributes you need to show in order to give yourself the chance of getting there? What are the beliefs you need to have to give yourself that chance? It is all about what you're like as an individual. The brain is a little bit like a satnav. If you don't put the right information in, it will just take you somewhere you don't want to go.

'"Resilience" is a buzzword at the moment. In Tommy's case, it meant coming back from a culmination of events that led to this feeling of helplessness. He looked in the mirror and didn't deny the brutal facts of being one hundred and eighty-eighth in the world and not knowing where his ball was going to go, but he had faith that he was going to pull through.

'That's not blind faith. It's authentic optimism. He didn't hide from what he needed to do technically, tactically, psychologically. That's his underlying grit. Tommy is a nice guy, but you don't get to where he is – at the top of a sport that demands inner drive – without being a tough cookie who is ruthless at times. I have to understand the human being.'

Athletes, in Young's experience, require information in different forms and intensity. A more structured personality might want notes to read, to digest a session. Someone more independently minded, with an expansive, looser view, might want only three points to remember. The impatient player might restrict the session to forty-five minutes; a more serene character might require three hours.

Young, who also works with Roberto Martínez and Belgium's national football team, prepares a twenty-six-page Personal Development Analysis for a client. In Fleetwood's case, he expanded it to include Ian Finnis because, in business terms, they are leader and direct report. It reflected the player's authority and the caddie's need to be assertive at certain times during a round.

'How does someone's humanity come out on a golf course? Tommy is seen as being quite relaxed and calm, because he is very friendly, patient and methodical, but he is also very analytical. He's always thinking. His brain doesn't switch off; he's always looking for something to activate him, because he is never really satisfied.

'He needs an element of focused practice, a direction to his day. We suit his personality by almost ticking things off, in terms of planning and progress. He uses his phone to instil certain drills, and to write down daily aims, but we do an old-school piece of reflection in a notebook, which covers what was good in that day's work, what needs to improve, what he has learned and what his targets for the following day will be.'

All elite athletes are conditioned to developing non-negotiable habits, ingraining so-called winning and losing behaviours that can include everything from dietary advice to temper training. Time management is as critical as a clear-eyed approach to the purpose of practice. Golf is complicated by the subtle power shifts in the relationship between player and caddie.

'We did a profile of Tommy and Ian, and they are opposites, basically. Ian is more direct, kind of aggressive, louder. He's straight to the point, an extrovert, so he talks a lot. You don't micromanage him; you allow him to set his own tone. Tommy's the opposite, but their relationship works because they think a lot of each other. Ian is almost family, really.

'Tommy is the boss, but Ian is not just carrying the bag as a mate, which might have been the perception when he first came out on Tour. He was a pro golfer, at Formby Hall, and is one of the hardest-working people out there. He's really invested in our work; he understands they are in a highly competitive, complex environment that involves playing for a lot of money in front of a lot of people.'

Fleetwood's personal life overlaps with his professional. He and Molinari were eager to partner each other in the Ryder Cup, as much as an expression of the bond between their respective families as a statement of faith in their complementary talents on the golf course. Their wives, Clare and Valentina, are close friends; Clare used to manage the Open champion.

Fleetwood began building his baby son into his Ryder Cup planning six months beforehand, since he realised it would coincide with Frankie's first birthday. Frankie gave him an emotional fulcrum on which to base his response to a new, uniquely diverting, sporting experience. His marriage is another indication of his free-spiritedness and strong moral compass, since it was not without opposition.

Again he is earnest, unflinchingly honest: 'I've dealt with stuff off the course. I fell in love with a woman who was a lot older than me. Nobody agreed with that whatsoever, but I followed my heart. Clare and I ended up getting married and having a son – that's bigger than anything to do with golf. It was another aspect of learning. You go with what you truly feel.

'Golf is all about self-awareness and self-perception. Some people do set really high goals, but you tend to end up where you see yourself. If that's number one hundred in the world, you will probably end up there. That's why you see guys who are amongst the most talented fail to get where they should be; and others, who aren't as gifted, push themselves to a level that logically they shouldn't maintain, but they do.'

Leadership is an intuitive, individualised process. Thomas Bjørn recognised Fleetwood's need for structure and spent hours with him, discussing philosophical issues within the context of a game that bent others to its will. They established a deeper connection than is possible in other, more hierarchical sports. 'We connected off the course,' Fleetwood acknowledged. 'Thomas dealt with us as people. He became very close to everyone. He did it perfectly, he really did.'

Having also been pulled into Bjørn's orbit, Young identified with the emotional intensity of the relationship. It matched Fleetwood's personality, in that it was based on mutual respect and an appreciation of something greater than propelling a ball into a hole in the ground. Each, in his own way, had the courage to follow his heart.

'If you look at human behaviour in general, people respond to someone like Tommy, who is quite calm and patient, in a certain sort of way. He's perceived as being a salt-of-the-earth guy. And that type of individual values things like honesty, loyalty, long-term relationships and trust. With that comes a moral code, doing things right, being authentic, being genuine, no bullshit – maybe sometimes to a fault, where he's a bit too open. You can't fake that. Yeah, he is very good at golf, but he's actually just a good guy.'

Certain places have a magnetic attraction because of the power of memory and imagination. Fleetwood's major pre-event session with Young was at Formby Hall, the club where, aged eight, he astonished his first coach, Norman Marshall, by hitting an archery-style target twenty-one times in twenty-five attempts from seventy-five yards. The previous record, held by Marshall himself, was sixteen.

Fleetwood stood with Young at sunrise on the morning before the Cup began, at the top of the grandstand overlooking the first tee at Le Golf National. He visualised walking down the steps to meet his destiny, and asked the psychologist to be with him inside the ropes before his opening drive in the match against Tiger Woods and Patrick Reed, because Young wanted to see him excel under pressure.

Moments of absurdity, such as on the team's first day in Paris, when Fleetwood was one of four European players to get lost on the way to the course because their drivers did not know the route from the team hotel in Versailles, were countered by immersive ten-minute consultations at nine-thirty each evening, when he FaceTimed Young to go through the events of the day.

Fleetwood had the foresight to understand that leaving the Ryder Cup bubble required forward planning. He ran out of mental and physical energy in his singles defeat to Tony Finau; less predictably, endless regurgitation of the Moliwood bromance complicated his comedown from such an emotional high.

He and Young had prepared for the Ryder Cup as if for a penalty shoot-out in football; they could not predict the outcome, but they could strategise the challenge. Fleetwood flew directly to Scotland on a private jet for the Dunhill Links Championship, 'without seeing anything or anyone', and had an hour-long meeting with his psychologist late on the Tuesday afternoon to reset himself for the rest of the year.

'It's not hit me yet,' he admitted when we met on the Wednesday morning. 'I haven't been into the outside world properly yet. Let's see what it's like. The most important thing is to stay on the same path. Stay the same person. You know your life goals are still there and keep working towards them.'

He identifies emotionally with the 'Auld Grey Toun' of St Andrews; one of his career goals is to win there, in the cradle of the game. He nearly did so, finishing as runner-up to Lucas Bjerregaard, along with Ryder Cup teammate Tyrrell Hatton. His body language was relaxed because, as Young remarked, 'You are not going to get many fan boys at St Andrews, are you?'

Fleetwood finally ran out of steam in his penultimate round of the 2018 season, in Dubai, where he fell out of contention by shooting seventy-four. His striking blue eyes radiated fatigue, he bit his lower lip and his voice was low and slow. 'The adrenaline might have gone now,' he acknowledged. 'I think you kind of know when your time's up. I lasted within two days of the season.

'You live and breathe the game, don't you, so there's going to be good bits and bad bits. But it is what it is. I'm fine. Fit and healthy. I'll play golf tomorrow, and that's it. I'll go home and I'll spend time with my son tonight. It's just golf, but it does hurt when you have days like that. It's tough grafting.'

He is operating on the finest of margins. His most obvious ambition in 2019 is to win a major; coming second at the US Open with a final-round sixty-three that stirred the blood of beer-bellied galleries has given him another glimpse of the summit. His intriguing relationship with the messianic Manchester City coach Pep Guardiola, whom he partnered in a pro-am at Wentworth, is mutually beneficial.

In his own environment, Guardiola has the assurance of a legend that links him to Johan Cruyff and the Catalan church that is Camp Nou, home of FC Barcelona. On a golf course, he exhibits deeply buried aspects of his character; he is one of golf's impatient perfectionists, a victim of the traditional amateur's trait of speeding up his swing under pressure.

Parallels between the sports are telling. One of the keys to England's unaccustomed success in a penalty shoot-out at the last World Cup was a conscious decision not to rush to respond to the referee's whistle before shooting, and Fleetwood has studied Manchester City's training methods to get an insight into the practical aspects of a high-pressure, high-performance environment.

Guardiola, who is coy about his handicap (fourteen, when last openly discussed, in 2016), appreciates the power of repetition that is central to a golfer's success. Fleetwood picked up on an obsessive attention to detail, and was introduced to the empathetic approach to mental-skills training adopted by Guardiola's long-term lieutenant Manel Estiarte, a former Olympic water-polo champion.

Guardiola accepts that football managers, like professional golfers, are 'very, very alone'. Estiarte's influence is incalculable: 'He helped me a lot in terms of the significance of understanding sport, by seeing it from above. I have my smell, but he helps me see things from a different perspective. Like in life, there are things that you have to treat differently.'

Fleetwood, as a singular man, is on the same wavelength. He turned twenty-eight on 19 January 2019, with a different set of challenges to face. He was around the world's top ten, a globally recognisable figure obliged to rationalise the need to make incremental progress at the highest level of his sport. Ask him about the future, and there are no PR platitudes.

'Let's see where we get to. The main goal in life is to have your family fulfilled and comfortable. My career goals are to win the

Open and become world number one. Say if I did that. I could stop and be happy. Literally, I know I could. I know, deep down inside myself, that I'm not like those who can't let go. I wouldn't stop, of course, but I have a life to live . . .'

Perhaps it was the rockstar vibe, the sweep of shoulder-length hair struggling to escape from the ubiquitous baseball cap, but I thought back to that scene in Paris, when 50,000 fans paid homage to a man cradling his child in the natural bowl beneath them. 'These times will pass,' Fleetwood said, in unconscious recognition of sport's unceasing carousel.

Molinari, his soulmate, also had a new life to reconcile.

Chapter Fourteen

HOW TO CREATE A CHAMPION GOLFER

'And with a score of two hundred and seventy-six, the winner of the gold medal, and the Champion Golfer of the Year, is . . .'

This was no self-congratulatory review of the sporting year, enacted to give terrestrial television editorial content. This was not yet another invitation to corporate canonisation on the rubber-chicken awards circuit. This was the real thing: the moment Francesco Molinari's name was etched into the history of the game.

Much more was to come, in that hot, extended summer of 2018. He would become the first European to win five points in a Ryder Cup match, and would be cheered through the Gare du Nord on his way to taking the 13.13 Eurostar back to London, like a triumphant Roman general progressing through Palatine streets before being hailed by Caesar.

Molinari would end the European season, which began with holding off Rory McIlroy in the flagship PGA Championship at Wentworth, as the winner of the Race to Dubai, the sponsored version of the old-school Order of Merit. But as he waited beside the final green at Carnoustie, he felt the weight of the occasion.

Though he had walked countless miles during a slow-burn career, the forty-one steps he took, up and through a guard of

honour, to receive the Claret Jug – awarded to the winner of the
Open Championship – were the most important. They were
dreamlike because he had taken them many times, over many
years, in his imagination, but they were very real.

He had removed his cap out of respect, to reveal the letterbox
of pale, lightly tanned skin across the forehead that gives away a
golfer's profession. He spoke with humility and occasional hesi-
tancy, glancing at cue-cards held in his left hand, but thanked the
right people, from the ground staff to the blazerati of the Royal
& Ancient Golf Club.

Only then did Molinari underline his gratitude to his nearest
and dearest. His wife, Valentina, hid moist eyes behind large
sunglasses as he paid tribute to his family. He expressed his appreciation of his coaching team, his caddie, Pello Iguarán, and his
manager, Gorka Guillén. All those mentioned knew the nature of
his journey. This is how they combined to create a Champion
Golfer.

Raw material

Sibling rivalry has shaped modern sport, from the Waugh
twins in cricket to the Williams sisters in tennis. The relationship can be flinty, as with football's Charlton brothers, or expe-
dient, as evidenced by the business model developed by the
Klitschko brothers in heavyweight boxing. The Molinari brothers, Edoardo and Francesco, conform to the classic model of
child psychology.

Edoardo, the elder by twenty-one months, is tall and meticu-
lous. He was an easy baby, a diligent scholar and a dutiful
son, who emulated his maternal grandfather by earning an
engineering degree. Francesco, shorter, more deeply driven
and the possessor of an economics degree, was the traditional
attention-seeking younger child. According to his father, Paolo,

his 'gypsy soul' led to regular temper tantrums, both on and off the course.

Paolo, a dentist, and his wife Micaela, an architect, were not the high-pressure parents that professional sport tends to attract. They recognised Edoardo's affinity with golf as a toddler, without seeing its long-term relevance; Francesco followed him into the game almost by default. The pair shared a set of clubs, respectively using odd- and even-numbered irons, but rarely squabbled.

Their closeness was captured by an anecdote told by their childhood golf teacher, Sergio Bertaina, in an illuminating profile of the brothers for *Today's Golfer* by Jock Howard. It related to Edoardo's qualification for his first Open Championship, at St Andrews in 2005, following his hallmark achievement in becoming the first continental European in ninety-four years to win the US Amateur title.

Francesco, standing in the shadow of the R&A clubhouse with his mother and Bertaina, burst into tears when Edoardo was announced on the first tee. Eyes in the gallery inevitably swivelled towards him, so Sergio swallowed him in a protective embrace. 'You don't want your brother to see you crying now, do you?' he said tenderly. Francesco sobbed: 'Nobody knows what playing this tournament means to my brother . . .'

He conformed to a childhood pact when he caddied for Edoardo at the Masters the following year, and partnered him to victory in the World Cup in 2009. They became the first brothers to play against the United States for forty-seven years in the 2010 Ryder Cup, staged in monsoon conditions at Celtic Manor.

Edoardo's manic victory dance in Wales hinted at a change in the relationship; he had matured into the more expressive, outgoing personality. Francesco, whose rebel streak extended to supporting Inter Milan in opposition to his father's beloved Juventus, was cultivating an enduring reputation for being shy and softly-spoken.

The fire burned within, without emitting much smoke. Francesco had announced himself by lifting his first European Tour trophy at the Italian Open in 2006. His widely admired ball-striking ability guaranteed a lucrative living, without making him a regular winner. The easy option was to bask in the admiration of his peers, maintain the status quo and use professional golf as an ATM.

His tipping point came at the Open Championship at Hoylake in 2014 when, in a third-round group with McIlroy and Dustin Johnson, Francesco fell out of contention by shooting seventy-five. Though he rallied with a final sixty-seven, he was taunted by a sense of inadequacy. He knew he had fundamentally to change the emphasis of his approach to match the best.

Having finally paused to reflect, he succinctly summed up his motivation: 'I don't look for perfection, but I do look to see where the limit is. Obviously you reach a threshold of performance, but you can move it up and up, little by little, especially when you have a team around you. It is about fine margins, finding a way. We are looking for that one per cent.'

Length and strength

Francesco's swing was economic, simple and concise. It was an open invitation for tournament organisers to write out top-ten cheques. In choosing to break it down and rebuild it, he was taking a huge risk. Locker rooms are littered with shattered strategies and the desiccated husks of players unwisely emboldened by a supposed need to change.

His swing coach, Denis Pugh, who first noticed him, aged twenty, in 2003, looked into the next decade and saw players booming the ball 375 yards from the tee. To put that into current perspective, Rory McIlroy led driving distances on the PGA Tour in 2018 by averaging 319.8 yards on all measured holes. McIlroy

'If I have to say the most special memory, it was right before I stood up to the putt, walking towards it. Somebody in the crowd thought it was a great moment to yell, just at the top of their lungs, "Do it for Seve."'

JOHN RAM

'Leadership is tantalising, because it promises nothing. No matter what you do it is still down to the talent, application and inspiration of others. My partner Grace lived it, as I lived it. I might have made the speeches, but we were One Family, players, wives, parents, children, caddies, support staff and vice captains.

'I told the players they would not be defined as golfers by the Cup, but they would be identified as personalities. Their philosophies, experiences, characters and approaches were different, but they responded collectively to one of the most pressurised environments in world sport. That team will never again play together but they will be with me for the rest of my life.

'Golf is all about self-awareness and self-perception. Some people do set really high goals but you tend to end up where you see yourself. If that's number 100 in the world you will probably end up there. That's why you see guys who are amongst the most talented fail to get where they should be.'

TOMMY FLEETWOOD

'In Paris I felt I was ready to compete and fight. In some ways, that inner confidence is even more special than that feeling you get when you sense you are going to win. It's great, very rare, and comes randomly, a few times a season if you are fortunate.'

FRANCESCO MOLINARI

'Can you ever be that kid who first fell in love with the game?
Can you ever retain that enthusiasm and excitement? We lose our
innocence. It is just how things happen. You don't get up in the
morning convinced you're going to find the secret of golfing nirvana
for the rest of your days. It just doesn't work like that.'

PADRAIG HARRINGTON

'Golf is one of the few sports where you see people giving other people lessons, giving fellow competitors a tip to make them play better. I doubt you'd see Ronaldo giving Messi a tip, or Federer giving Nadal a tip on the practice courts. It's a strange sport like that.'

LEE WESTWOOD

'As a team, we related to the concept of Europe as an indication of humanity, rather than a political framework. It drew us closer together as a group, gave us a distinctive identity. It was about how we saw ourselves, how we channelled our passion and celebrated our differences. We were one, formed from millions.'

THOMAS BJØRN

was also the best driver on the European Tour, gaining 1.2 shots a round from the tee.

Mark Broadie, the godfather of golf's analytical movement through his invention of the Strokes Gained statistic, estimates that three strokes a round can be gained by hitting the ball an additional twenty yards from the tee. Within the limitations of his physique, Molinari – officially five feet eight inches tall, and eleven stones four pounds in weight – had to gain length. His days as a self-confessed couch-potato were done.

Pugh describes Molinari as being the hardest worker, in terms of intensity, that he has seen. Again, for context, he has coached around 200 Tour pros, including Colin Montgomerie during a hugely successful twelve-year spell. He works with Molinari at The Wisley, a members' club in Surrey that has three loops of nine holes, designed by the acclaimed course architect Robert Trent Jones, Jr.

'We've been working for a long time for this to come to fruition,' Molinari explained. 'Denis was making sure I was at the top of my game, technically. My swing has always been consistent, in terms of ball flight, but he noticed little breaks in its motion. Obviously my mobility was limited. I was not using all my strength and speed. Our concept was to remove those breaks, swing more freely and use bigger muscles. We were getting rid of anything that was slowing the clubhead down.'

In such cases, mentality is as important as technical purity. Subtle changes, such as Pugh's suggestion that Molinari rid himself of the habit of starting his preparation on the range with wedge shots, since his hands were more active in the shorter swing, were undertaken as part of a broader overhaul of approach and attitude.

Molinari's description of the change is revealingly precise: 'We looked at our pre-round warm-up and started to think more deeply about why we did things in a certain way. We used to go into the gym first, have a few putts and hit balls. It wasn't exactly random, but it lacked a bit of intensity and purpose.

'When you're about twenty-five to thirty minutes away from teeing off, you want to feel that sharpness and anticipation building. You know you need to perform at your best from the first shot, because there is no margin for error. I spend between thirty-five to forty minutes on the range – most people are out there for between an hour and seventy-five minutes. Nothing is wasted. That slight lack of time forces you to be sharper, and stops you from switching off. It saves mental energy.'

The golf swing is an athletic, coordinated sequence that requires strength, power, speed and flexibility. Molinari's gym sessions were concentrated, designed to increase muscle mass and enhance balance, and became a talking point among his peers. As Jordan Spieth said: 'He works his butt off. I see him in the gym all the time, going through his routine, grinding on the range, doing his own stuff.'

A technical assessment of Molinari's swing, on pgatour.com, noted that, to create greater speed, he makes a bigger turn on the backswing. This is said to involve a conscious attempt to 'feel his sternum turning as far and as high from the ball as possible. He lifts his left heel off the ground to increase his turn.' Logical enough, biomechanically, but the process of recalibration was not without its price.

Adrian Rietveld of TaylorMade, the club manufacturers, appreciated the physical stresses as he oversaw a complementary research and development programme: 'He constantly spoke about how hard he was working with Denis on his swing and in the gym with his team. Some days he would be just too tired from the strength work to produce long equipment sessions.'

Some of those sessions required Molinari to wear a motion suit, with twenty-seven sensory markers. 'We are getting closer to getting an exact idea of what is going on,' he explained. 'There are so many elements, so many parts of the body involved, and any little difference results in a change. Before, we were guessing, going on feel, but now we are getting a lot more feedback. It's immediate. It's objective. It's numbers.'

The numbers didn't lie.

Numbers

Edoardo Molinari was one of the first players to pick up on the significance of Mark Broadie's theories, expressed in his book *Every Shot Counts*. Broadie, whose role as the Carson Family Professor of Business at Columbia Business School incorporates research into financial risk management, keeps statistical records for both brothers.

He calculates that Francesco gained 1.9 strokes on the field, per tournament, from the tee between 2015 and the transcendent end to 2018. The statistic is adjusted for such variables as course layout and depth of field, but is supported by an in-depth review, conducted by Sean Martin of the US PGA Tour.

Before Molinari's re-evaluation of his game, in 2015, he was ranked 153rd in driving distance, with an average measured drive of 281.6 yards. He improved consistently, from 286.7 yards the following year, 129th on Tour, to 291.9 yards and a ranking of 99th in 2017. Accelerated progress in 2018 elevated him to 52nd, with an average distance of 301 yards.

He was ranked seventh in terms of strokes gained off the tee that season, with a score of +0.72, His ability to find the fairway consistently enabled Molinari to be ranked eighth in total driving, the statistic that amalgamates driving distance and accuracy. His tee shots covered 64 per cent of the yardage on par fours and par fives, almost 5 per cent more than in 2015, when he was ranked 168th out of 184 players.

The impact has a practical and psychological dimension. Molinari has the confidence to use his driver with greater ambition and frequency. He no longer trails the longest hitters by fifty yards; greater length contracts the golf course, so that he can use a bigger range of calibrated wedges in his approach play. When he misses the fairway, he does not do so by much; his average distance from the fairway – twenty-four feet three inches – was ranked fifty-seventh.

Martin's research found that the average PGA Tour player takes 2.98 strokes to hole out from 160 yards, and 2.91 from 140 yards. Molinari's iron play has changed markedly; during their final round at the Open Championship, Tiger Woods noticed that Molinari's shots were longer, hit on a higher trajectory and with increased spin.

'You could see him actually try and hit a couple with cut spin, a couple of draw spin,' Woods said. 'You know, he was working the ball around the greens, and that was cool to see. He chipped it beautifully. I know he made a couple of putts here and there for par, but to get it to where it was basically kick-in from some of the spots he put himself, that was impressive. Great touch.'

The other element of the equation concerns speed. During one of Rietveld's first tests, in October 2016, Molinari's clubhead speed averaged 107.1 mph. His ball speed registered as 158.5 mph. That improved, by February 2018, to 112 mph and 166 mph respectively. Three months later he recorded speeds of 114 mph and 169 mph. The last test of the year, in October, revealed another step change: 118 mph and 174.5 mph.

These figures may pale alongside those of the freakish American newcomer Cameron Champ, whose swing and ball speed have been measured at 130 mph and 192.6 mph respectively, but they are the bedrock of an overall improvement that extends to performance on the greens. To adapt and personalise the old golfing maxim, Molinari no longer drives for show, and he putts for dough.

Man in black

Thursday, the final practice day at the Ryder Cup, provided a last chance to commune with nature and bathe in the beauty of the treeline's autumnal colours before the madness hit. Spectators still arrived as if fresh from ransacking the local fancy-dress shop, but it was an opportunity to concentrate on golf, rather than indulge in theatrics.

A large gallery followed Molinari to the signature eleventh hole at Le Golf National, a 178-yard par three. They stood or sat, singly or in small groups, on the hill surrounding a green with a double slope, from the left edge to the right edge. The mood was relaxed, and was further eased by a surprisingly warm sun.

It took perhaps a second for the quality of Molinari's shot from an elevated tee, over a lake reintroduced in 2016, to seize the imagination. A low hum, from those following it through binoculars, grew in intensity when the ball pitched on the green and rolled unerringly towards the hole. By the time it stopped, less than a foot short, fans were bouncing on their toes in anticipation.

A short, muscular man, carrying a notebook and clad in black, in contrast to the European team's canary-yellow, was first to reach the ball. He picked it up, as if retrieving litter from his front garden, and tossed it casually to the Italian, who bashfully acknowledged the acclaim before following the instructions of his performance coach.

Dave Alred, the man in black, measured three extended paces above and below the hole, tossing two balls down with a flourish that defied the soporific circumstances. He had been delighted by the intensity of Molinari's practice with a driver and three-wood earlier in the week; this drill involved a series of putts from between nine and eleven feet. He set specific targets throughout the fine-tuning process.

'We usually do this type of work on the putting green, but because of the nature of the Ryder Cup, there is less time to practise,' Molinari explained. 'Going into the week, we both thought that, because of the pressure it applies, the Cup is the ultimate test of whether you can make marginal changes under stress. In those circumstances you tend to revert back to your happy thoughts, your more natural approach.

'For me, it was a case of embracing the challenge and playing more aggressively than I was used to. That's what is required in match play. In Paris I felt I was ready to compete and fight. In some ways, that inner confidence is even more special than that feeling you get when you sense you are going to win. It's great, very rare and comes randomly, a few times a season, if you are fortunate. It is strange. I felt nothing special during the practice round at the Open; I wasn't flushing every shot, but gradually the energy grew.'

His putting at Carnoustie was nerveless, testament to the influence of Phil Kenyon, a former pro with a masters' degree in sports science who has acted as a specialist coach to six other members of the triumphant European team: Tommy Fleetwood, Rory McIlroy, Henrik Stenson, Justin Rose, Thorbjørn Olesen and Alex Norén.

Molinari approached him at Arnold Palmer's tournament in Bay Hill in March 2018. Kenyon spoke with characteristic candour: 'Technically there was a lot he could improve on,' he told Rick Broadbent of *The Times*. 'Players don't often want to hear that, but he's one of the most professional I've worked with, in his attitude to getting better.

'He was struggling to start his ball on line, which was a lot down to his set-up and how his body worked around the stroke. We changed his grip, his posture, the concept of how he moved his putter. We changed how he aims, some aspects of how he read greens, how he practised. It took time to get going, but once he could see positive signs, his confidence grew.'

Molinari also changed his putter, with Kenyon's assistance, to a customised Bettinardi blade model, 32¼ inches in length, with a loft of 2.5 degrees. A single dot aids alignment and the club-head weighs precisely 372 grams. It has a skull-and-crossbones stamp in the rear cavity, with a colour scheme based on the Italian flag.

There are no marks for artistic impression on the green, but statistics gathered by the European analytic team in Paris underlined putting's importance. Molinari gained 3.7 strokes relative to the rest of the field over the first two days, when his partnership with Fleetwood flourished. In that sequence, Europe gained a six-putt advantage over the Americans.

The human chemistry of Molinari's support team is fascinating, since his three principal advisers, Pugh, Kenyon and Alred, work in isolation. A discernible creative tension between them understandable, since they are leaders in their respective fields – has, over time, been diluted. But golf at the highest level is no place for naïvety; the pressure principle applies.

The Ugly Zone

The first time Dave Alred met Molinari he was direct, and to the point: 'You are going to be fucked-off with me. You are going to get pissy, annoyed and frustrated. You need to be in that space, and if I can get you there, and we work within it, you can take that resilience onto the course. This is about contextualising what is almost a random game, for you as a player. It is not bullying. It is believable.'

Robert Bjork, Distinguished Research Professor of Psychology at UCLA, is a globally renowned expert in the science of learning and the impact of memory on the educational process. He may not be as acerbic, but he agrees that 'when embarked on any substantial learning enterprise, we should probably find the absence, not the presence, of errors, mistakes, and difficulties to be distressing'.

In 1994 he introduced the concept of 'desirable difficulties', in which challenges are intentionally created to enhance long-term retention of knowledge and skill sets. Academics have isolated five such examples. One, testing from memory to strengthen memory, is more suited to conventional education in the classroom. A second, varying practice conditions, has greater relevance to an indoor sport like basketball, where shooting distances and angles are easier to alter.

Three of the five have some substance in golf. Dr Bjork argues that feedback, provided too regularly and too quickly, can act as a crutch. Far better to allow a player to consider and correct their own mistakes; this builds self-reliance in competitive situations, where external influences cannot be imposed immediately during a fluid, ever-changing challenge like an important round of golf.

Alred's adaptation of the principle began in rugby, coaching goal-kickers like Jonny Wilkinson and Jonathan Sexton: 'They go into the arena for ninety minutes, when it will basically be World War Three. It's snotty, relentless, but you will have six kicks at goal. It is quite possible you will miss one. You need to work out on your own what went wrong. You need to correct yourself when you are under the pump.

'Sometimes coaches jump straight in and say things like "Put your shoulder forward." The player very quickly parrots this, and when he misses again he asks, "What happened there?" That's not a road I go down. To give you an example, I will tell a player, "There are times when I am going to watch you mess up a kick, and watch you dig yourself out of the dirt." That has far greater value than simply giving an answer.

'The art of coaching is at what stage do you give feedback and, more importantly, what are you – the player – going to do with it? That's really important. You might miss again, and I'll ask you what went wrong. You'll say something like "My shoulder was open and I kicked the ball with the inside of my foot." Well done. Your awareness is spot-on.'

Dr Bjork's concept of spacing opposes the traditional student model of cramming for examinations. Research suggests it is deemed better, for instance, to hit twenty five-iron shots a day for five days than 100 five-iron shots in a single session on the range. The amount of practice time is identical, but gradual honing of the skill encourages better retention.

In Alred's words, 'Long-term learning is enhanced by little and often. Let's say Denis wants Fran to work on a technical issue. We might hit twenty-five shots. The twenty-fifth shot will be based on the other twenty-four. You are not learning much, if at all. But if you do only five repetitions, on the fifth you will be beginning to feel comfortable with the process.'

Perhaps the most relevant notion is that of Bjork's 'interleaving practice'. Instead of what he calls 'blocked practice' – in golfing terms, hitting balls with a single club until the shot is perceived to have been mastered – he believes the brain retains information more effectively by recalibrating when it is forced to adapt to a variety of different situations.

Alred has taken this a stage further, by adding the element of pressure. Once he has warmed up, Molinari is accountable for each practice shot. Drills are target-specific; to give one example, he is tested on how many wedge shots it takes to get ten balls within ten feet of the flag. Golfers regard their yardages for individual clubs as holy writ; by using TrackMan radar technology during a practice round to randomly select a target and distance, Alred seeks to put Molinari under the real-time pressure of being between clubs.

'Say your stock yardage with a fifty-six-degree wedge is eighty-six. Fine. Hit ten. You are calibrating distance, understanding the club. The art is being able to flick backwards and forwards between clubs. If I said to you, "Chip three balls to the pin. and then add 'Tell you what, putt the worst ball." all of a sudden you are in match-mode, because there is a consequence to failure.'

In a variation on the principle, both Phil Mickelson and Colin Montgomerie are known for forcing themselves to sink 100 three-foot putts in a row before they can leave the practice green. In technical terms, this is a relatively straightforward exercise, but the sense of jeopardy, the dread of having to go back to the start, increases the heart rate.

Alred's mantra is stark, and suggestive: 'No second chances. Match intensity. You can't do it again.' This is all part of taking a pupil into what he calls 'The Ugly Zone', a consciously uncomfortable environment where improvements are made 'when execution doesn't match intention'. He looks at behaviours through a three-word formula – Repair, Training, Match – and creates conditions relevant to each phase.

He explains: 'Both player and coach have to understand what practice means in performance terms. In the match phase during a practice round I'm looking at one shot, and saying, "This is it. Deal with it." Players have to want to achieve. Some will argue, "When I'm comfortable I play well", but when you're playing, things happen and you get in areas where you're uncomfortable, so wouldn't it be better to practise in those areas, so you can cope with whatever the tournament throws at you?'

Alred established his reputation by unravelling the complexity and insecurity of Wilkinson, a World Cup-winning England fly half. A definitive drill, designed to counter a mental blockage with his place-kicking, involved visualising a spectator in the stands, whom he christened Doris. Wilkinson was challenged to kick the ball through the uprights and dislodge her imaginary magazine; once that task was completed, he was ordered to aim for the drink supposedly held in her other hand.

The beauty of the process lay in its simplicity, and its prioritisation of process. By being obliged to focus on a tiny target, Wilkinson pushed damaging thoughts of technique into his subconscious. Alred has created what he terms 'the pressure dome', where he makes similar use of distractions. He complicates practice with loud music, wind-machines that create a blizzard of empty crisp packets, or teammates throwing balls across the field of vision.

'The principles we use are very similar, both in rugby, golf and maybe other sports,' Molinari acknowledged. 'Obviously there are technical differences, and the mentality is different, but there are skills that can be enhanced and transferred. The work I do with Dave is part of a long progression.

'We started little by little, and this is our third season together. He knows me better, so he can tailor drills and exercises. My practice is less pleasant, to be honest. It is more challenging, and though I have loved every minute of the last few years, it has been hard. The best time is on the course, where you see the quiet, unpublicised work you do pay off in the toughest moments.'

Alred's influence extends to Molinari's caddie, Pello Iguarán, who is urged to 'get really fussy', to the point of forcing the player to focus on tightly defined landing areas, such as a specific shadow. The coach explains: 'You almost displace any concentration on what you want to avoid, because if the target is small enough, you haven't got the spare mental capacity to focus on anything else.'

He pushes Molinari into sensory shutdown in moments of pressure, and regards language as 'the ultimate performance-enhancing drug'. He teaches through numbers, but is prepared to be unorthodox; when I was following him inside the ropes at the Ryder Cup, Alred left to join the galleries for a stretch of holes, to see Molinari work from a different perspective.

Alred used golf techniques to turn British modern pentathlete James Cooke from supremely talented underachiever to world champion. The creation of mental images – he convinced Luke Donald to adapt an assassin's mindset when they worked together – is consistent across sports, but tailored to individual personalities.

'Dave is an explorer,' reflected Pádraig Harrington, a former pupil. 'He gets guys to practise what they don't like. It can seem so easy. You can be the best ball-striker, so you never practise chipping and putting. I'm generally in the top five in bunker play. If I stop practising that, and put my effort into something else, I might slip from five to six in rankings but I won't go down to one hundred.

'Dave puts numbers and logic into the process. A performance coach is more important than a swing coach to a player, out there on Tour. At the end of the day we have all got a certain level of physical ability. We've got our swing. Everything else after that is mental. People see what they expect to see.'

The key to Molinari is stimulating his sense of excitement. Spark that, and a fire rages.

Present tense

The day after the Ryder Cup, Molinari could not tie up his shoe-laces. That had nothing to do with the mother of all hangovers, and everything to do with his commitment. He had kept his discomfort from Thomas Bjørn throughout the week, dealing with the pain through anti-inflammatory tablets. Ambition and adrenaline did the rest.

Like many of the world's best players, Molinari's response to the revised global calendar in 2019 has been to concentrate on the PGA Tour. He has compartmentalised 2018, because of his deep-seated belief in the process of progress. He knows that, to win more majors, he must continue to work on the finest margins.

Where is he, in his life and in his game?

'You get used to the travelling, the airports. It's more the people around you – your family – that find it harder to adjust. We have the joy and pleasure of doing something we love and want to do. The off-season was busier than ever before. People recognise me in the street, but that is the greatest compliment. I have to embrace the new level of interest, and feel grateful for the prizes they want to give me.

'I have learned two lessons. Number one: it is hard to keep your priorities in check. I have always said my family comes first, but it is not as easy and straightforward as you think. As the demands multiply, you need to disappoint people by saying "No". I know the biggest players, like Rory, are dealing with that, but it was never a challenge I had before.

'Number two: I have surprised myself. I never believed my own publicity, and have always been uncomfortable with praise. Looking back, I can understand why in the past people were telling me I was better than I thought. I suppose they were right . . .'

Chapter Fifteen

FIRE AND FEAR

The badly weathered sign, held fast on a rusting pole, stood sentinel in the rocks on St Andrews Bay. 'Danger,' it read, barely discernibly, as a fierce west-north-westerly wind sand-blasted a solitary horserider on an otherwise deserted beach. A silver sheen of water, whipped off sets of waves sprinting to the shore, captured the bleak beauty of the scene.

A matter of yards away, in the Old Course caddie shack beside the first fairway, a man with an official black waterproof jacket summed up conditions with a single word that sounded like a sermon: 'brutal'. The unfamiliar wind direction – more usually south or south-westerly on this fabled stretch of Fife coastline – was causing havoc. It was cold, forbidding and as nature intended.

Matt Wallace was out on the links, absorbed in his art. He had been hitting the ball too high in Portugal a fortnight previously, and had missed the cut when the wind blew hard, at the Irish, Scottish and US Opens, in what was a breakthrough year. He experimented with a lower ball flight as the tempest raged. It was like trying to arm-wrestle a ghost.

He was the new kid on the block, a four-time winner on the European Tour making up for lost time. He worked in a clothing store at nineteen, played 'shit golf' and applied unsuccessfully for a job at seven sports-management agencies at twenty-five. At twenty-eight, suddenly prominent and understandably insatiable, his self-confidence affronted those who failed to recognise the contrasting humility of his desire to learn from his betters.

The most persuasive example he followed was that of Ian Poulter. Wallace was similarly unafraid of the strength of his opinion, conscious of the modesty of his background, and capable of channelling unfiltered emotion into streaks of irresistible play. He was an outsider, eager to acquire inside knowledge. The generosity of spirit encouraged by the game's vicissitudes worked in his favour.

He had solicited a lesson in wedge play from Thomas Bjørn. Brett Rumford, an acknowledged expert, provided personal advice on the intricacy and strategy of bunker play. Robert Rock, an early role model because of the single-mindedness with which he rose from assistant club pro to European Tour winner, had agreed to be his swing coach during a 7 a.m. session that demonstrated mutual intent.

Wallace had secured a practice round the following day with Louis Oosthuizen, whose seven-shot victory in the 2010 Open Championship at St Andrews was characterised by an underdog's opportunism and a trawlerman's comfort with elemental extremes. Though contrasting characters quiet farm boy from the Western Cape and driven schoolboy from west London – Wallace recognised in the South African the intensity of a winner.

Having removed two layers of protective clothing and partially unbuttoned a black long-sleeved shirt to reveal a white thermal vest, he nursed a pint of Coca-Cola in the corner of the dining room in the Links clubhouse and stated his case. 'I'm still learning from everyone,' he said. 'You've got to have the character to ask for help, even if it is not immediately forthcoming.

'I'm always trying to push myself beyond my natural ability. I don't think there is a level. I've always wanted to be the best I can be, but I want to be better than that, if you get what I mean. That feeling of doing all the work, being in the situation to win and then winning, is what drives me. I'm not scared. It's golf. Let's put it this way: I haven't missed a shot when I've been in with a chance to win.

'I know the bad shot will come, and one day I'll lose a tournament because of it. If you come out here and think, "Oh, okay, I can do this, no bother", you're wrong. Practice and preparation gets you in the position to see what your body and your mind does under stress. You can't teach that. No management company, no coach, can ever help when you've got a chance to win a tournament on the eighteenth. Let's see how you react.

'You can teach the stuff that I do, but you can't teach what's inside, my make-up. I can't explain that feeling, deep down, of knowing how to win. The closest I can get to it is telling my team to do their job, and then I'll take over and do mine. It's like in cycling, where the domestiques set up the main man, or the sprinter is worked to the front. I'm the finisher, the guy who gets it over the line.'

Wallace won ten titles across three tours in three years, taking his world ranking from 1,156 to forty-four by the end of 2018. Considering that the first of six victories on the Alps mini-tour in 2016 came in the surreal setting of Pyramids Dreamland, a dressage centre in Egypt, his awe at testing himself at the home of golf was unforced and affecting.

'This is only my second time here. Last year, on Sunday morning, I walked down through the town, saw the first hole and got a little bit emotional. I was like, "I'm a professional golfer, playing on tour, playing St Andrews on a Sunday in a tournament." The only thing that gets better than that is if it's the Open, you're leading it and you go on to win it.

'I was like, "This is mental." Only two years ago I was flying Ryanair, staying in Airbnbs. Now I'm getting hotels paid for, and

I'm playing the best courses in the world. The only way I might get tired of it is if I start playing bad golf, but I don't think I'll ever let myself get to that position. I always tend to catch things before they get too bad. I'm a newbie out here, so I'm riding the crest massively.'

Competitiveness is in his genes. Rackets would be thrown in family tennis matches. His parents were PE teachers; his mother played international hockey and his father played rugby for Wasps. Matt played schoolboy cricket at a high level, excelled in hockey and football, but was ultimately unsuited to team sports because of the fundamentalism of his approach. He could rationalise the weaknesses of others, but refused to compromise for them.

'I love winning so much that it has lost me friends over the years, especially at school. We argued, because they didn't understand why I wanted to win so badly. Everyone was: "Why are you so serious about it?" They didn't get it, because they didn't care really. They knew their path was different. I knew what I wanted and, to be honest, that was unhealthy for a time. I just hated losing.'

Wallace has made his peace with Bjørn, who excluded him from his Ryder Cup team, despite watching him play on a higher plane in the final qualifying tournament in Denmark, where he birdied ten of his last thirteen holes to win in a four-man play-off. Wallace followed the European win on television at home, unlike his veteran caddie, Dave McNeilly, who could not bear to watch. Wallace's immediate response was to go to the range. He sent a hasty, heartfelt and not-entirely-grammatical WhatsApp message to his manager, Andrew 'Chubby' Chandler, and his support team: 'I ain't missing 2020 so we're not going to miss 2020 and we're not going to miss the one after that.'

The parallels between golf and boxing may not be obvious immediately. One inflicts mental punishment, the other physical, but both require supreme self-control. Sitting across from Wallace as he leaned forward to articulate the determination generated by disappointment, I was bizarrely reminded of the street wisdom of Cus D'Amato, the legendary boxing trainer and manager.

A strangely delicate, compulsively driven man, he did not live to see Mike Tyson become world heavyweight champion in 1986, but D'Amato created him, as surely as a potter moulds clay on a wheel. 'I fan the spark until it becomes a flame,' he once explained. 'I feed the flame until it becomes a fire. Then I feed the fire until it becomes a roaring blaze.'

One of the many harsh truths he expressed to the delinquent fighter acts as a legacy: 'You must understand fear so you can manipulate it. Fear is like fire. You can make it work for you: it can warm you in the winter, cook your food when you're hungry, give you light when you are in the dark, and produce energy. Let it get out of control and it can hurt you, even kill you.'

Wallace speaks of fire, but not of fear, though they coexist in professional sport. For the only time in a ninety-minute conversation, the stridency of his words is not matched by the certainty of his body language. It is easy to overlook the fact that his learning curve has been steep. Though the gradient is becoming less onerous, fear of regression is understandable, almost inevitable.

Wallace admits he must rationalise his schedule. He played 'too many' tournaments in 2018: thirty-five in twenty-one countries. Though he ended the season as runner-up to Danny Willett in Dubai, and in the top ten on the European Tour, he had acquired a tendency to periodic brilliance, undermined by the occasional indifferent round.

'I'm the type of character that's going to use disappointment as fire. I've had many ups and downs in my career. I wouldn't say it was a down, as such, but not making the Ryder Cup has given me the fire to make the next one. I need to get better as a golfer and a human being. I think there's something written in the stars telling me that it wasn't my time.

'I deserved to be in Paris. I deserved it, for what I've shown this year. I wasn't the best player in Denmark. I didn't play the best, but I wanted it way more than anyone else. I had so much on the line. I wanted it badly and I won. I'm not going to shy away from anything, once I know what I need to do.

'I know I need to learn more about links golf. I know I need to have a different mentality to win a US Open. I need to be a little like Brooks Koepka. I played college golf with him in the States. He wasn't that good, naturally, but as a competitor he was unreal. He's fearless, bombs it, couldn't give a fuck. He goes for it and wins.

'I know I need to control that fire. I recently spoke to Chubby at Heathrow about it. We were flying off somewhere, I can't remember where, and I was so angry. I wasn't playing well, and that fire was burning in my head. Chub was like, "Mate, do not lose it. It's what makes you a winner. You've just got to try to be cosy around it."'

Lessons can be expensive. Wallace was fined for swearing four times in a sequence that was inevitably captured by the television cameras. His initial instinct, in discussing the incident with his psychologist Lee Crombleholme, was that it was a by-product of cumulative exhaustion. On further reflection, it was a fundamental failure of process, a short-circuiting of the brain.

'I had a seven-footer for birdie. I knew I had to make it, to give myself a good run on the back nine to bump up the leader board and get back into contention. I lost the process and didn't control the fire. I told myself I just had to make it, created unnecessary pressure and missed it. I was so fired up, everything came out. I should have said, "Right, where do I need to hit this, for it to go in the hole?"

'It's like an expert penalty-taker in football. They don't say, "Right, I need to score this." They ask themselves the question, and decide where they are going to hit it. I hadn't sworn in ages, but I boiled over because I allowed myself to dwell on what I convinced myself I needed to do, rather than how I was going to do it.'

If the fire singed him at that point, it provided warmth and security in Denmark. Wallace is revealingly descriptive about the tranquillity that settled on him that afternoon, when his ruminative smile, following a bogey on the twelfth hole, triggered the senses of Dave McNeilly, the cancer survivor who has caddied for Nick Faldo, Nick Price and Pádraig Harrington, among others, over thirty-four years on Tour.

'I smiled because I thought, "That's it, the tournament is finished." The moment that changed everything came on the next hole, when Dave said, "I know you can make this putt." It was about a forty-footer up the hill, and it's gone in dead weight, dead centre, perfect. I was like, "Oh, okay." I also birdied the next and was pretty chilled when I parred fifteen.

'I knew I hadn't quite zoned out, but on sixteen I hit a nice tee shot and everything became heightened. I realised the crowds were building around me, and knew I had to birdie every hole coming in. When I walked to the tee on seventeen, I saw people, but didn't see their faces. It's weird; they become like silhouettes. You sense they are there, but you're fully focused on the next shot.

'What am I going to do? The wind was slightly down, so driver. Boom! Hit a good one up the left-hand side. Then I saw the shot with a nine, underneath the tree. Stiffed it in there. The crowd went mental, but I could hardly hear anything, I was so in it. The same down eighteen. Smashed driver down there, got a really good number for a wedge and had the perfect putt, just outside right. It was my time.

'There's no way I'm losing the play-off. On the first hole Steve Brown hit it close. I had an eight-footer, downhill, and did something I'd never done before. I crouched down behind my ball, looked at the floor with my putter in my hand and started tapping it on the ground. I was saying to myself, "You are going to make this – you *are* going to make this."

'I rolled it in, and picked the ball out without fist-pumping. I knew it was huge, and I knew I'd probably have him at the next. It was pretty crazy. I sat with my elbows on my knees in the buggy going back down eighteen, feeling myself breathing slowly. It's that inner calmness that comes when you are confident you have done everything in your power to be ready.

'It's funny. Over the years I've come to realise I do certain things in those situations, without consciously thinking or talking about them. When I putt I open my mouth, because if it is closed and I'm breathing through my nose, I might just stop breathing. That sounds stupid, but it is natural and it helps.'

He is working with Crombleholme on visualising two targets, a left and a right post, with his approach shots to the green. They use a railway line as a symbol of the symmetry they are attempting to exploit. Rather than aiming directly at the pin – the most logical strategy, especially with shorter clubs – Wallace aims to land the ball between two pre-assigned points.

Crombleholme is a master-practitioner in Neuro-Linguistic Programming and holds a diploma in clinical hypnotherapy, but Wallace feels most benefit from the simplicity of his asking the right question at the right time. Wallace knows the answer, but the intellectual process is one of revision or, to use the psychologist's phrase, 'drawing them out and getting rid of the rubbish in their heads'.

The psychologist's approach was best summarised in an interview with Steven Shorrock for *HindSight*, a magazine aimed at air-traffic controllers and professional pilots. Their susceptibility to stress obviously carries far greater consequence, but professional golfers can identify with the importance of maintaining mental and emotional equilibrium. Crombleholme reflected:

> Sport is multifaceted. Golf is quite a technical, physical movement. So they have to be very competent in their basic golf swing, or the way they chip the ball, or the way they putt. They are constantly tweaking and changing their technique. The more elite the player is, the more competent they are from a technical, physical point of view.
>
> From a mental point of view, the difference between a top 20 player in the world and someone who is 500th in the world would be that they would have a much quieter mind. Things are more subconscious, more automatic. They have a better ability, generally, to manage their emotions, sometimes their expectations.
>
> They are thinking less about the technique because they are more competent with that. They just stay focused on things that are relevant. And they keep the direction of their thoughts more 'towards'. They focus on things that they want to do as opposed what they don't want to do, if that makes sense.

His principle of a 'three-level' approach was directly tailored to a distinctive audience:

> Level three is the top level, the behaviours and processes. With a golfer it might be their course management, decision-making, pre-shot routines, effective questions. But in order for level three to function, level two needs to function.
>
> I call that the attitude level. Within that you've got different types of motivation, whether it's mastery or ego. A mastery-motivated individual would be into learning about the nuances, the game. It would be me versus me, me ver-

sus the golf course. The money side, and playing against other competitors, would be the ego side.

Within the attitude level we've got the 'towards' goals and the avoidance goals. So with air-traffic controllers I would guess we need to be more 'towards', more 'mastery', focusing on the task. Then we go into level one, which I call biological level, because it's about how the blood is flowing around the brain, so it's more the emotional management.

With air-traffic controllers, generally you would want them to be emotionally calm, clear, a nice quiet mind, so they can make the right decisions. If you can get all three levels functioning really nicely, that's when you get that peak flow state. That's almost when the behaviours on level three just happen automatically.

When Abraham Maslow formed his 'Theory of Human Motivation' in 1943, he identified five levels of motivation, or five needs, that humans have, as pack animals. They are: Survival, Safety, Social Needs, Esteem and Fulfilment. Like many golfers, Wallace finds them in a self-created team environment. The biggest lessons were learned in the most humble setting.

'When I first got out there on the Alps Tour, I was basically paying to play. I had no mates, didn't know where I was. I saw the walls of my room and might have seen the bar downstairs, where I'd have a pizza and a beer on my own. That was it. Luckily you got Netflix now and then, where you could just chill.

'Time is quite precious to me now. I have a feeling for my team. I know what to ask. Lee, give me the knowledge. You are my mind. Are we prepared to grind out there on hard golf courses in the wind? Are we ready to accept bad bounces and all sorts? Rocky, get my swing pure. You were my swing idol for years. It's so cool to talk to you every day. When I asked you to be my coach,

I thought you were going to say, "No, your swing is shit." You help me out, massively.

'Rob, my trainer, get my body ready. Dave, be ready for the course. You are the best. In India, I told you, "You are going to win us the tournament this week. It's a really hard and quirky golf course, and you will have it mapped out right." We aimed thirty feet left of the flags, got out with two putts and made birdies elsewhere. We hit a driver when the commentators were saying, "What's he doing that for?" I ultimately won because of that. Dave was ready, prepared. I finished it off. That's how it goes.'

How good can Wallace become? Chandler, CEO of Cheshire-based International Sports Management, knows of which he speaks, having worked with Rory McIlroy, Graeme McDowell, Darren Clarke, Lee Westwood and South Africa's three most recent major winners, Ernie Els, Louis Oosthuizen and Charl Schwartzel.

When I bumped into Chandler, after interviewing Wallace for this book, he simply smiled and said, 'He's got it, hasn't he?' He predicted privately to Wallace that he would win a major, after watching the maturity he showed in the idiosyncratic setting of New Delhi's DLF club, where feature holes were set in a quarry, and bunkers resembled the North Face of the Eiger, but that failed to satisfy Wallace's ambition.

'Chubs said it quite nicely,' he stated, earnestly. 'I thought about it and I was like, "I'm not just going to win one major." I can see myself putting on a Green Jacket. I can see myself lifting up the Claret Jug, though I need to learn more about playing the Open. You've got to learn how to win around US Open courses, and I probably couldn't do that at the moment, but I can see myself eventually lifting up the Wanamaker Trophy.

'I know I can win at least two majors – the PGA and the Masters – because I've got Dave on the bag. He knows Augusta like the back of his hand. The Ryder Cup is where names are made, and I want some of that. I want to be pushing. I want to do things that I'm not capable of doing, basically. Why not win two or three majors in a row. Why not? I love that stuff. That's why I was waiting for Oli Fisher, to spray champagne over him when he shot fifty-nine. He's history. I want a piece of history . . .'

Golf encourages conservatism, because of the punishment it can inflict. Wallace has the aura of a natural winner, but must overcome the deeply ingrained scepticism of cautious souls who recoil at his ebullience. He has the attention of the golfing world, not least from two men with storied pasts, who are seeking to shape a successful future for European golf.

Chapter Sixteen

NEXT MEN UP

Just in case you were wondering, the good news for Matt Wallace is that Pádraig Harrington and Lee Westwood, earmarked as Europe's next two Ryder Cup captains, know what they are dealing with and like what they see. He's not the finished article, and results will ultimately sweep away the froth of conjecture, but the vital signs are good.

'Matt delivers the performance,' reflected Harrington, whose personable nature, impeccably disguised cynicism and compelling sense of curiosity will inform his leadership style in Whistling Straits, Wisconsin, in September 2020. 'When he gets comfortable he seems to be able to deliver. Players like him use anger to get back into the zone.

'Anger is a huge energy, but I'm not so sure that is a good thing. I once was at loggerheads with Paul McGinley. When things go badly, he's wanting to knuckle down and fight. I believe when things are going badly you've got to smile, be happy and find another way. When you get that bad break, you've got to take a step back and see the bigger picture.'

Westwood, quietly influential as a vice-captain in Paris, is by common consent the best choice to take charge in Rome in 2022. His leadership style will be direct, laced with humour and reflective of the resilience he showed in emerging from a sustained struggle to become world number one for twenty-two weeks. He speaks as a winner of forty-three tournaments, across five continents.

'Matt's hungry, he wants it. He's got that something about him I don't see in others, who might have more game than him. When push comes to shove, and the heat is fully on, they back off. They don't really feel comfortable being there. They don't really want to be in there. Maybe they are just afraid of failing, rather than being excited about having the chance to succeed.'

He and Harrington are survivors, products of a hard school. Little can surprise them, and their attitudes say much about them. Captaincy will oblige them to be diplomatic, but it is unlikely to be at the expense of a refreshing sense of realism. They embody the essential honesty of the seasoned athlete; their lessons have been occasionally harsh, cumulatively invaluable and are willingly shared.

Harrington won his three major titles in thirteen months between July 2007 and August 2008. He became the first European to win back-to-back Open Championships since James Braid in 1905–6, and three weeks later ended a seventy-eight-year wait for a European victory at the US PGA Championships. The roots of that stellar sequence can be traced back nearly thirty years, to a traumatic experience at the Irish Youth Championships in Dundalk.

'My ability to seize the moment was definitely developed. As a kid, I was very determined. My role models were in my family – my dad and my four brothers. I wasn't one for watching TV or collecting autographs. I was particularly driven, and had a few pivotal moments. At eighteen, I lost the Irish Youths tournament by losing a two-stroke lead by bogeying the last three holes.

'Kids can be harsh. I was called a choker, and shed more than a few tears. From that moment on, I knew that I needed a sports psychologist to help me understand what had happened and how to deal with it. I lost because I relaxed, not because I was under pressure. I'd got through the tough holes. There were no leader boards, and someone came out and told me I was two ahead. I thought I had it won, and relaxed.'

The memory, initially rationalised by Aidan Moran, Professor of Cognitive Psychology at University College Dublin, helped Harrington to win his first major, at Carnoustie: 'On the third play-off hole, I had an eight-footer to go three shots ahead. I rolled that putt down there with zero intensity, a total lack of focus. It's amazing, but I realised the moment I hit it that it was the exact same feeling as Dundalk.

'I thought I had done it. I thought I had it finished. I had to give myself a talking-to, putting myself under pressure on the final hole. Dundalk had taught me that I perform better with a bit of intensity. I need to be hyped up, to have that buzz at the end of the round. That's a great thing to find out early.'

Doubt lingers like a faded stain. Harrington became accustomed to having his nerve questioned because of twenty-nine second-place finishes – precisely half the number of runner-up positions taken by Jack Nicklaus on the PGA Tour. Shallow assessments that he had succumbed to pressure failed to take into account differing circumstances, and the positive aspects of a narrow failure to win.

'People wanted to pigeonhole me into a certain category. The media assumed it was due to something similar. There were a few clusters, but it in fact there were half a dozen categories. Some of them I lost through being ahead and relaxing. Some I lost to hitting bad shots under pressure. Some I shot a great round to finish second. In others, somebody holed a putt to beat me, and I could do nothing about it.

'All twenty-nine second places were learning experiences. You understand how to read a situation, and that's the one thing I can do really well now, coming down the stretch. I can understand what the other players are doing, how they are feeling, what's likely to happen, who is the threat. What do I have to do? Do I need to push on, or is that guy going to come back to me?'

Harrington talks engagingly and intelligently, with an element of self-deprecation not always found in professional sport. Listening to him speak in Ireland, months before our more formal interview in the aftermath of the Ryder Cup at Le Golf National, I was struck by the comfort of his storytelling, and by the way he used easily relatable images to get his points across.

The borderline eccentricity of his resolve never to be 'half-arsed' about his trade has shaped opinion, to the extent that Thomas Bjørn affectionately describes him as 'a little bit of a nutty professor'. Yet winning is capricious. It is not a simple case of joining the dots, colouring in the pictures or enacting the theory. There are random components that cannot be replicated.

'People seem to think that it's a hundred per cent under control of the player. You can get yourself into a state of mind that could lead to you being in contention, and could lead to you winning, but the things that fall into place – and I could list a million of them – are bizarre. So, the first play-off hole at Carnoustie in 2007, I hit my tee shot down the fairway. Sergio's hit an iron short-right of me in the rough.

'As we walked up, a small, really dark thundercloud came across the sun and the temperature dropped five degrees. I had been playing the week before in the Irish PGA Championship at the European Club, and was amazed how much the modern golf ball changes its performance in temperature. It goes for ever when it gets warm, but without being at the European Club I wouldn't have seen the backside of that: how short it goes when it gets cool.

'I had one hundred and sixty-eight yards into the pin, when the temperature dropped. I took an extra club, hit it harder than I wanted to hit it and just got it to pin-high. Sergio was two clubs short, with where he landed his second shot. So, because of that one little cloud, I had the advantage. I had seen what could happen with the weather.'

Experienced players embrace insecurity as an ally, since it is so familiar. They look beyond lazy criticism and loosely delivered platitudes. As a keen student of North American sport, Harrington was struck by the bombast of a young basketball player competing in March Madness, the month-long tournament designed to crown college champions and create a conveyer belt of NBA stars.

'He said, "There is no place for fear in this team." Well, most successful athletes acknowledge their success is based on the fear of losing when they're ahead. People look for the easy solutions in sport. Speed is one. They look at a footballer and say, "Hey, he's very fast. That's why he scores so many goals." It is an important asset, but it is only part of the picture.

'When I was twenty-five years of age, everybody was my competitor. Now I've mellowed out quite a lot, and I'd be quite happy to give advice to the young guys on Tour. I'm not as competitive, in that sense. If I thought I had the secret to the game twenty years ago, I would have guarded it. Now, look – everybody can know everything. It's up to them to do it.

'Around ninety-eight per cent of players over-prepare for a major. If you want to be competitive, you've got to figure a way of taking it somewhat easy during the week. The goal is to turn up and be ready. You certainly don't do more practice that week. You do less. You do less work in the gym. You do less work on the range. You actually take it easier. You really taper down.'

This, remember, is a man who practised for up to ten hours at a stretch through the pain of blistered hands during the eight years he was under the tutelage of Bob Torrance, the coach's coach. Harrington can be wary of strangers, and those around him are sensitive to his moods. His battle scars are discoloured; he is perfectly imperfect.

'Can you ever be that kid who first fell in love with the game? Can you ever retain that enthusiasm and excitement? We lose our innocence. It is just how things happen. You don't get up in the morning convinced you're going to find the secret of golfing nirvana for the rest of your days. It just doesn't work like that.

'There is a tipping point where experience and cynicism take over from the eternal questions of our game. I don't get angry. I worked with Dr Steve Peters [the clinical psychiatrist who operates across sports] and my chimp didn't get angry. He was a much more devious chimp, who asked me much more leading questions.

'I put players like Ernie Els on a pedestal when I turned pro. I would have been amazed, then, to realise how much more cynical I would become. Now you see someone come out here with a competitive game and you think to yourself, "Wait until the Tour gets hold of him."

'I look to enjoy tournaments more. I'm still pretty driven, intense and committed to working hard, because that is just my personality. But I enjoy playing in Europe, because of the connections to what is going on around us. I'll make a point of going to a local Irish bar, wherever we play, so I can have a drink and watch the Champions League on TV.

'The guy who will never make it heads to his room instead, to look at those four walls. That's not a good place to be. When I first came out here in 1996 there were fourteen Irish players on tour. We'd all be down in the lobby at 7 p.m., ready to go out for dinner. It gets you away from the game, from mulling over the frustrations of the day.

'You are two distinctly different people, on and off the course. On it, you are a focused competitive individual. That never changes. It is all about believing that what you are doing is right. If you are working with your coach, you have to believe he is the best in the world. You have to have a great perception of where you are with your game and your life.

'We are self-managed, self-motivated individuals. Some people practise for twelve hours a day, if they get the chance. Others think half an hour is enough. I think this is the best sport in the world. There are thousands of players with natural talent who will never make it. If you look at the US Tour, think of how few players have a job each year – it is the equivalent to two and a half NFL teams.'

He people watches from a privileged position. We, behind the ropes, second-guess the significance of personality, and imagine issues disguised by skin-deep self-confidence. Part of Harrington's truth is his awareness that there is no one way to win – both in terms of technique and of temperament – and no one way simply to be. He is as curious as the rest of us.

'It is fascinating to watch the guys who are successful. There are some funky swings out there. It is not about surface talent. It is far more to do with hidden talent that cannot be quantified or measured. If you look at Jordan Spieth, you can't see why he is the great player he has become. He has that X-factor.

'It is the same with Brooks Koepka and Dustin Johnson. There are thousands of more naturally talented players. Sure, they hit the ball a long way, but others hit it further. There has to be something more about them than that one feature of their game. Whatever system you use, you have to believe in it.

'Tommy Fleetwood has managed to keep his sense of innocence. His approach to golf, and life, works for him. We've had successful players in the midst of tumultuous divorces. Another player might be horrible off the course, but on it he puts his shoulders back and tells himself, "I'm the man." Deep down, he believes this way is right for him.

'Bryson DeChambeau is successful because he feels doing something different gives him an edge. He has systems in place that he believes in. Others find that difference in the gym. They tell themselves, "This is where I look after my life." Some of the greatest physical talents never make it because they don't have that deep belief. I have seen some of the most beautiful players give it all away.

'It took me thirteen years before I could have a winter break, without that fear that everything would be gone when I got back to work. It's experience, I suppose. I've realised it's not going to change that much, is it? Even if it did disappear, I've done what I set out to do. It wouldn't be the end of the world. Life would still go on.

'So what keeps me going? I'm fortunate, because I am still fascinated by the game. To another person, I might seem obsessed. I get a lot of grief because I'm out there looking for the nuances. I remember watching Arnold Palmer, playing the Champions Tour at seventy. He was getting giddy with excitement that he had suddenly found something. I know I'm cynical, but sometimes golf is pretty good, isn't it?'

Levels of judgement vary. Harrington believes that winning a major 'possibly makes golf harder', because momentum is difficult to maintain. He argues that external appreciation of his career would have been kinder, had his three wins been spaced out, every five years, instead of being crammed into that hyper-concentrated phase of thirteen months.

Westwood currently figures prominently in golf's double-edged debate about the identity of the best player never to have won a major. That narrative cheapens his achievements – he is, after all, the European Tour's biggest all-time money-winner, having accumulated in excess of £36 million – but it is dangerously seductive.

I have rarely asked an athlete a more stupid question than the one I posed to Westwood as we sat in the members' lounge at

Walton Health, opposite the antique roll-top desk on which James Braid did his correspondence until his death in 1950: 'You're forty-five now. Would you consider your career a successful career?'

He couldn't quite conceal his understandable irritation: 'Yeah, massively successful. I've been the best player in the world. Not many people can say that, can they, about anything? I think people like me for having struggled and come back. I was four in the world, went down to two hundred and sixty-sixth. Some might have given the game up, but I battled away, and got to number one in the world.

'Week in, week out, you've got to be very thick-skinned. You've got to be able to take knocks, bounce back from them straight away, so that they don't get you down. You've got to be very single-minded, selfish and committed to what you're doing. You can listen to everybody, but in the end you've got to make up your own mind what you think is right and what you are comfortable with.

'My biggest lesson has been about trusting myself and trusting my intuition. Take the responsibility. When things were going wrong in my swing, I didn't take responsibility for what I thought was wrong. I looked for other people to sort it out for me, rather than sorting it out for myself, and ended up kind of hitting rock-bottom.

'I had weeks and weeks of just turning up and not wanting to be there. Not wanting to do what I love was worse than shooting eighties. I went to see David Leadbetter in Florida and he said, "You know, we're going to have to start again from scratch, and you're going to have to lead it. I'll tell you what I think, and give you a few keys you should work on, but you're going to have to be comfortable with them, turn them into your thoughts and feelings."

'Sometimes, when you think you've got it, it vanishes, just like that. Sometimes you have got it, and the results still won't come.

Sometimes you can hit it crap on the range and go out and shoot sixty-three, sixty-four. There's no logic to it. You can't figure golf out. People can send themselves mad, searching for something that's not there.'

Westwood's tears, on winning his first European Tour event for 1,666 days – the Nedbank Golf Challenge at Sun City in South Africa in November 2018 – confirmed the intensity of that search. As is the way of things in modern sport and society, the achievement was sprinkled with the holy water of Jack Nicklaus's praise on Twitter: 'Crying doesn't show weakness. Crying shows you have a heart! @WestwoodLee, you showed the heart of a competitor!'

It had been a difficult period, both on and off the course. Golf's global village was drawn into his divorce from Laurae, sister of the popular former Tour player and TV commentator Andrew Coltart. Westwood's split from his manager, Andrew 'Chubby' Chandler, after twenty-four years was sealed by the sort of confidentiality clause that incites speculative, ill-informed whispers.

There is a strong sense of renewal. Westwood parted from his long-term caddie, Billy Foster, the week before the win in South Africa, where his bag was carried by girlfriend Helen Storey, a fitness consultant from Newcastle. His son Sam caddied for him at the Andalucia Valderrama Masters, where a top-five finish presaged the end of his barren spell.

He speaks of the importance of a broader perspective, 'because golf beats you up in your head and I see people who become totally consumed by it'. His seamless transition from a ten-time Ryder Cup player to one of Bjørn's vice-captains in Paris highlighted his maturity and perceptiveness. Westwood's captaincy will not be dull.

'Being vice-captain taught me a lot about reading people. Obviously you have to treat different people in different ways. You can say something to one person and it makes them tick, and you can say the same thing to another person and it has no effect; they don't even hear it. You have to say the same thing, but in different ways they can relate to.

'Certain players like it kept very simple. All they want is for the whole scenario to be mapped out for them, from what they are going to do to who they are going to be with. Other players don't want to know certain things. You don't have to know what makes them play well, really. They are all talented individuals, who know what they are doing.

'You just have to lighten the load as much as possible. I thought that's what Thomas did well. He took all the residual stuff, kept it to a minimum. All the players had to do was be ready. You can also learn from Jim's captaincy and the mistakes that it looked like he made. I don't know how much he got right, but I certainly didn't see Phil as a pick around that golf course.

'It was a bit like Sir Alex Ferguson picking a player for a big game who didn't fit, tactically. It was a golf course for Xander Schauffele, or Zach Johnson, or Matt Kuchar, somebody that keeps it in play all the time. It's a black-and-white job. You're a bad captain if you lose, and you're a good captain if you win. That's not necessarily true, but golf is a results thing, isn't it? You're defined by whether you win or not.'

Harrington, the next man with his head on the block, begs subtly to differ. The Ryder Cup is important, but as another punctuation mark in a story that will enter a new chapter in August 2021, when he passes fifty and enters the nostalgia market by qualifying for the remarkably lucrative Champions Tour in the United States.

'The captaincy comes at an ideal time,' he admits. 'It is all-encompassing, but I am prepared to make that sacrifice. My legacy isn't dependent on it. Nick Faldo thought it was, and failed. Monty's legacy did depend on it: if he'd have lost, it would have taken something from his individual playing career. We are all different. For Ollie, for instance, it was a big, big deal.'

It remains golf's greatest draw card, because of the humanity it enshrines. I first got to know Westwood just before his Ryder Cup debut at Valderrama in 1997, where he partnered Faldo in four matches, before losing to Jeff Maggert in the singles. Europe's victory, by a single point, was secured by Colin Montgomerie halving with Scott Hoch.

Westwood had set the tone on the opening day, when he was approached on the range by captain Seve Ballesteros, who held out some balls of cotton. 'Lee, I want you to put these in your ears before you go to the first tee,' he said. 'The noise there will be deafening.' Westwood replied: 'I've worked a long time just to hear that roar. No thanks, Seve.'

His sangfroid on the Saturday was so pronounced that he wandered across the fairway to ask the foot soldiers in the media army how his beloved Nottingham Forest were getting on. It transpired they were in process of successfully protecting a Kevin Campbell goal against Stoke City at the City Ground. Westwood's memory is still vivid.

'I was looking for the Forest score when somebody came up behind me and said, "Can you tell me how Stanford are getting on against Notre Dame?" It was Tiger, looking over my shoulder. So you know, we're all the same. Whilst you are in the heat of battle – and that's the most important thing in your life at that time – we still know there are other things going on in the rest of the world that are important to us.

'It's a good distraction sometimes. At the end of the day, it's just a game of golf. It's a sport. It's about getting a little white ball into a little hole. It's ridiculously stupid, and we all get to do it every day for fun, really, and make loads of money out of it . . .'

Chapter Seventeen

MATCH MADE IN HELL

A gentleman named Adam Lefkoe, who on closer inspection turned out to be a video host with a voice as soothing as a dentist's drill, was in little danger of underselling his wares. 'This is going to be awesome,' he promised. 'The side-action is going to be flowing.' After what seemed a century or so, he handed over to 'the main man, the superstud, David Levy'.

Gamblers in the cavernous betting warehouses of Las Vegas turned their rheumy eyes towards the president of Turner, the media conglomerate. Levy had the decency to appear embarrassed by his billing, but quickly descended into synthetic enthusiasm about the 'tremendous amount of vision, collaboration and creativity it took to make this historic match a reality'.

Levy thanked 'key stakeholders' with as much grace as he could muster, before introducing Tiger Woods and Phil Mickelson, billionaire golfers with nineteen major championships between them. They had 'The Match' to sell: a $9 million winner-takes-all contest, staged for pay-per-view television on a specially tailored, hermetically sealed course fifteen minutes from the Strip.

Woods vowed the microphones would pick up 'the snide little remarks I make under my breath'. Mickelson, his partner in a jointly owned company set up to manage the project, looked forward to 'sitting in the champions' locker room at Augusta and talking smack'. Evidently pleased with the image he had created, he smiled his doughboy smile and added: 'FOMO is real. The fear of missing out is real.'

The excitable Lefkoe inveigled them into posing for boxing's most crass pre-fight cliché, the nose-to-nose confrontation. He posited, 'These two are going toe-to-toe. Keep it straight. Keep it straight.' The golfers dissolved into a fit of giggles, before doing penance by being photographed ogling mountains of money.

Hucksters talked history, but Eddie Pepperell, the Descartes of Didcot, spoke common sense. 'This is everything golf shouldn't be doing right now,' he posted on his Twitter feed. 'One man earning $9 million isn't attractive. This putrid attempt at attention will turn out to be futile for everyone. Pathetic.'

Buy that man a Montrachet.

Mickelson won on the twenty-second hole of a match of such relentless mediocrity and shameless artificiality that token NBA rebel Charles Barkley, one of many discordant voices on a commentary team that also included actor Samuel L. Jackson, was excused the flash of insight that led him to observe: 'This is some crappy golf.'

The final hole, a par five, was reduced to a ninety-three-yard par three during the play-off or, to be more precise, chip-on. Woods, who somehow managed to miss the green twice, failed to deliver on his undertaking to talk trash. 'Nice speed' was his biggest put-down, as Mickelson misread the birdie putt that cost him a $200,000 side-bet on the first.

The enduring impression left by the players' radio microphones was the sound of Woods's congested nasal passages and Mickelson's heavy breathing. The camera-carrying drone, supposedly the world's biggest, sounded like a Chinook helicopter.

The decision to ban the general public, in favour of a nebulous collection of self-styled VIPs, seemed a small mercy.

The business model didn't stack up. Technological problems led to Turner refunding pay-per-view subscribers $10 million. No official figures were made available, although, according to *The Wall Street Journal*, the event drew 750,000 unique views through a live stream on Bleacher Report, a Turner subsidiary. For comparison, the final round of the 2018 Masters on CBS TV in the US averaged thirteen million viewers.

They were literally playing with House Money, since MGM Resorts were in on the deal. Levy, whose company lost the ability to process payments minutes before the broadcast, accentuated the positive in being forced to offer free coverage. He highlighted sponsors' satisfaction, without producing supporting evidence, and insisted, 'We are in this for the long haul.' It emerged that Woods and Mickelson had signed a three-year contact.

As an award-winning TV executive, Levy lives in a world where, to use his well-worn phrase, 'content is king'. The PGA Tour was not slow in recognising this; their 2019 bonus pool was doubled to $70 million, in return for players giving live interviews during rounds. As 2018 came to a close, entrepreneurs doubled down on Tiger's market value.

Plans for a personalised energy drink were unveiled. Most significantly, GOLFTV, an on-demand streaming service developed by Discovery and the PGA Tour, announced that Woods had agreed to collaborate 'on a wide range of programming, content creation and storytelling opportunities that will offer fans an authentic and regular look into the life, mind and performance of the game's ultimate icon'.

It remains to be seen whether weekly programmes, promising exclusive access and insight, will rise above airbrushed trivialisation. Woods's role as US captain in the Presidents Cup, due to be staged at Royal Melbourne in December 2019, will offer the chance to atone for yet another Ryder Cup in which he was introspective and ineffective.

Stage-managed promises, on his first visit to Australia in eight years, that 'It's going to be exciting, it's going to be electric' are all very well, yet questions about the limitations of Woods's individualism and the strains upon a battered body are justifiable. Golf needs Woods to maintain a redemptive narrative; images of evangelical fervour, created by crowds that flooded the fairway as he closed out the Tour Championship at East Lake in September 2018, are pure box-office.

That eightieth win, his first in 1,876 days and after four major spinal surgeries, drew immediate comparisons with Hogan's comeback from near-fatal injury, and Vardon's endurance of tuberculosis. In broader terms, it was likened to Magic Johnson's inspirational response to an AIDS diagnosis, and Muhammad Ali's recovery from exile and opprobrium, as a perceived Vietnam draft-dodger.

A sinner had saved himself; the scandals and psychological scars, the police footage of Woods as a rambling, prematurely aged, over-medicated wreck, were cleansed. A T-shirt picked out in the throng at East Lake – 'Make Sunday Great Again' – seemed to say it all. It is never that simple, of course, but it was impossible not to warm to Woods's unaccustomed humanity. The man whose luxury yacht, moored in the Bahamas, is pointedly called 'Privacy' spoke powerfully and emotionally about the impact of physical and mental struggles on him, and on those around him.

'Probably the low point was not knowing if I'd ever be able to live pain-free again. Am I going to be able to sit, stand, walk, lay down, without feeling the pain that I was in? I just didn't want to live that way. This is how the rest of my life is going to be? I was beyond playing. I couldn't sit. I couldn't walk. I couldn't lay down without feeling the pain in my back and my leg. That was a pretty low point for a very long time.

'I think my kids understand a little bit of what Dad does now. I hadn't won any tournaments they can remember, so I think this will be a little bit different for them. A lot of times they equated golf to pain because every time I did it, I would hurt, and it would cause me more pain. And so now they're seeing a little bit of joy and seeing how much fun it is for me to be able to do this again.'

Players identified with the moment; many contemporaries, including Rickie Fowler, Zach Johnson, Davis Love III and Matt Kuchar, waited behind the final hole to pay homage. The embrace with Rory McIlroy, his playing partner, was warm and suffused with similar respect. 'They've seen what I've been through,' Woods said. 'They know how hard it was just to get back playing, forget at an elite level.'

Yet, within a week, his world was out of kilter. Invited to engage in the traditional self-flagellation of a loser's press conference at the Ryder Cup, Woods was listless and lost, pulling his baseball cap low over his forehead and hunching his shoulders until he had the appearance of a tortoise, recoiling its head into its shell.

His teammates, lined up along the platform as if they were about to be served an unholy Last Supper, exchanged knowing glances and idly checked their phones, before Jim Furyk, their captain, reeled off the pieties expected in such circumstances. The one moment of authenticity was his response to a suggestion that his team had suffered a traumatic defeat. 'It's just golf,' he said, sadly. 'Golf isn't traumatic.'

Fowler bristled at the understandable assumption that Thomas Bjørn had done a better job. Apart from a brief, poignant reflection on whether he had played his last Ryder Cup match, Mickelson wore a cheerleader's painted smile and contributed a saccharine summary of events. An 'awesome team' with 'phenomenal leadership' and 'great vice-captains' couldn't wait to get out of Dodge.

Inevitably, they didn't do so without Woods being called to account. He sighed deeply, leaned forward into the microphone and delivered words without meaning, shaped sentences without substance. 'We obviously didn't win the Cup,' he said, in a mono-tone that contrasted with the vibrancy of the renewed figure who had walked with the gods the previous Sunday. There was no light in those piercing eyes.

'We didn't execute like we had planned and wanted to. For me personally, I went 0–4. Obviously very disappointing. Those are four points that aren't going towards our side. It's going towards their side. To have a Ryder Cup end that way, for me personally, it doesn't feel very good, because I didn't help my teammates earn any points. At the end of the day, we came here as a team and we win or lose, and unfortunately we lost this one.'

He didn't get off that lightly. The elephant in the room was summoned by a follow-up question about 'the effect on your game and your health' of a busy schedule. His eyes flicked right and focused on his interlocutor. Again, the words flowed slowly, like molten steel extracted from the furnace. Here, for context, is his unedited answer.

'Yeah, I mean, I played seven out of nine weeks because I qualified for Akron and you know, all of those are big events, starting with the Open Championship. You've got a World Golf Championships, you've got another major championship, you've got the Play-offs and then you have the Ryder Cup on the back side. So a lot of big events, and a lot of focus, a lot of energy goes into it.

'I was fortunate enough to have won one, and we were all com-ing here on a high and feeling great about our games, about what we were doing, and excited about playing this week. For me, it's been a lot of golf for a short period of time. I'll have a better understanding of what my training needs to be for next year so that I certainly can endure the entire season, because this year was very much up in the air of how much I would play or if I would play at all.'

With that, he entered emotional hibernation. His failure to respond when Jordan Spieth invited him to contribute to analysis of the Americans' 'fire team' concept of an internal cell consisting of four interconnected players was met with a sad 'Too tired to talk, Tiger?' The nuance was lost in the subsequent meltdown about Spieth's dysfunctional relationship with Patrick Reed, but it seemed a significant fissure.

Furyk ultimately failed because of a lack of sophistication in preparation and a lack of depth in decision-making, but American Ryder Cup teams tend to be the Republican Party at play. Wealth sanitises; cliques form and institutionalised individualism distorts. European golf has a unity that European politics is incapable of matching; it has a balancing sense of democracy, and a willingness to embrace responsibility beyond braying sloganeering.

There are times when Woods seems bigger than the game. When a 208 per cent rise in viewing figures for his triumph at East Lake was relayed to him, he laughed and said, 'Against [American] football, that's a big deal.' The TV ratings he generates are venerated, and are shared as an indication of golf's health. Eyes are averted from his uncomfortable singularity of purpose. Suspicion that if there is a benefit of the doubt to be given, Woods generally receives it, is periodically replenished.

A strange sequence in his own tournament, the Hero World Challenge staged in the Bahamas in late November 2018, highlighted the potential moral dilemma. Following a lengthy review, Woods was not penalised for hitting his ball twice in the same movement from beneath a bush on a sandy surface beside the final green at Albany golf club.

The tournament, eventually won by Jon Rahm, was an invitation event in which eighteen players shared a prize fund of $3,500,000 and an excessive number of world-ranking points. In such circumstances, most players would have taken a penalty drop and played the ball from a more advantageous lie. For someone of Woods's character, that was anathema.

It appeared that his ball had stuck to the face of the club and had been scooped out of trouble. Mark Russell, the PGA Tour's vice-president of rules and competitions, ruled in Woods's favour after reviewing high-definition, ultra-slow-motion TV pictures. 'When you slow it down, you could see where the ball did stay on the clubface quite a bit of time and it looked like he might have hit it twice,' he acknowledged. 'But there's no way he could tell that.'

Russell's decision was based on his application of rule 34-3/10m, dealing with 'limitations on use of video evidence'. He explained: 'Basically, it says if the player did not know that he did that, and the only way you can tell is by using this type of slow-motion technology, he's exempt from the rule. There is no penalty there.'

Woods added: 'It was such a short little shot, I was just trying to hit it sideways there. In slow motion, you can see I did hit it twice, but in real time I didn't feel that at all.' He seemed oblivious to the purist's belief that the letter of the law had been adhered to, but the spirit of the game had been compromised.

He had inadvertently provided an insight into his self-regard on arrival in France when, as part of the US team's pre-event PR push, he was asked to name the four icons who would form his golfing version of Mount Rushmore. He named himself alongside Sam Snead, Bobby Jones and Jack Nicklaus.

Paris is associated with the joys of spring, but it signalled the onset of winter for Mickelson, who coincidentally completed twenty-five years inside the world's top fifty in the week of Woods's tournament. Anyone with such an astonishing record of prominence and consistency does not deserve to be dismissed casually, yet there is an unmistakable sense of diminishment.

There was a forbidding symbolism in Mickelson's ball finding the water on the sixteenth at Le Golf National, confirming his loss to Francesco Molinari and the US team's overall defeat. He was alone on the tee when he conceded; his wife Amy had walked ahead, assuming the drama would play out on the green. There were no teammates or vice-captains to offer immediate succour and sympathy.

Alan Shipnuck, a prominent and perceptive American golf writer, captured the scene vividly in a despatch for GOLF.com:

As the game versus Francesco Molinari slipped away on the back nine, Mickelson's wife Amy had been greeting him between every green and tee, to give him a high-5 and a few encouraging words. But now she was in a crowd down the hill from the 16th tee box and Phil had no one. This proud champion has been a part of every US Ryder Cup team since 1994, a dominant force in the team room if not on the golf course.

There have been a couple of thrilling victories, a defining controversy and more than a few inexplicable losses. Mickelson has rarely brought his best golf to the Ryder Cup, but he's always been there, in the middle of it all. It was jarring to see him now – face flushed, eyes watery, looking utterly lost. Finally he spied Amy and they embraced on the hillside. 'It's okay, I'm fine,' he said, squeezing her tight.

European captain Thomas Bjørn suddenly materialised. He pulled Mickelson in for a manly hug and then recoiled, to look in his eyes. Bjørn patted him tenderly on the cheek but said nothing. It was the shared respect, and empathy, of two men who have been in the arena many times together. Now US captain Jim Furyk put a hand on Mickelson's neck and brought him in for a squeeze. He whispered hard in Phil's ear and Mickelson answered back, 'You did a great job this week. It was an honour to play for you.'

If only others obeyed such courtesies and conventions. The rift between Spieth and Reed was exacerbated by Janet Kessler

Karain, mother-in-law of the Masters champion: 'He [Reed] is one of the best match player's [*sic*] in the world,' she tweeted. 'Unfortunately the Buddy System is what the Ryder Cup has become for US team. Politics over winning. Being popular over winning! That's all it is now. 6 buds for vice captains? Like how many buddies does one captain need? Lol! Such a joke!! Big mess! One big mess.'

Reed is renowned as a loner, and seems more at ease in the less presumptuous surroundings of the European Tour. He has not spoken to his parents, Jeanette and Bill, and his sister Hannah since his wedding in 2012 to Justine, a former nurse who spent two years as his caddie before she became pregnant with their first child, a daughter named Windsor-Wells, in 2014.

He has a small, closely knit team around him. Lowell Taub acts as his agent, Kevin Kirk grooves his swing and Kessler Karain, his brother-in-law, is his caddie. Josh Gregory, his performance coach, first worked with him at Augusta State University, where Reed won two national titles after a single season at Georgia, where he was dismissed in disputed circumstances.

Bitterness lingers. He was described as being 'full of shit' by an anonymous Ryder Cup teammate. An article in *Golf Digest* in December 2018, quoted by Reuters, featured PGA Tour pro Kevin Kisner, who gave a scathing summary of the impression Reed left in college golf. 'They all hate him,' he said. 'I don't know that they'd piss on him if he was on fire, to tell you the truth.'

The image-makers of American golf recoiled from such crudity, yet their determination to massage the news agenda invites scorn. An excruciating video featuring Koepka and Dustin Johnson, supposed combatants in an altercation at a Ryder Cup after-party that remains shrouded in mystery, did neither any favours with its transparent brittleness.

Koepka was significantly more comfortable when he defended himself at St Andrews, where he was playing in the Dunhill Masters immediately after the rumours surfaced. 'There was no argument,' he insisted. 'There was no fight. I'd be curious, though, who would win in a fight. I feel like it would be pretty interesting.'

Michael Gibbons, a senior and widely respected member of the European Tour's media team, interjected: 'Fifteen Rounds?' Koepka laughed and replied: 'Yeah, rough and rowdy. We've never fought. That's not our relationship. We're two even-keeled guys.' A point had been made, in more ways than one.

In Europe, Koepka is regarded as a popular, sociable figure, shaped by the privations of life on its second-tier Challenge Tour, where he learned self-sufficiency. He doesn't consider himself a 'golf nerd' and is 'not big on the history' of the game, but caddies – a breed unaccustomed to dispensing idle praise – speak glowingly about the humility he demonstrated, sleeping in a hire car during a tournament in Kazakhstan.

He survived a chaotic auto-rickshaw ride in India and enjoys the absurdity of recounting an aborted kidnapping attempt in Kenya: 'We were in a taxi. We were supposed to go left, and went right into what wasn't the best part of town, to put it that way. I mean, he took us on a joyride. A bunch of guys hopped out of the gas station and tried to get in the car. I even called my family to try to turn my location services on. I thought the guy was going to kill us.'

Koepka is a global force, having won twelve tournaments in seven countries, and was named PGA Tour Player of the Year in 2018, when he won two majors, the US Open and the PGA Championship, in fifty-six days. He overcame what was a career-threatening injury, according to his coach Claude Harmon, to become the first repeat winner of his home Open since Curtis Strange in 1988 and 1989.

In the United States, Koepka has a tense relationship with a magisterial minority of the media. His rise to number one in the world has been pockmarked by regular references to the respect he feels routinely denied. At his US Open champion's press conference he insisted: 'I always feel like I'm overlooked. I could care less. It doesn't bug me. I just kind of keep doing what I'm doing, keep plugging away, kind of hide behind closed doors.'

At the PGA, he took offence at not being interviewed after his opening round, and subsequently stressed: 'I don't care what anyone thinks about me. There's always going to be people that hate you, but you've just got to move on with it and use that as motivation.' The creation of a siege mentality is a common self-defence mechanism in sport, and is often contradictory.

Time offers perspective; asked to return to the subject at the HSBC Championship in Abu Dhabi in January 2019, he reasoned that 'I was mad for all of five minutes when I said that, and it just took on a life of its own.' He is more concerned with the minutiae of continual improvement, a range of personal targets that involve being in bed before 10 p.m. on the road, and putting himself through at least five gym sessions a week.

Koepka, whose brother Chase was ranked 671 in the world at the end of 2018, admits he is 'very focused, very disciplined'. His insistence that 'maybe I've matured off the course over the last few years' was supported by the sardonic emoji he used to comment on his exclusion from a list of the United States' twenty most dominant contemporary athletes. (LPGA golfer Ariya Jutanugarn was ranked fourth.)

Additional context is provided by his response to two testing moments of adversity. He was incapacitated for the first ten weeks of 2018 by a severely damaged tendon in his left wrist, which was in danger of separating muscle from the bone. Rest was the only cure; though Koepka could do limited lower-body work in the gym, dark thoughts were inevitable.

'Sitting on the couch made me really appreciate how much I actually love this game and love competition,' he said. 'I don't want to say I was depressed, but I was definitely down. And to finally have the chance to come back and play, I can't tell you how excited I was. I couldn't wait to get up in the morning.

'Some of those days I don't think I moved off the couch at all. I got fat, gained about fifteen, twenty pounds. That's never fun. I just kind of talked to myself, "All right, one day at a time. Keep going, keep going. You're getting closer and closer." Finally to get the okay from the doctors, I've never been more focused, more driven, more excited to play and really embrace what's around me.'

That was a largely private struggle. A traumatic episode on the sixth hole at Le Golf National on the first morning of the Ryder Cup, when his errant shot struck a spectator, Corine Remande, in the face and cost her the sight in her right eye, was played out in public. The impact fractured her eye socket and damaged the eyeball.

Koepka was living through the golfer's worst nightmare, the morning after speaking privately to her, at St Andrews. His remorse was genuine, heartfelt and deeply affecting. 'It's a tragic accident,' he said quietly, as if subdued by shock. 'I mean, I'm heartbroken. I'm all messed up inside. Just because I hit a golf ball, someone lost the sight in their eye. If you break it down to the heart of it, it's not a good feeling.'

Life doesn't need the pre-packaged artificiality peddled by the likes of Adam Lefkoe, who do their job well, without dwelling on the finer details. Will the future of golf be defined by the rigour of a major championship, which brings the best out of a complex character like Koepka, or by the fairground frenzy of 'The Match', which hardly embellished the legend of Woods and Mickelson?

We shall see . . .

Chapter Eighteen

THE ART OF SURVIVAL

A senior sports-management executive was awoken by the incessant vibration of his mobile telephone on the bedside table in his hotel room. He recognised the name displayed on the screen instantly and was alarmed by the time, just past 3 a.m. His unease was justified when he answered the call.

'You've got to get me out of here,' said a prominent client, through loud, deep sobs. 'I can't do this any more.' The agent was relieved to learn that he was, at least, in his suite, one of the perks of that week's tournament, on the Florida swing of the PGA Tour. He thought quickly, dressed even quicker and prepared to deal with his worst nightmare.

There had been tremors before, because his client missed his young family and the quiet certainties of his rural, deeply religious upbringing. But this was a full-blown panic attack. The agent stayed with the golfer for the rest of the night, talking him down.

Both knew that withdrawal from the event on the morning of the opening round could lead to awkward questions. It was relatively easy to invent an ailment or an excuse, but he was a popular figure, who had apparently been fully fit and carefree in his final practice round. The player resisted any suggestion that he should get medical help; he was even reluctant to allow his caddie into the circle of trust.

He could not face breakfast, ordered and ignored room service, and recoiled from his normal practice regime before his tee time just after 10 a.m., because 'I can't stand the thought of people watching me.' He hesitantly agreed to a compromise: his agent would escort him to the range and putting green, where he would go through a minimal warm-up routine, and then take him to the first tee.

I was told the story by the executive, on the strict promise of confidentiality, in the early stages of research for this book, and I have done my best to disguise the player's identity. For the avoidance of doubt, he is not European. Though on edge emotionally throughout the tournament, which drew daily crowds in excess of 20,000, he finished in the top ten and won around $150,000. The golf course was his sanctuary.

The episode spoke on several different levels, most notably to the astonishing complexity of the human condition. The rituals of professional golf can be a blessing, because they are so embedded in a player's psyche; or a curse, because the game's capacity to trample through the subconscious is terrifying. Most players are on first-name terms with their demons.

They can re-emerge suddenly, catastrophically. Suspicions about the brittleness of Sergio Garcia's behaviour, and the complexity of his character, appeared to be confirmed by the sustained lack of self-control that led to his disqualification from the inaugural Saudi International in early February, 2019.

His offence, in damaging five greens by dragging the sole of his shoe across the putting surface or, on one occasion, leaving a divot mark, was unprecedented in modern Tour history. His public apology was accepted by those players affected, though it challenged unwritten rules of solidarity with fellow professionals.

Brooks Koepka, an increasingly emboldened voice, hinted at the broader implications when, speaking on the Playing Through podcast, he commented: 'It's not setting a good example and it's not cool to us, showing us no respect, or anybody else. That's just Sergio acting like a child.'

Garcia subsequently referred to 'emotional, personal news' in attempting to rationalise his behaviour. He insisted: 'What happened is not an example I want to set, and it's not who I truly am.' This is not directly linked to the strain on Garcia's rehabilitated reputation, but we live in an age in which sport is obliged to take account of the mental health of its participants.

One tragedy is too many, but golf has endured relatively few. Wayne Westner, who won the World Cup with Ernie Els for South Africa in 1996, shot himself with a 9mm handgun in front of his second wife in January 2017; Erica Blasberg, a pro on the LPGA Tour, took her own life in 2010, after leaving a note that revealed she had made several unsuccessful suicide attempts because of loneliness and depression, at poor results.

Golfers have an intimate knowledge of their faults. Some camouflage them better than others. As a breed, their resilience is remarkable and doesn't require the over-protective culture established around them. They are capable of small, redeeming acts of kindness and solidarity, such as the one recounted by Laurie Canter when Oliver Wilson qualified for the 2019 Open Championship.

'In 2012 I played with Oli on the Challenge Tour in Norway. I shot seventy-nine and marked his sixty-two. At the end of the round, I was alone in the players' lounge and he came and sat with me, despite there being other tables with his mates on. He told me to keep my chin up, and that gesture meant a lot to me, starting out as a pro.'

Lee Westwood recognises the incongruity of players helping their rivals: 'Golf is one of the few sports where you see people giving other people lessons, giving fellow competitors a tip to make them play better. I doubt you'd see Ronaldo giving Messi a tip, or Federer giving Nadal a tip on the practice courts. It's a strange sport, like that.'

Yet golfers are not paragons of virtue. The game cannot realistically expect to be hermetically sealed from the ills and excesses of modern life. There have been murmurs of the use of beta blockers, to slow down heart rate. There is an element of the worthy charade about anti-doping campaigns being conducted across professional sport and the Olympic movement, but golf has been notably slow to respond to the formalities of the cause.

The 2018 Open Championship was the first to feature blood-testing, following pressure applied by Rory McIlroy, amongst others. Around 20 per cent of the field gave samples. Gary Player marked his sixty-third successive appearance by announcing to *The Times*: 'We have had players who have used performance-enhancing drugs. Are we ever going to be able to stop it? No. There's too much involved. That's the world we live in.'

Player's seer-like status, at the age of eighty-three, is another indication of the double-edged nature of a game transfixed by tradition. It is easy to belittle nostalgia, and golf is struggling to make the current generation as relevant and relatable as its living legends, but there is something wonderfully unique about someone like Player holding court, as he did at Carnoustie.

'This championship is a test of patience, of never feeling sorry for yourself, of courage, almost teaching yourself to enjoy adversity because you're going to be inundated with it,' he said. 'It doesn't matter who you are. We are coming back here in memory of Ben Hogan. I never saw a man swing a club like Ben Hogan, nowhere close.

'He was the best striker of the ball that ever lived, bar none. No question. I've played with them all and I've never seen anybody like it, with an inferior golf club and an inferior golf ball. What would have happened if he played under today's conditions with these clubs? Heaven knows. If I was a young man, I'd get that tape of him swinging, because he was on the perfect plane. He had the perfect move. He had the perfect balance. He had every ingredient.'

With that, Player was off, reminiscing about the first of his nine major wins, the Open at Muirfield in 1959: 'It is a special memory to me because my wife had just had a baby, and unlike today, with the guys with their jets and all the money, I couldn't fly home. I saw my daughter when she was three months old. I thought, "I've got to win this to make some money." I arrived at the clubhouse at Muirfield and didn't know it was as sticky as Augusta.

'I walked in and said, "Good morning, sir" to the secretary. His name was Colonel Evans-Lombe. He said, "What do you want here?" It was quite a shock. I said, "Well, I've come to practise." He said, "You're not practising here, boy." I thought very quickly. I said, "Look, I don't have much. My wife is coming with our baby. I need the money, and I'm going to win the tournament."

'He said, "Not only are you not welcome here, you're an insolent little bastard." So I was put back, to say the least, and humbled, but I befriended him, and he was fantastic. He was instrumental in me winning, because I was hitting a driver and a wedge to number fifteen every day, and he came out to me and said, "If the wind changes, you could be hitting a three-iron."

'Those days in the US Open and the Open, we had to play thirty-six holes the final day. Not to digress, but we also faced a thirty-six-hole play-off. The wind blew hard. I had a three-iron in the morning and birdied fifteen, two-iron in the afternoon and birdied it. I went to thank him, and he stood there at the prize-giving as though he'd won it.'

These are the sort of press conferences where a writer is tempted to stop taking notes and absorb the history lesson. Player is a man of such unashamed, unfashionable courtesy that he once sent me a handwritten note, thanking me for what was an unremarkable feature piece. I readily forgave him the sin of pride out of respect to his status, as the embodiment of the game's heritage.

'You know,' he mused, 'I'm so blessed. Wherever I go in the world, I really don't know there's a man on this planet that gets more love than I do. I go into China, India, Europe, Africa – black, white, Muslim, Christian, Jews – and these people come up and hug me. I get quite tearful. They come up, and say, "My father knew you." I say, "Is he alive?" They say "Yes." I say, "Get him on the phone. I want to talk to him."

'I'm hoping I can contribute to this game, now that I'm not a champion any more. I can still play very well, and I enjoy it, and I play in a few tournaments, and I can still beat my age by ten shots. I'm proud of the fact that I promote fitness. I'm proud of the fact that I can play well, because I want young people to see what you can do if you look after your body and stay healthy and have a good education.

'It is an honour for me to go to these places and try to raise a lot of money for underprivileged people, because I had nothing as a kid. I suffered like a junkyard dog and lay in bed every night of my life – well, for several years I was wishing that I was dead, and that's the reason that I became a champion. So I knew what adversity was, and it was the greatest gift bestowed upon me.

'I don't believe in legacies. Probably the greatest leader that ever lived is Sir Winston Churchill. You can go to schools today that don't know who he is. If it wasn't for him, we wouldn't be sitting here today, folks. So I don't know if they're going to remember who Gary Player was, who Arnold Palmer was, who Jack Nicklaus was. Life goes by. Do your share when you're here, and make room for others to fulfil and continue what you did.'

Golf's problem is twofold: it must woo a new audience from a generation accustomed to urgency, superficiality and interactivity, while weaning its traditional demographic off its Tiger fixation. Woods can only do so much; no one can predict with any certainty how long, or how successful, his comeback will be.

His social importance, expressed by his role in the restoration of an historic, heavily discounted golf course in Chicago in conjunction with President Barack Obama, is critical if the game is to reach urban youths who are as apparently unwelcome in American country clubs as they are in the starch-collared middle-class enclaves of traditional golf clubs in the UK.

Thomas Bjørn is unequivocal: 'If you want to grow this game, you've got to get into the inner cities. You've got to have little golf courses in parks, in big cities. It's the only way to grow it. Imagine if you could stick a nine-hole golf course in the middle of places like Islington. That's obviously very difficult, because of the lack of land, but you would have a whole new group of people playing the game.'

Tony Finau, one of the few American Ryder Cup successes in Paris, highlights the potential of a greater social mix. Born in Salt Lake City, of Polynesian descent, he was culturally pre-programmed to play rugby, but fell in love with golf aged eight, watching it on television with his brother, Gipper. The game was alien to his father, Kelepi; the solitary course on his home island in American Samoa has seven holes.

Nevertheless, Finau bought second-hand clubs from a pawn shop and a Salvation Army store, and tied a mattress to the beams in the garage, at which the boys hit balls from a roughly carpeted floor. He studied the game through a library copy of Jack Nicklaus's book, *Golf My Way*. Tony turned pro at seventeen, after turning down a basketball scholarship, and lived hand-to-mouth through six attempts to qualify for the second-tier Web.com tour.

'Basically, I had very humble beginnings,' he explained in Paris. 'Golf is an extremely expensive sport and, growing up, my parents sacrificed a lot for me to compete. We really didn't have the funds to play, but my goals were their goals. It's been cool. I'm really proud, seeing a lot of the kids that have been inspired by me, just through similar backgrounds.

'I definitely think the game can grow in those areas, in the States, Third World countries. There are a lot of great athletes all over the world, and some of them don't have the access or opportunity to play the game of golf. I grew up with a lot of friends that were abused, who dealt with drugs, alcohol, gangs, single parents, no parents, so I know what it can be like. To be a role model for some of these kids, to tell them they can make it, I love that.'

The financial rewards will echo through the ghetto. As 2019 began, Finau had made $14 million on the PGA Tour, just enough to squeeze into the top 130 on the all-time money list. For someone who has won only one tournament, and whose first physical activity was the Samoan pursuit of fire-knife dancing, that is a life-changing level of reward.

The dynamics of the professional game are driven by the player. Finau has the power of patronage, beyond contemporaries in other sports. This leads to complications, outlined by Hugh Marr, Thorbjørn Olesen's coach: 'In every other sport, by and large the player is the employee. The coaching culture dictates the player's behaviour.

'Why? Because we, the club, are paying you. You bring your talent, do what we ask you to, and you'll become a multi-millionaire and a megastar. Here, in golf, the employer is the player. It takes a very special player to entirely trust his team or the individuals who are involved with his development. That's why the hire-and-fire rate within coaching and caddying is huge. It is always the player who is in charge.'

His realism brought to mind the immortal observation of fellow coach Pete Cowen: 'I spend my share of time around miserable millionaires. If you assume tour players are unimaginably happy and content, I assure you that is not the case. Many are, but most aren't. They are healthy, rich and living the dream, but something in them – the perfectionist tendencies, perhaps – leads them to not being happy people.

'When you think about it, there are only two things in life that are essential: food and shelter. Beyond that, it's all window-dressing. A new iPhone? New car? Bigger house? You've got to be kidding. If there's a fact of life I see hit home on an almost daily basis, it's that money and fame do not bring happiness.'

As preparation becomes more sophisticated, and golf is shaped by practically applied data as much as by personal relationships, coaches can follow their players in real time through the PGA Tour's ShotLink system. Each tournament venue is mapped beforehand, so that a digital image of each hole can be used to calculate exact locations and distances between two coordinates.

A largely volunteer workforce of around 350 records every shot, by every player, each week. Their mission statement – to 'turn data into information, information into knowledge, and knowledge into entertainment' – leads to the dissemination of statistics, given focus by the Strokes Gained concept pioneered by Mark Broadie, to media and support staff.

Broadie is in the early stages of developing a new metric, which measures the impact of competitive stress. It has yet to be named, and has no agreement to be used by the Tour, but his idea is to 'measure performance in the clutch or performance under pressure'. He envisages that this would cover obvious pressure points, such as struggling to make the cut or being in contention on the back nine on Sunday.

Performance would be broken down into traditional statistical areas, such as driving, approach play and putting. 'I think that's of great interest, because if a player does or does not wilt under pressure, what part of their game is most responsive is quite interesting,' Broadie told Josh Berhow of GOLF.com. 'Some of the results I think will be completely obvious, and that's fine, but it's the twenty per cent not obvious that's often the most interesting.'

Golf's great attraction lies in the diversity of character of its leading players. Tyrrell Hatton was the only one I came across who admitted to feeling uncomfortable expressing deeper emotions. He was friendly, engaged by the 'incredible' experience of his Ryder Cup debut, but simply said, 'I don't really like talking about that sort of thing.'

His reticence was understandable, on several levels. He had been criticised previously, told to 'grow up' by self-appointed guardians of the game's conscience. At twenty-seven, he was still prone to volcanic outbursts of temper, such as his atomisation of a tee box with his driver at the World Cup in Australia in late November 2018.

Inevitably, he popped into the contemporary confessional, his Twitter feed: 'Not my finest moment on a golf course. Well aware that I've made a mistake here and I should have at least cleaned up the tee box. That was poor to walk away! I will always be fiery, just need to find a way to control my emotions better!!'

Hatton reminded me of a modern footballer, since he was a product of concentrated development from the age of three. He was driven straight from school to the driving range by his mother; his father, Jeff, a management executive and single handicapper who had been beaten, on gross score, by his son at the age of six, changed careers to become his coach at the age of eleven.

The gamble, which involved Jeff establishing a customised club fitting business to supplement his income, has been successful. Tyrrell turned pro in 2011, and was named Rookie of the Year on the third-tier EuroPro Tour in 2012, when he won his first title, the Your Golf Travel Classic, at Bovey Castle, Devon. He retained the Dunhill Links title in 2017, when he also won in Italy.

He no longer travels on Tour with his father, though they continue to work to simplify his swing, when necessary. 'We have our moments, but it works,' Hatton reflected, with a grin. 'It's strange. Sometimes you don't know what you've learned. It takes time to adjust to the life. Your confidence comes from dealing with a completely different type of pressure.'

Hatton finished tied for fifty-sixth in the 2019 Masters, two strokes behind Eddie Pepperell and Martin Kaymer, and twenty-three places adrift of Tommy Fleetwood and Henrik Stenson. Matt Wallace had won the preceding par-three tournament, but missed the cut. Most conspicuously, Rory McIlroy was never in contention. Their names were easy to overlook in the small print of history.

Tiger Woods unforgettably fused his personal and professional lives by winning his fifth Masters, fourteen years after the fourth, on a stormy Sunday afternoon in Georgia. The public humiliation and private pain he had endured in the 3,955 days since his previous major championship win made it a contender as the greatest sporting comeback.

Forgive me for a name-drop that registers on the Richter scale, but my eyes are drawn to a photograph on the wall above the laptop on which I am typing these words. It depicts me interviewing Muhammad Ali in the middle of Park Lane in central London; he simply stopped the three-lane traffic to hold court. Ali was in his prime, a force of nature who transcended sport. He had survived nearly four years out of the ring and had been denigrated as a social and political outcast. Argue at your peril against Ali's victories in the Rumble in the Jungle and the Thrilla in Manila, against George Foreman and Joe Frazier respectively, but this is the company Woods now keeps.

There is something self-consciously prim and proper about Augusta, its clinical courtesies, manicured acres and arboreal beauty. Woods's celebrations on that April evening were earthy, elemental, stained with sweat and tears. His body tense, his eyes closed and his arms aloft, he screamed at the sky, a comic-strip superhero given licence to roam.

Spectators reached out to him as if the merest touch would be a benediction. Unseen millions melted when Woods swept up his son, Charlie, in his arms. You didn't have to understand, or even like, golf to appreciate the joy and solidarity of a fractured family, when he held his daughter, Sam, and his mother, Kultida – greying, and seeming suddenly so small – close.

Great players, from several generations, formed a guard of honour outside the clubhouse, not embarrassed to wait in line like superannuated autograph-hunters. The royal family of North American sport – Serena Williams, Magic Johnson, LeBron

James, Steph Curry, Tom Brady and Kobe Bryant – paid homage on social media. Presidents past and present, Obama and Trump, sent their congratulations.

Woods seemed more human, less corporate, without losing his contradictions. He had seized the day with a cage-fighter's savagery and a portrait painter's flourish. Journalists cheered him in the media centre, abandoning conventional objectivity in deference to the magnitude of the story. *Sports Illustrated* was preparing the rare tribute of a wordless cover, dominated by an image of an exultant Woods.

Two years previously Tiger had confessed to his enduring friend Mark O'Meara that he contemplated never being able to play again. He could not bend to tie his shoelaces. When he fell, he needed help to rise to his feet. A cocktail of five drugs, pre-scribed to combat anxiety, insomnia and persistent pain, left him in such a haze that he literally did not know where he was when he was arrested in Jupiter, Florida.

'I had serious doubts after what transpired a couple years ago,' he acknowledged at a victor's press conference that had all the hallmarks of a state occasion. 'I could barely walk. I couldn't sit, couldn't lay down. I really couldn't do much of anything. Luckily, I had the pro-cedure on my back, which gave me a chance at having a normal life.

'But then all of a sudden I realised I could actually swing a golf club again. I felt if I could somehow piece this together, that I still had the hands to do it. The body's not the same as it was a long time ago, but I still have good hands.

'I think the kids are starting to understand how much this game means to me, and some of the things I've done in the game; prior to comeback, they only knew that golf caused me a lot of pain. If I tried to swing a club I would be on the ground, and I struggled for years, and that's basically all they remember. We're creating new memories for them, and it's just very special.'

Golf – the game to which Woods meant so much – wanted desperately to believe in the power of redemption. In a crowded marketplace, it needed his legend. Now, suddenly, it had a morality play that Broadway producers would kill for. It could revive a cherished backstory and bar-room debate: can Tiger, with fifteen majors to his name, equal or overcome the eighteen major titles won by Jack Nicklaus?

Mental strength, and associated fallibility, shape the characters in this book. The combination of masochistic commitment and sadistic trial makes championship golf uniquely compelling. Someone as seemingly impervious to pressure as Francesco Molinari became the latest golfer to succumb on Augusta's back nine, where it would be appropriate to have tombstones as tee boxes.

Woods remains self-aware, arguing that 'I've driven a lot more youth to the game.' He sees players 'getting bigger, stronger, faster, more athletic. They are recovering better. They are hitting the ball prodigious distances, and a little bit of that's probably attributed to what I did.' But exercise protocols and nutritional nagging cannot explain what lie in a man's heart.

Thomas Bjørn knew what he was watching that day. He texted me when Woods took a lead that he would never lose: 'I told you he would recognise this world,' he said, referring to the alchemy of a champion rediscovering himself. 'Unbelievable.' When Tiger speared an eight-iron to within three feet of the hole at the iconic short sixteenth, there seemed no point in holding back.

'This is the best moment in the history of the game,' wrote Thomas, summing up in eleven words the sales pitch for countless as-yet-unwritten books. When someone of his experience exudes a childish sense of wonder, you know he is in the presence of greatness.

Golf's pressure comes in various forms, and in contrasting circumstances. It can be imposed by external scrutiny or internal insecurity. But when all is said and done, in the life of a professional golfer, only one person truly matters.

The man in the mirror.

EPILOGUE: THOMAS BJØRN ANSWERS

Eventually, the mirror relents. It respects persistence, rewards diligence. The answers it provides may not be uniformly encouraging, but they are burnished by honesty. Thomas Bjørn stands before the mirror as a successful Ryder Cup captain and a more fulfilled human being. His search for clues will never truly be over, but it is time to take stock.

Listen in . . .

'Why are you crying?'

Golf has been my life. I got emotional with my kids in Paris because I watched them discover who I am and why I do what I do. I won a lot of tournaments when they were very young – too young to have an understanding of what it feels to be right in the middle of it. Until that moment my life had been more of an illusion for them.

That's why picking them out in the crowd, and sharing that sense of realisation, was so special. I also became emotional seeing other people's success. I welled up a couple of times watching the video of the week. This was never about me, though the job of captain probably brought out the best in me. It was about

Sergio finding himself, Thorbjørn and Jon proving their points by winning their points.

On a personal level, you cry when you are a lost soul, wandering aimlessly, wondering what you have become. You are crying because you lose yourself. You feel that everything you are is running through your fingers, like grains of sand. You ask yourself, 'What am I holding on to? Am I prepared to do all the things I need to do to get back in control?'

You cry because nothing comes back when you ask the mirror those types of questions for the first time. You are completely lost in a world that seems cold and stagnant. You can turn to your wife, or your better half, you can turn to your friends. But they don't understand. They may try, bless them, because they want to help. But they don't get it.

They can't understand the sportsman's dilemma, the sportsman's drive. At home, you play a certain role. When you get into the car to drive to the airport, you become a subtly different person. A lot of people find it extremely difficult to reconcile the personal and the professional. The person coming towards the end of his career is not the person who started out.

He comes with baggage, complications. Marriage and kids are a great part of life, but everyone has to be very accommodating to make it work. When you talk to the greatest players, they all refer to the support they have from home, but everyone has their bumps along the way. That is part of the turbulence of a professional sportsman's life.

Aspects of life change. When you are in your early forties, your children tend to be coming to terms with changes in their own lives, as they enter their teenage years. A more traditional sportsman, whose career tends to end about a decade earlier, in their thirties, is better placed to respond. When you remain relatively inaccessible, because you are still on the road, it puts a lot of strain on the family.

'Why do you put yourself through this pain?'

It is the idea of understanding what the end-goal is, and what it means to you. When you are out there, in the arena, living through the big moments where everything gels, there is no better feeling. It is the greatest joy in life. All the hard work, all the private fears unfolds. It comes together, right in front of you.

The dream you had as a child becomes a reality. You realise the dream is so much bigger and better when you live it. I've done it a few times and you never lose the urge to drive yourself towards that moment, again and again. For me, it has never been about the external pleasures of being successful, the patting on the back, the congratulations and the 'Aren't you great' sort of stuff.

It is about self-realisation, the internal conversation you have when it dawns on you that 'Yeah, I'm gonna win this.' The sensation that surges through the body is difficult to describe and hard to share, because you become a little selfish and want to keep it for yourself. You have to put yourself through the pain, the hours of thought, the hours of work that no one sees. It's yours. Own it.

Push yourself towards, and through, boundaries. You meet different problems, different people, along the way. You have challenges, balancing your game with your family. Then you emerge on the other side and realise: 'This is what I live for. These are the things that drive me.' Why do you put yourself through the pain? Because you know that on the other side of that pain barrier there is something special, something secretive that fulfils you as a person.

'Why do you play this game?'

It's not the scene on the eighteenth green at Le Golf National, when Alex holed that fantastic putt and everyone stampeded towards him. It's not Francesco jumping into the crowd when we realised we had won. Those are the moments everybody sees. They're great, but I treasured sitting in the locker room with the team, having them all looking at me and feeling their faith. That was a really intimate scene. I realised I had got them. They knew I meant business.

Professional sportsmen and women must be self-critical, but they also develop peripheral vision, because they have a unique insight into the struggles and successes of their rivals. Golf demands so much of an individual that when you see them rise again, as Danny Willett did in winning the World Tour Championship in Dubai at the end of the 2018 season, the bonds of brotherhood tighten.

You could see how much that win meant. He held his family close, and held himself together. The statistical summary of his achievement – it was his first win in sixty-three tournaments and 953 days, in which he had descended to 462nd in the world – merely skimmed the surface. The Masters champion of 2016 had mastered himself.

I had never doubted him; I expressed my confidence to Michael, during the early stages of research for this book. It's about understanding the scale of achievement. Danny got back because he didn't try to hide. He put himself in the middle of it. He believed. I have never seen anybody work that hard, that well and that strongly.

There was no fear in the way he presented himself to the world. It is when you try and cut corners, retreat from the reality of the struggle, that you fail. There is no hiding place, no alternative to gritting the teeth and pushing through. We felt for him, and lived a little through him. Perhaps that is the highest form of praise.

'Who are you?'

That's always an interesting question to be asked, isn't it? When you are on this planet, what is it that you are here to do? When you delve into the detail, it becomes pretty simple. I am a professional golfer, in my blood, soul and heart. That is everything I am. I am a player. I am not a politician. I am not an administrator.

I am the boy aged two, planted at a golf course when my mum and dad played two or three times a week. Everyone knew everyone else, and the people who worked at the club were unofficial nannies, who kept an eye out for me. I am the boy aged six, eight or ten who found a simple joy in playing a game with his friends.

The boy becomes a competitor. You want to win. You are trying to be an alpha male on the golf course. That feeling never leaves you. A lot of sports people struggle once they get to the end of their careers, because nature takes away their essence of being the guy who stands there, tall and unyielding, in the arena.

That's why some struggle with their mental health. It is so easy to lose focus, lose track of who you are. That makes it harder to perform, and before you know it, you are locked into a downward spiral. You are whoever you want to be, whether that's a businessman, a family man or someone who directs his attention in a thousand different directions.

Once more, with feeling: I am a professional golfer.

'Where are you in your life?'

I'm at a crossroads. Can I continue to put down the work over six to eight months, to get back playing at a level where I can understand where I am going? Am I willing to do that? Or do I embark on a completely different route, on the back of a successful Ryder Cup? Have I a mission to explain? Have I the courage to make a leap of faith? Do I go into a different world, to help others lead, or to manage through my own experience?

The Ryder Cup gave me inspiration. It is not about wallowing in the glory of it all, but when you have a successful moment in your career, why don't you live that moment? There are lessons in being with twelve highly talented, hugely motivated guys who showed up, wanting to do a job. I don't think I can play to the level of those guys week in, week out, but at times I can be competitive. That gives me the motivation to get out there and do the work. It involves withdrawing into a solitary world, retracting myself from pretty much everything else.

Leadership is tantalising, because it promises nothing. No matter what you do, it is still down to the talent, application and inspiration of others. You can put all the pieces in place, but if your team is not prepared to respond, you can fall flat on your face. There are no guarantees, but we created the right environment for the right players at the right moment in time.

There was change needed, a revision in focus required. In modern sport it is no longer possible to indulge the old-school certainty that 'we've always done it this way'. That leads you to look at how golf is. What do players crave? What do they need, to breathe freely in the rarefied air at the top of the game? We have to be realistic. Most golf fans are only interested in the famous few.

I consider myself a sports fan, and look at other sports for signals. Take tennis: there is an understandable concentration on the champions, Federer, Djokovic, Nadal, Murray. New generations will provide fresh challengers and renewed impetus, but that quartet set the standards for their sport and must be approached accordingly.

Look at Formula One, and the flair and single-mindedness of Lewis Hamilton. There may only be twenty-two drivers, but how many can you name? It is the age of the individual and, as a sports fan, it makes me wonder how outsiders look at golf.

'What do you want to achieve?'

Golf has a problem. It is a very popular sport and offers something unique through a pro-am system that allows the weekend hacker to play alongside experienced pros. That is corporately attractive, and there is a potential to play in every corner of the planet. The flipside is that the situation over-produces golf tournaments. That makes it extremely difficult for the top player. There is too much choice, too much dilution.

All they want to do is drive themselves towards the top. They want to play against each other, and that doesn't happen enough. Money is a subsidiary issue; majors and world-championship events matter. There may only be three or four other tournaments where most of them show up. There are so many tours, so many conflicting interests. Golf ends up fighting itself, looking internally, when it should be looking externally to gauge our position in the world.

It is a naturally introspective sport, because it is probably the most individual sport there is. You have always to look after the top players; you are driven to do so by fans, sponsors, TV and media. Their success trickles down. There will always be a championship in Denmark, or France, or Sweden; there will always be an outlet for the player who is number 100 in the world.

The French Open will no longer be one of the top events in 2019. I can understand it when people say Le Golf National has been dumped because it has served its purpose. Look back at recent history: the same thing has happened to other great venues, like the Belfry, the K Club, Celtic Manor and Gleneagles.

The Ryder Cup is successful in its own right, but because the process is so long, does it suck the life out of golf in that region? That is not healthy. You want to leave a legacy, not only for the professional game, but for the amateur sport, the junior player. The leaders of today's tours, Jay Monahan and Keith Pelley, have a huge responsibility.

How is the game of golf going to look in two years, five years, ten years, twenty years? That's a precarious prediction. No one really knows, but it will definitely be better if those guys are working hand-in-hand, rather than fighting for their own narrow self-interest. We need a plan to sell to players and the public.

Golf has historically had so many 'them and us' scenarios between the US and European tours. I've been a member of the American tour, but I've been European, by instinct and inclination, all my career. When I look back, at the Eighties and Nineties, we weren't welcome in America. The players didn't want us there. The environment didn't give you the confidence to think, 'This could be my Tour.'

That changed with the likes of GMac, Luke, Henrik, Poulter and Rosie. Their heart may still be in Europe, but they became part of the US Tour. They see it as their home; we didn't have that level of acceptance in the Nineties. Younger players, like Matt Wallace and Matt Fitzpatrick, will go there. So they should. That's how they progress, in the biggest tournaments against the best players. You can't hold it against them.

It is no secret that my relationship with Pelley was severely tested during the build-up to the Ryder Cup. We had, and have, a good working relationship, but I felt keenly the loss of Guy Kinnings, my long-term manager, who will, I am sure, provide long-term leadership in his new role as the European Tour's Deputy CEO & Ryder Cup Director.

I will never apologise for wanting the best for my team. I will never apologise for protecting the concept of a Tour that fuses Europe's different cultures with those of a wider world. Sometimes my patience is overwhelmed by my passion, but I understand the principles of progress. Europe is the heartland of golf, but it needs to be part of a bigger scene.

'Do you really want to continue?'

Watch this space. To be honest, I'm eager to take stock and see what 2019 brings.

'Why does it mean so much to you?'

I have learned that every person you meet along the way forms you. They make you who you are, what you are. They all plant seeds. Then it is down to you to trust who you are, and what you have become. The person I am today is not the person I was when I came on the main Tour in 1996. I have different beliefs, a different system of judging not only what I do, but what others do around me.

I have learned that people don't get to see everything I am, and how I think, very often. The person I really am is the person who came out that week in Paris. I think I've been misunderstood because of my intensity as a golfer, and I promise to smile more easily, but my view of the world aligns with how the greats of the Ryder Cup – Seve, Ollie, McGinley – see it.

I learned so much from them, even without consciously sitting down to pick their brains. I lived it, as they lived it. They helped me to understand how players like to be treated in Cup week. They taught me the importance of observation and adaptation. It wasn't how I did the job for me, but how I did it for the players.

I saw them when they were tired, uncertain. I noticed when they were sitting in the corner, hanging their head a little bit, for whatever reason. I let them know we were there for them. Sometimes, when you are tired, you just need space to chill out. Other times, the conversation needs to be a little longer, a little deeper.

The ability to bring people together is one of the things you learn through life, but once everything is in the pot, you have to make the most of it. This is who I am. This is what I can do. Let's run with that. Don't be tempted to tap into someone else's world. Don't try and be anything other than the man in the mirror.

Be true to yourself.

ACKNOWLEDGEMENTS

You never forget your first time, they say. Nearly twenty-eight years on, memories of watching my first Ryder Cup match on American soil, the so-called War on The Shore at Kiawah Island in South Carolina, have lost none of their power and peculiarity.

Mark Calcavecchia, who hyperventilated after losing the last four holes to halve his singles match against Colin Montgomerie, needed oxygen to recover. Bernhard Langer, whose face was embalmed with grief when he missed the six foot par putt to retain the Cup, was eventually persuaded he needed a drink or ten.

So much for golf as a sedate pastime, that allows men of a certain age to wear absurd trousers and tell tall tales about their grace under pressure. This had the lot – cartoon patriotism, camouflage gear, and callousness personified by Nick Faldo's indifference to his European playing partner, David Gilford. In the immortal words of Hale Irwin, who was rescued by Langer's lapse, "the sphincter-factor was high."

There had to be a book in such a scenario. The case became stronger, as the game's ability to inflict misery and inspire unlikely achievement became more obvious down the years. The catalyst for Mind Game was an approach by Thomas Bjørn in late 2017, to collaborate on an authentic summary of the sport that looked beyond the Ryder Cup. His raw honesty and emotional intelligence underpins our project.

Given strategic support by Scott Crockett and Guy Kinnings, we were off and running. I'm grateful for the candour and clarity of my interviewees, and indebted to Sarah Wooldridge, Vicky Cuming, Adrian Mitchell, Laurie Potter, Gorka Guillén, Philip Kaymer, Rory Flanagan, Andrew Chandler and Graham Chase for helping to organise access.

I knew the late Glenn Gibbons as a brilliantly acerbic football writer, a man of warmth, wit and integrity. His son Michael, a senior member of the European Tour's media team, shares those traits. No wonder he has the trust, respect and friendship of leading players. I thank, also, his colleagues, Clare Bodel, Briony Carlyon, Kate Wright, Frances Jennings, Neil Ahern, Steve Todd, Tom Carlisle and Maria Acacia Lopez-Bachiller.

The press conference transcription service provided by ASAP Sports was an invaluable source of information and insight, especially on the PGA Tour. I have attempted, wherever possible, to acknowledge external sources; if any have been inadvertently overlooked in what has been an exhaustive research process I apologise and will make amends in later editions.

Closer to home, Caroline Flatley and Christine Preston patiently transcribed interviews, and provided pertinent commentary on aspects of character. Thomas, for instance, was quickly christened 'Yoda.' Rory Scarfe, my literary representative at the Blair Partnership, was a familiar and much-valued source of faith and advice.

This book would not have been possible without the foresight of Tim Broughton, Editorial Director at Yellow Jersey Press. As a golf fan, he understood the potential of the game's hidden narrative. I'm grateful for the professionalism of his team, Mandy

Greenfield, Chloe Healy, Mia Quibell-Smith, Stephen Parker, Phil Brown and Hassan Musto.

Finally, I don't know how my family put up with my grumpiness and inability to sleep beyond 4 a.m. when I'm in writing mode. This is for you, Lynn, Nicholas, Vicky, Aaron, Jo, William, Lydia, Joe, Marielli and Michael. You make my world go round.

Michael Calvin, January 2019

INDEX

penguin.co.uk/vintage